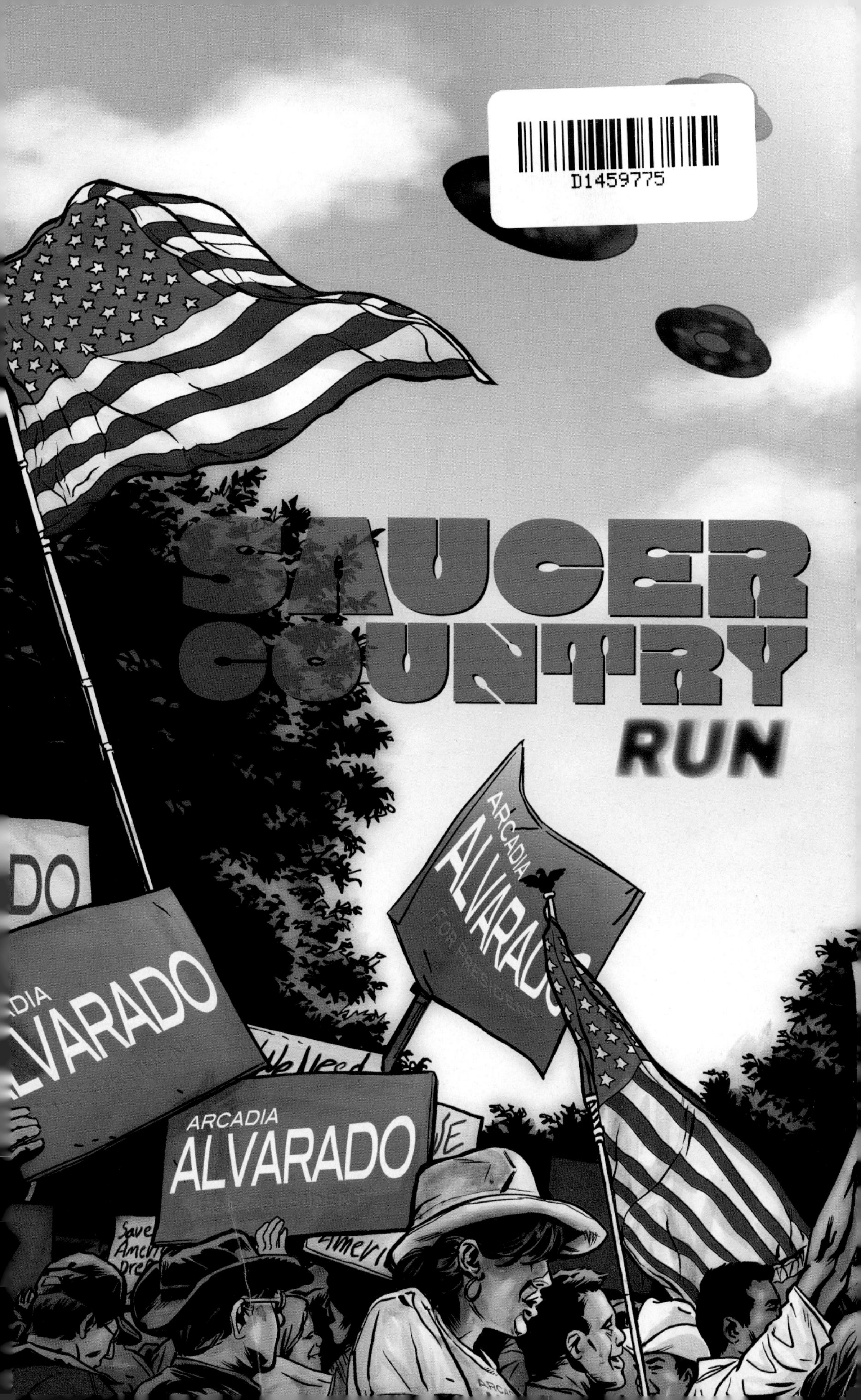

SAUCER COUNTRY
RUN
ARCADIA
ALVARADO
FOR PRESIDENT
DO
ADIA
ALVARADO
ARCADIA
ALVARADO

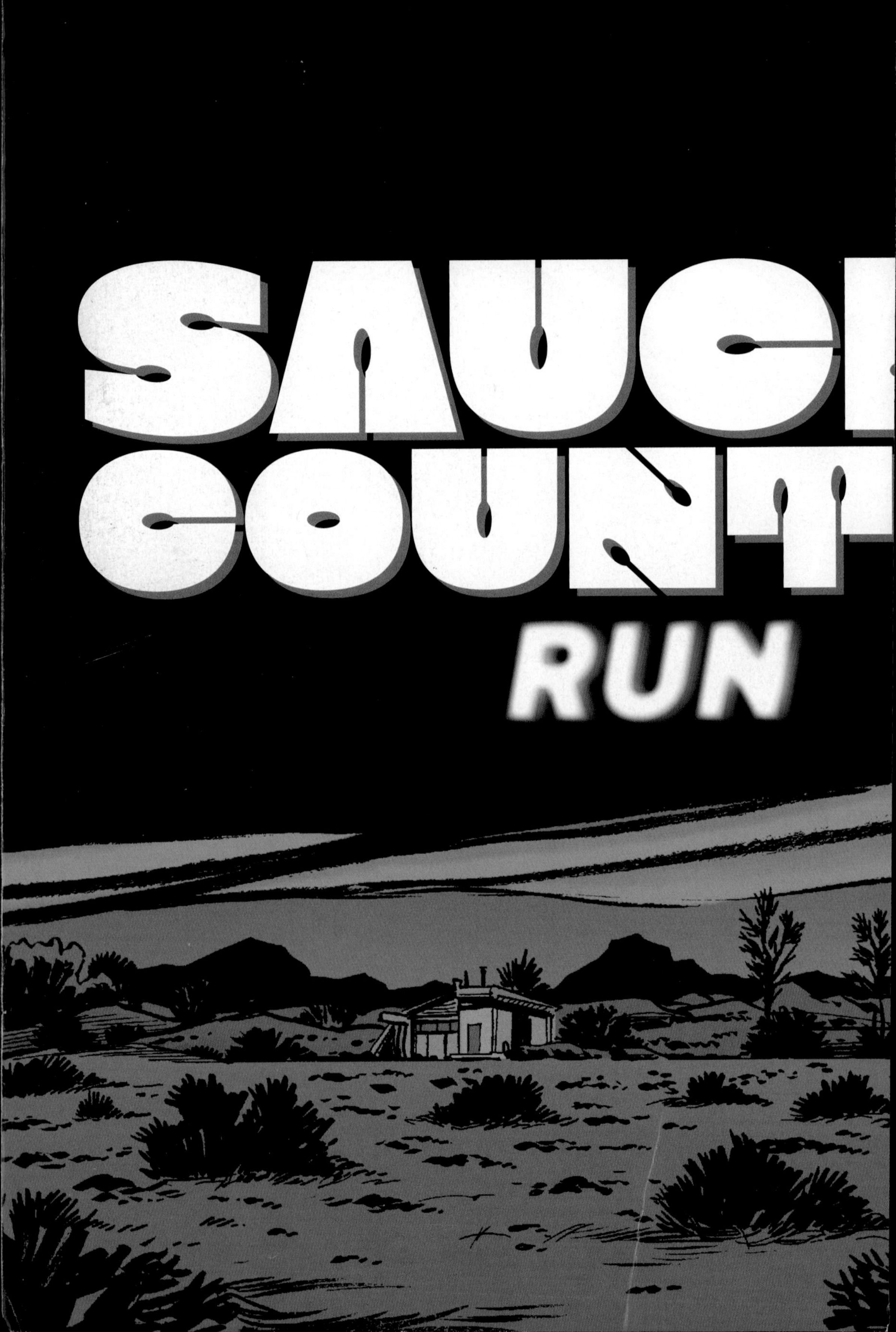
SAUC
COUN
RUN

PAUL CORNELL
WRITER

RYAN KELLY
JIMMY BRAXTON PGS. 117-136
GORAN SUDŽUKA PGS. 138-143
ARTISTS

GIULIA BRUSCO
LEE LOUGHRIDGE CRIS PETER
COLORISTS

SAL CIPRIANO
LETTERER

RYAN KELLY
SERIES & COLLECTION COVER ARTIST

SAUCER COUNTRY CREATED BY CORNELL & KELLY

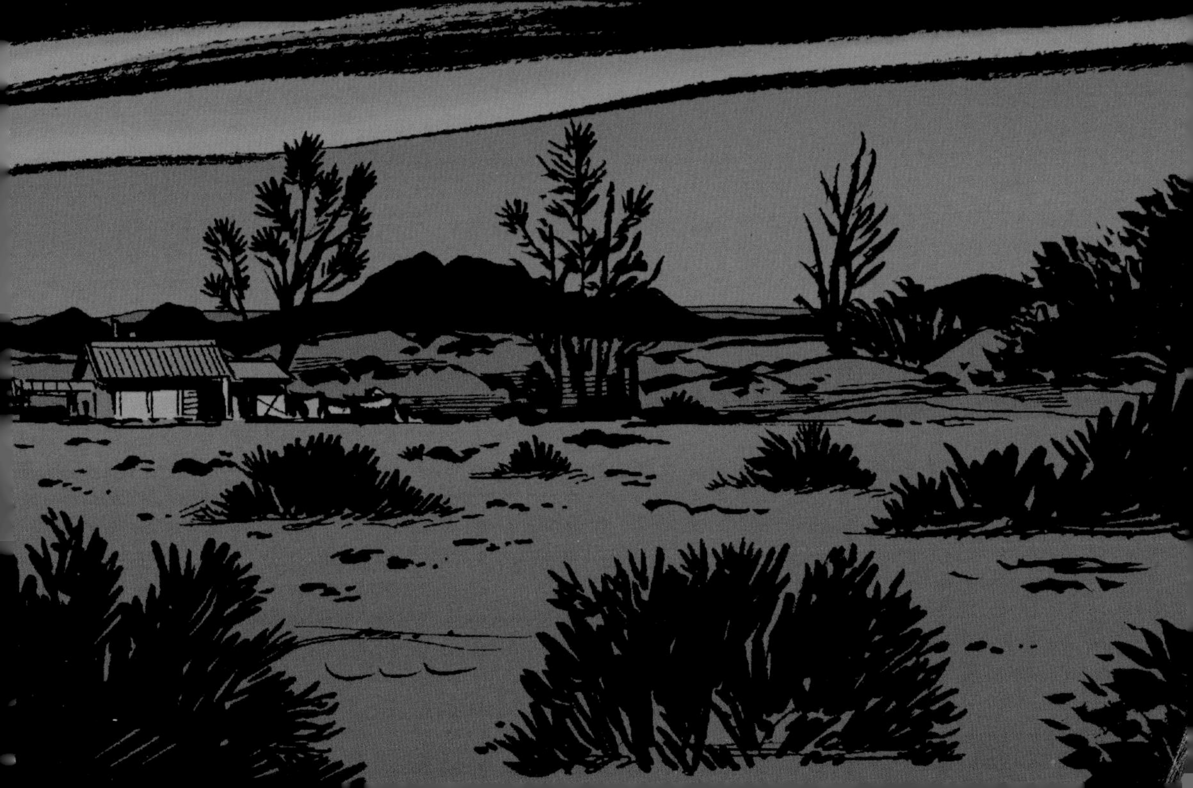

WILL DENNIS   EDITOR - ORIGINAL SERIES
MARK DOYLE   ASSOCIATE EDITOR - ORIGINAL SERIES
ROWENA YOW   EDITOR
ROBBIN BROSTERMAN   DESIGN DIRECTOR - BOOKS
CURTIS KING JR.   PUBLICATION DESIGN

KAREN BERGER   SENIOR VP - EXECUTIVE EDITOR, VERTIGO
BOB HARRAS   VP - EDITOR-IN-CHIEF

DIANE NELSON   PRESIDENT
DAN DIDIO AND JIM LEE   CO-PUBLISHERS
GEOFF JOHNS   CHIEF CREATIVE OFFICER
JOHN ROOD   EXECUTIVE VP - SALES, MARKETING
             AND BUSINESS DEVELOPMENT
AMY GENKINS   SENIOR VP - BUSINESS AND LEGAL AFFAIRS
NAIRI GARDINER   SENIOR VP - FINANCE
JEFF BOISON   VP - PUBLISHING OPERATIONS
MARK CHIARELLO   VP - ART DIRECTION AND DESIGN
JOHN CUNNINGHAM   VP - MARKETING
TERRI CUNNINGHAM   VP - TALENT RELATIONS AND SERVICES
ALISON GILL   SENIOR VP - MANUFACTURING AND OPERATIONS
HANK KANALZ   SENIOR VP - DIGITAL
JAY KOGAN   VP - BUSINESS AND LEGAL AFFAIRS, PUBLISHING
JACK MAHAN   VP - BUSINESS AFFAIRS, TALENT
NICK NAPOLITANO   VP - MANUFACTURING ADMINISTRATION
SUE POHJA   VP - BOOK SALES
COURTNEY SIMMONS   SENIOR VP - PUBLICITY
BOB WAYNE   SENIOR VP - SALES

DC COMICS, 1700 BROADWAY, NEW YORK, NY 10019
A WARNER BROS. ENTERTAINMENT COMPANY.
PRINTED IN THE USA. FIRST PRINTING.
ISBN:978-1-4012-3549-9

                    LIBRARY OF CONGRESS CATALOGING-IN-PUBLICATION DATA

CORNELL, PAUL.
   SAUCER COUNTRY. VOLUME 1, RUN / PAUL CORNELL, RYAN KELLY.
      P. CM.
   "ORIGINALLY PUBLISHED IN SINGLE MAGAZINE FORM IN SAUCER COUNTRY
1-6, STRANGE ADVENTURES 1."
   ISBN 978-1-4012-3549-9 (ALK. PAPER)
   1. HUMAN-ALIEN ENCOUNTERS — COMIC BOOKS, STRIPS, ETC. 2. WOMEN
GOVERNORS — COMIC BOOKS, STRIPS, ETC. 3. GRAPHIC NOVELS. 4.
POLITICAL FICTION. I. KELLY, RYAN, 1976- II. TITLE. III. TITLE:
RUN.
   PN6728.S28C67 2012
   741.5'973 — DC23
                                              2012026761

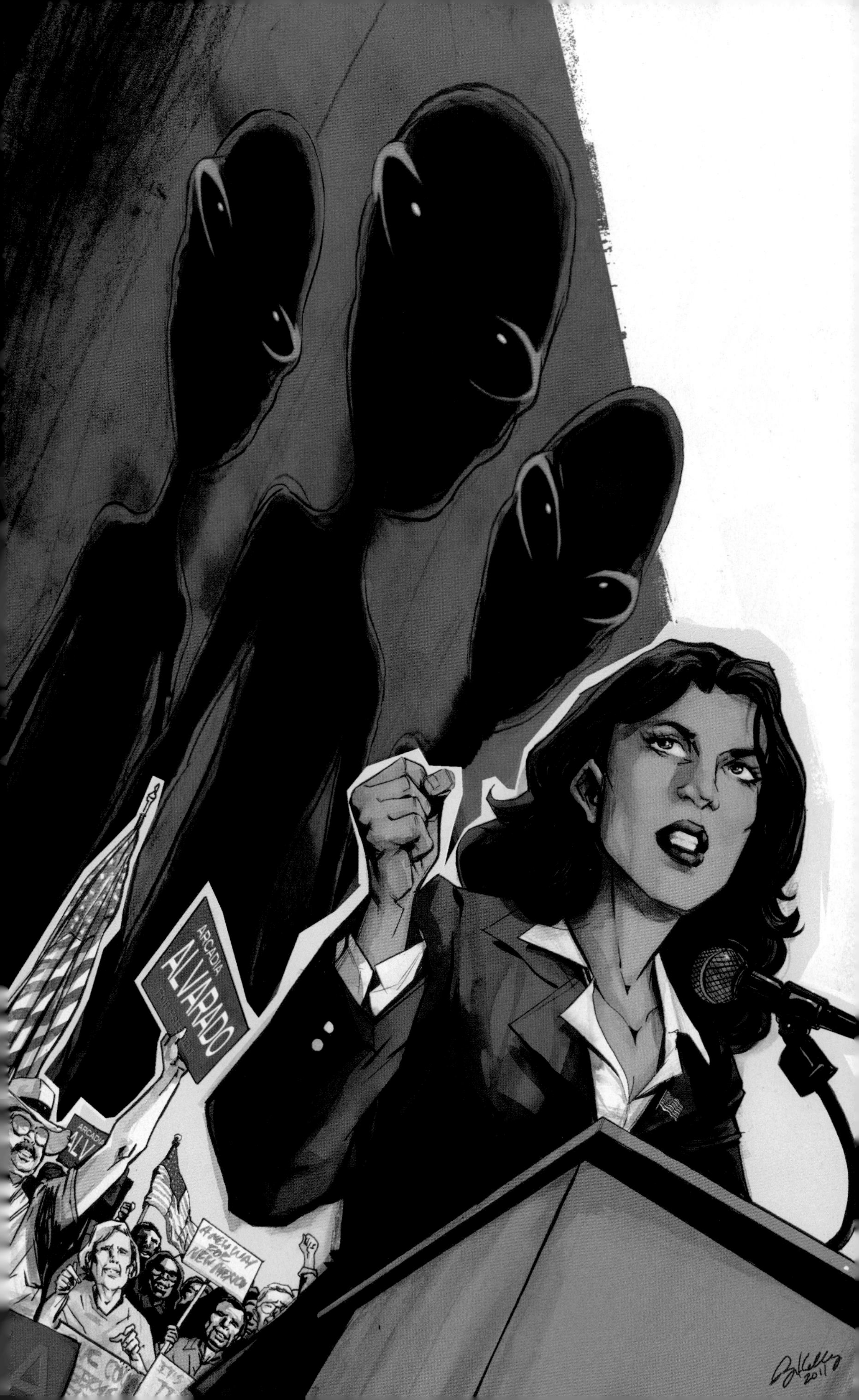
ARCADIA
ALVARADO
ARCADIA
ALV
A NEW WAY FOR NEW MEXICO

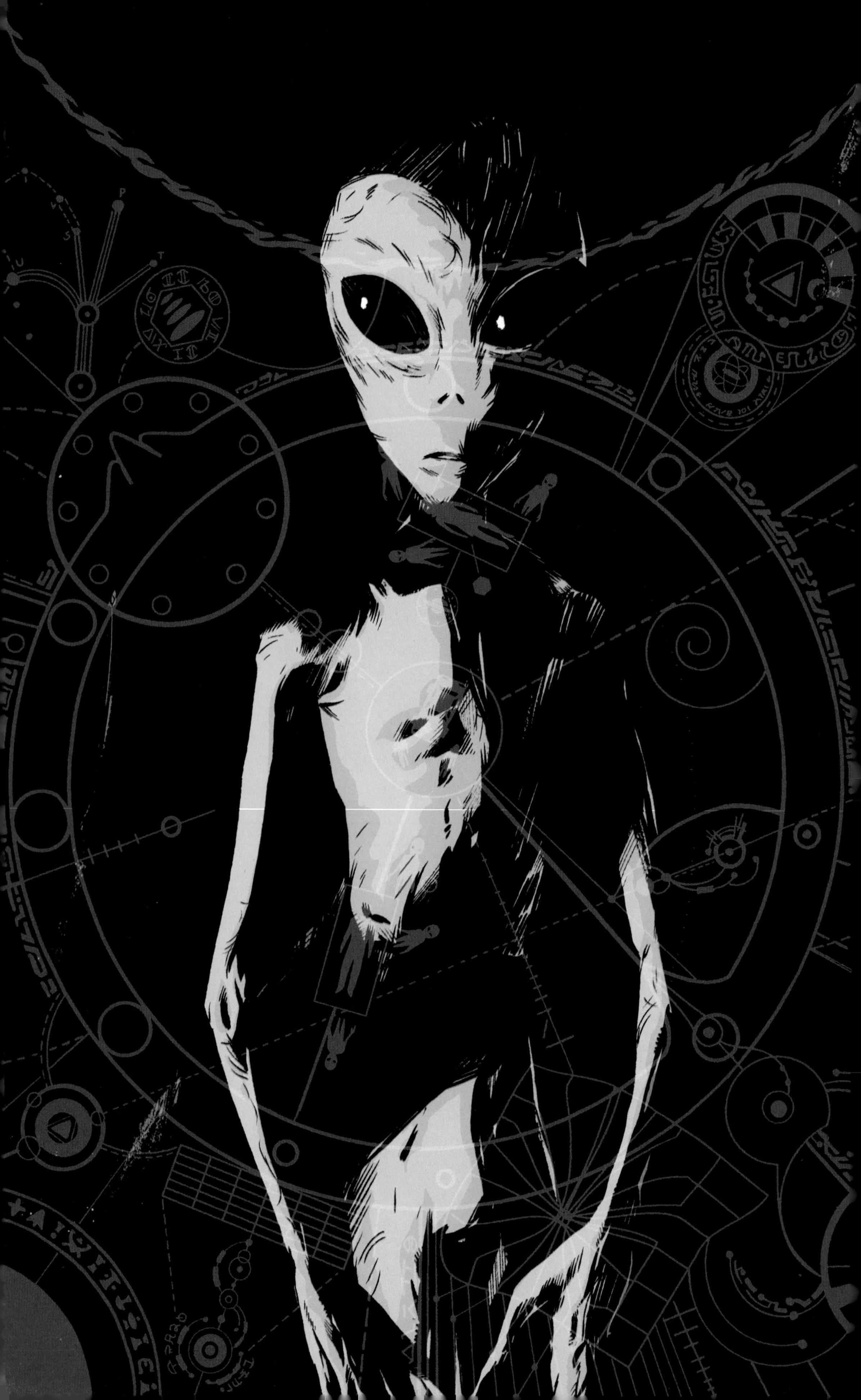

STAY ASLEEP.

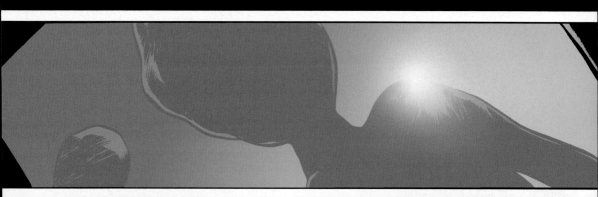

BORTED FETUSES, MONKEYS USED IN LAB EXPERIMENTS, THE CHILDREN OF BELSEN...

DOES *ANYONE* ACTUALLY BELIEVE *ANYTHING* ANYMORE?

I THINK THERE'S... SOMETHING...OUT THERE. BUT ANY TIME ANYONE TRIES TO PUT THEIR FINGER ON EXACTLY WHAT...

LOOK WHO'S HERE TO SEE YOU!

STAY ASLEEP.

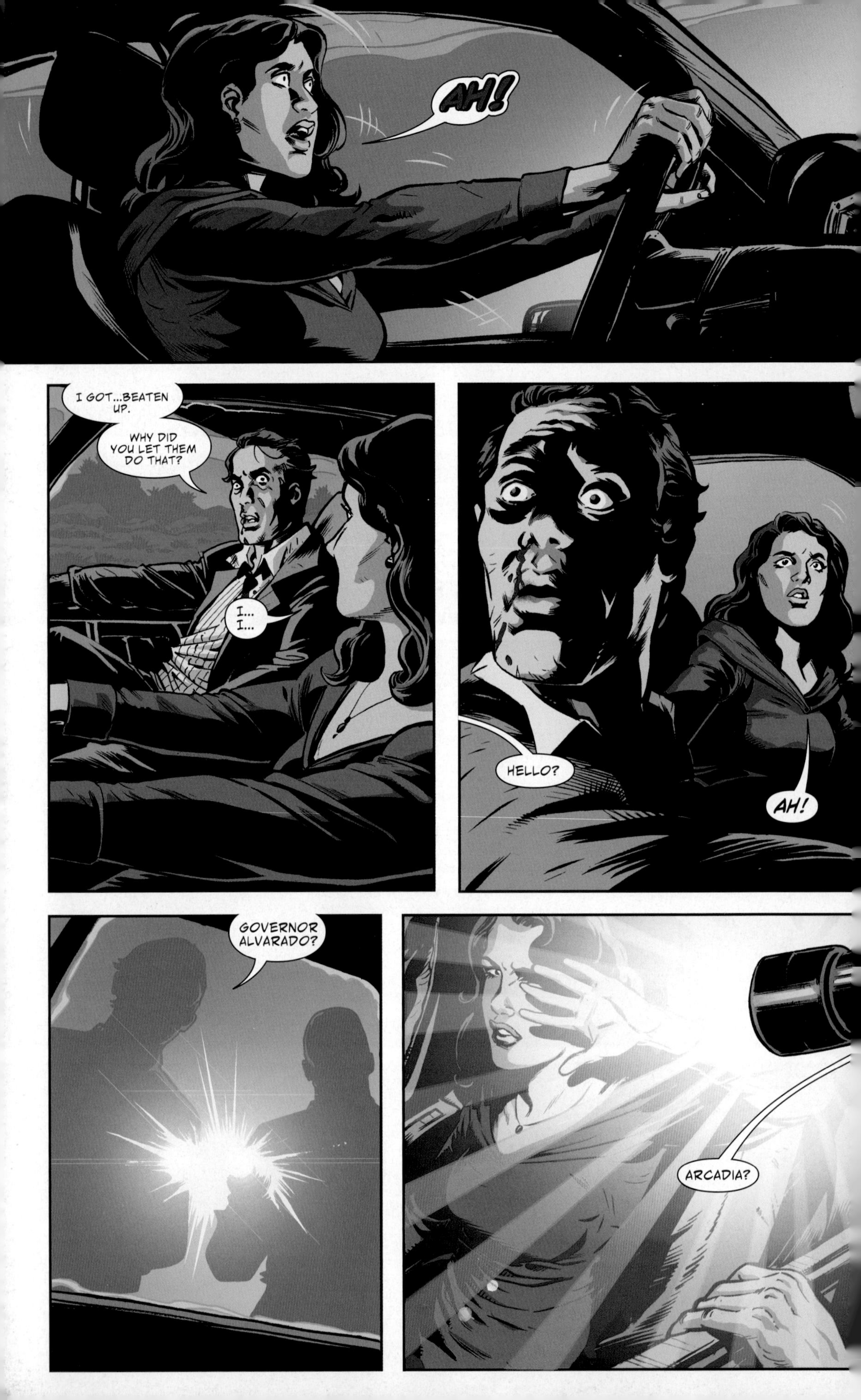
AH!
I GOT...BEATEN UP.
WHY DID YOU LET THEM DO THAT?
I... I...
HELLO?
AH!
GOVERNOR ALVARADO?
ARCADIA?

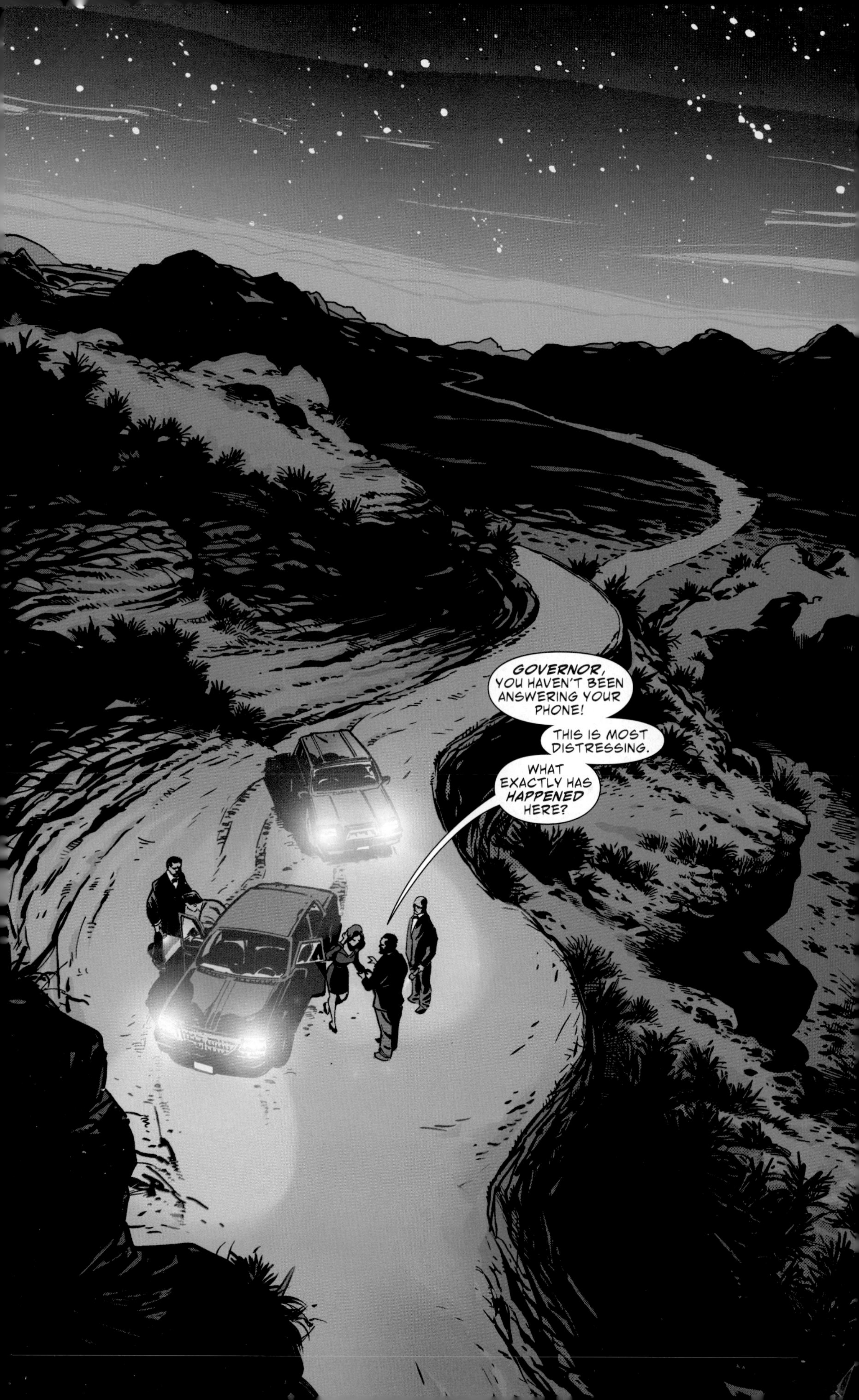

GOVERNOR, YOU HAVEN'T BEEN ANSWERING YOUR PHONE!
THIS IS MOST DISTRESSING.
WHAT EXACTLY HAS HAPPENED HERE?

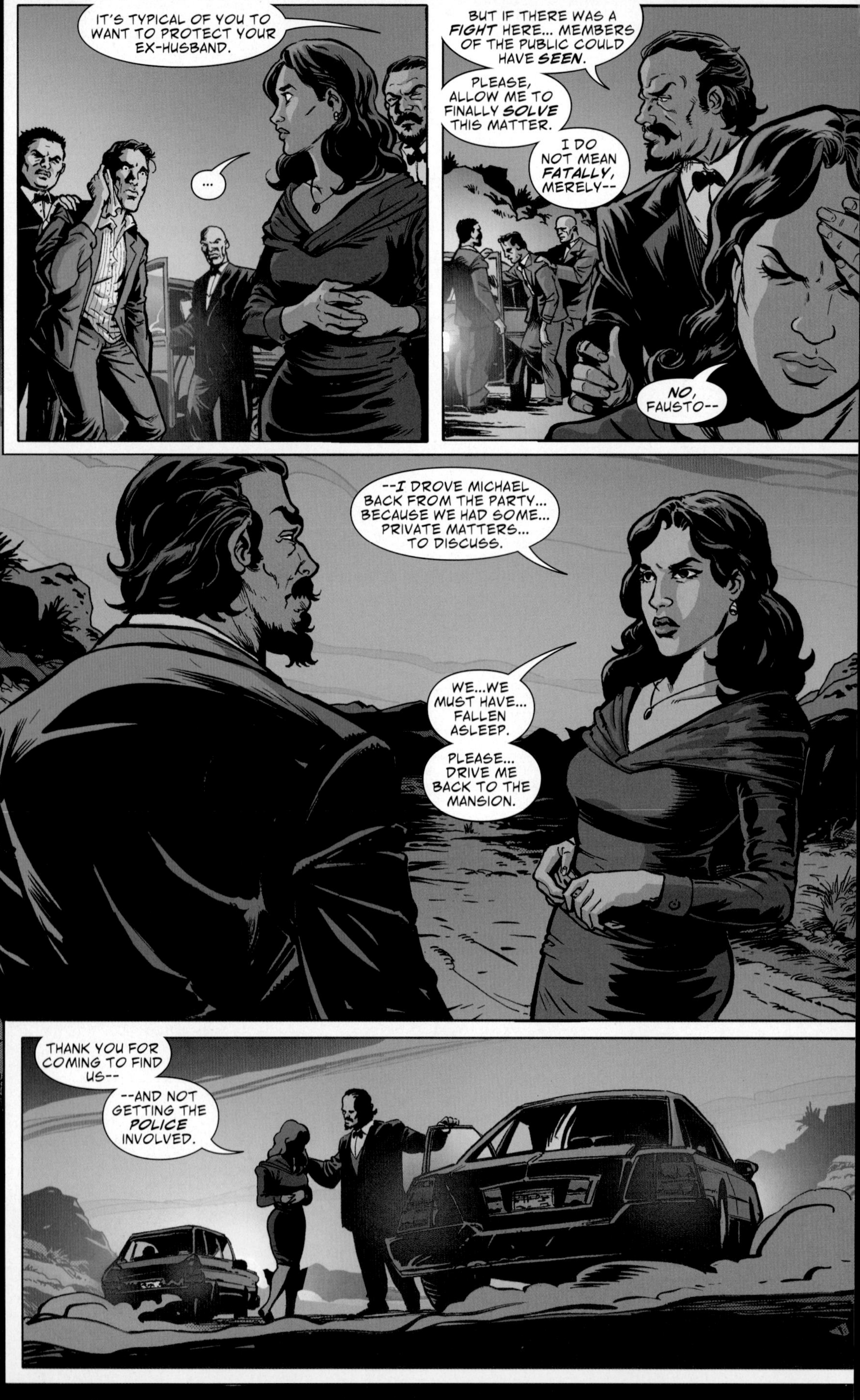
IT'S TYPICAL OF YOU TO WANT TO PROTECT YOUR EX-HUSBAND.
...
BUT IF THERE WAS A FIGHT HERE... MEMBERS OF THE PUBLIC COULD HAVE SEEN.
PLEASE, ALLOW ME TO FINALLY SOLVE THIS MATTER.
I DO NOT MEAN FATALLY, MERELY--
NO, FAUSTO--
--I DROVE MICHAEL BACK FROM THE PARTY... BECAUSE WE HAD SOME... PRIVATE MATTERS... TO DISCUSS.
WE...WE MUST HAVE... FALLEN ASLEEP.
PLEASE... DRIVE ME BACK TO THE MANSION.
THANK YOU FOR COMING TO FIND US--
--AND NOT GETTING THE POLICE INVOLVED.

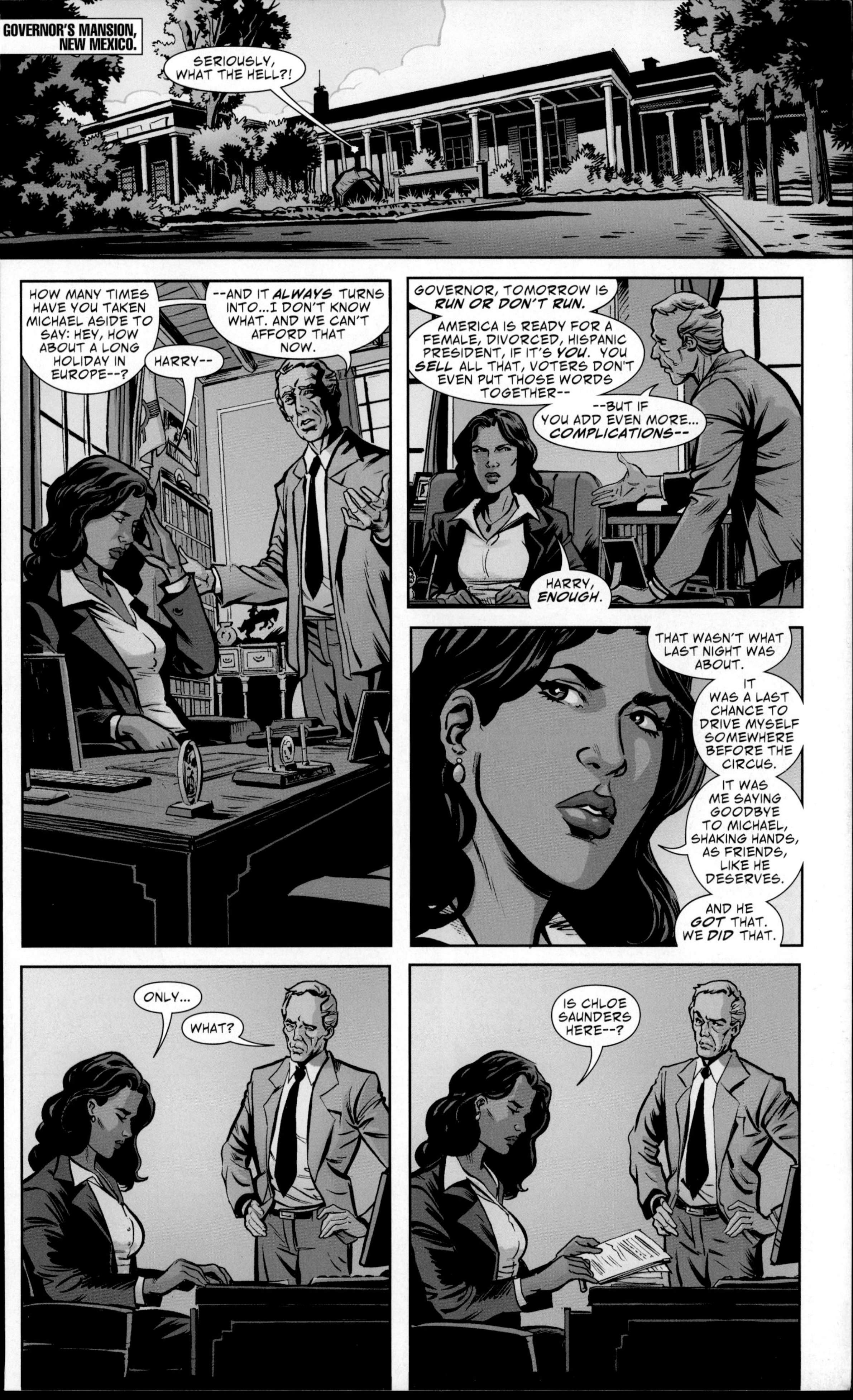
GOVERNOR'S MANSION, NEW MEXICO.
SERIOUSLY, WHAT THE HELL?!
HOW MANY TIMES HAVE YOU TAKEN MICHAEL ASIDE TO SAY: HEY, HOW ABOUT A LONG HOLIDAY IN EUROPE--?
HARRY--
--AND IT ALWAYS TURNS INTO...I DON'T KNOW WHAT. AND WE CAN'T AFFORD THAT NOW.
GOVERNOR, TOMORROW IS RUN OR DON'T RUN.
AMERICA IS READY FOR A FEMALE, DIVORCED, HISPANIC PRESIDENT, IF IT'S YOU. YOU SELL ALL THAT, VOTERS DON'T EVEN PUT THOSE WORDS TOGETHER--
--BUT IF YOU ADD EVEN MORE... COMPLICATIONS--
HARRY, ENOUGH.
THAT WASN'T WHAT LAST NIGHT WAS ABOUT.
IT WAS A LAST CHANCE TO DRIVE MYSELF SOMEWHERE BEFORE THE CIRCUS.
IT WAS ME SAYING GOODBYE TO MICHAEL, SHAKING HANDS, AS FRIENDS, LIKE HE DESERVES.
AND HE GOT THAT. WE DID THAT.
ONLY...
WHAT?
IS CHLOE SAUNDERS HERE--?

"--I FEEL LIKE A *WORKOUT*."

GOVERNOR ARCADIA ALVARADO... TO *PRESIDENT* ALVARADO.

IS IT POSSIBLE? YES. BUT ONLY RIGHT NOW, WHILE THE PARTY OF WHICH I AM A MEMBER IS COURTING NUTJOBS WHO POLL 15% WITH MIDDLE AMERICA.

BUT IT'S GOING TO TAKE SOME *HARD* CHOICES.

HERE'S THE TOP *ONE*.

MICHAEL *BEAT* YOU.

WHAT?! I'M NOT GOING TO--!

OH, I'M SORRY--

--I THOUGHT YOU WERE BRAVE ENOUGH TO CONSULT A *REPUBLICAN* STRATEGIST BECAUSE YOU WANTED TO HEAR THE *UNCOMFORTABLE* STUFF.

"BEAT YOU" IS SHORTHAND. YOU WOULD *NEVER* SAY, OR EVEN *IMPLY*, THOSE WORDS.

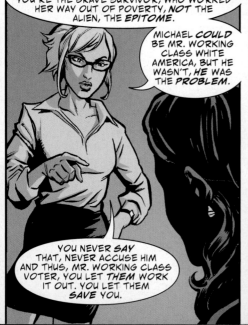

YOU'RE THE BRAVE SURVIVOR, WHO WORKED HER WAY OUT OF POVERTY, *NOT* THE ALIEN, THE *EPITOME*.

MICHAEL *COULD* BE MR. WORKING CLASS WHITE AMERICA, BUT HE WASN'T, *HE* WAS THE *PROBLEM*.

YOU NEVER *SAY* THAT, NEVER ACCUSE HIM AND THUS, MR. WORKING CLASS VOTER, YOU LET *THEM* WORK IT OUT. YOU LET THEM *SAVE* YOU.

AGREE TO THAT USEFUL SEXISM, AND I HAVE A WHOLE LIST OF SUGGESTIONS, EVERY ONE EQUALLY BARBAROUS.

WHAT DO YOU SAY, GOVERNOR?

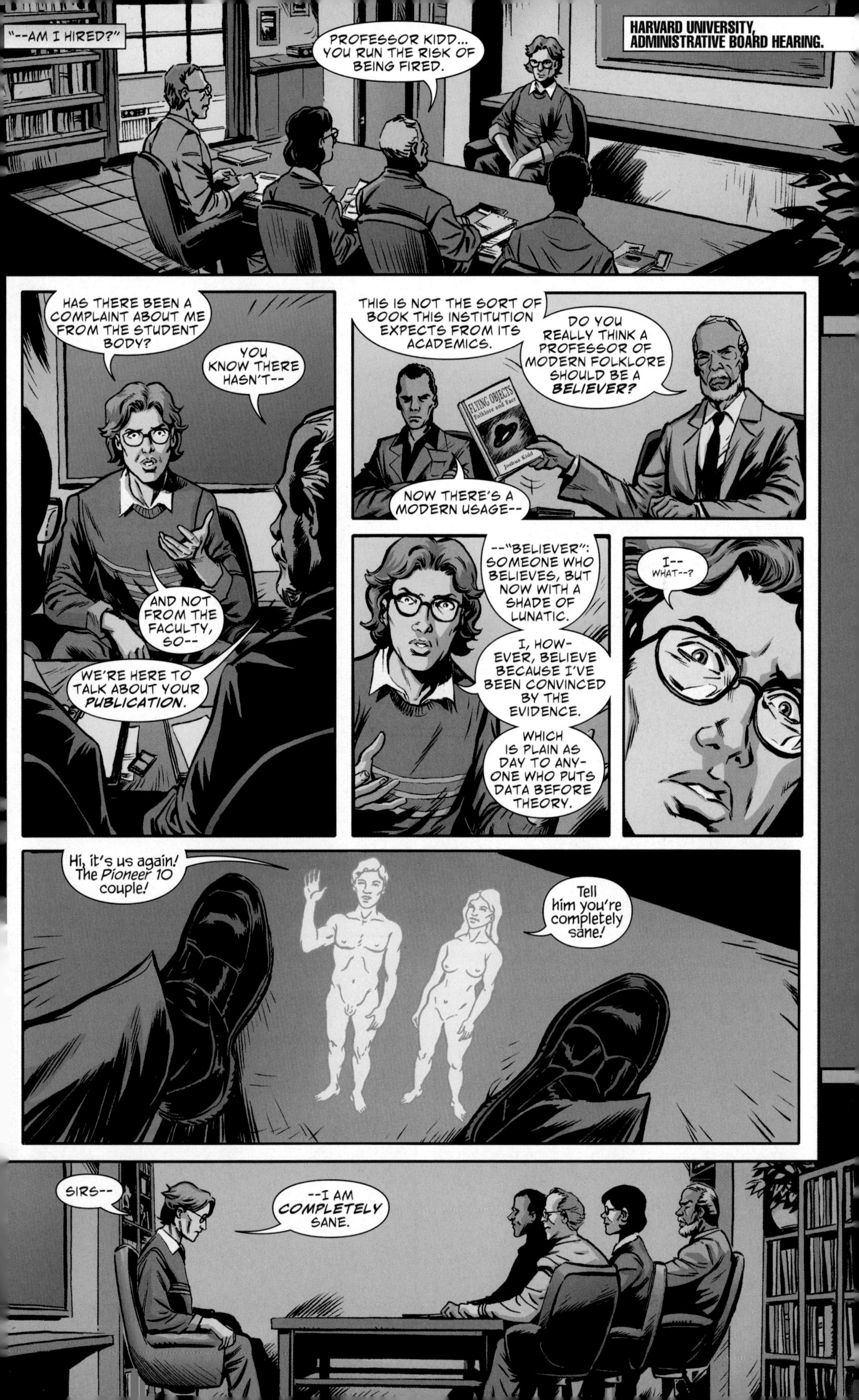
"--AM I HIRED?"
HARVARD UNIVERSITY, ADMINISTRATIVE BOARD HEARING.
PROFESSOR KIDD... YOU RUN THE RISK OF BEING FIRED.
HAS THERE BEEN A COMPLAINT ABOUT ME FROM THE STUDENT BODY?
YOU KNOW THERE HASN'T--
AND NOT FROM THE FACULTY, SO--
WE'RE HERE TO TALK ABOUT YOUR PUBLICATION.
THIS IS NOT THE SORT OF BOOK THIS INSTITUTION EXPECTS FROM ITS ACADEMICS.
DO YOU REALLY THINK A PROFESSOR OF MODERN FOLKLORE SHOULD BE A BELIEVER?
FLYING OBJECTS
Folklore and Fact
Joshua Kidd
NOW THERE'S A MODERN USAGE--
--"BELIEVER": SOMEONE WHO BELIEVES, BUT NOW WITH A SHADE OF LUNATIC.
I, HOWEVER, BELIEVE BECAUSE I'VE BEEN CONVINCED BY THE EVIDENCE.
WHICH IS PLAIN AS DAY TO ANYONE WHO PUTS DATA BEFORE THEORY.
I-- WHAT--?
Hi, it's us again! The Pioneer 10 couple!
Tell him you're completely sane!
SIRS--
--I AM COMPLETELY SANE.

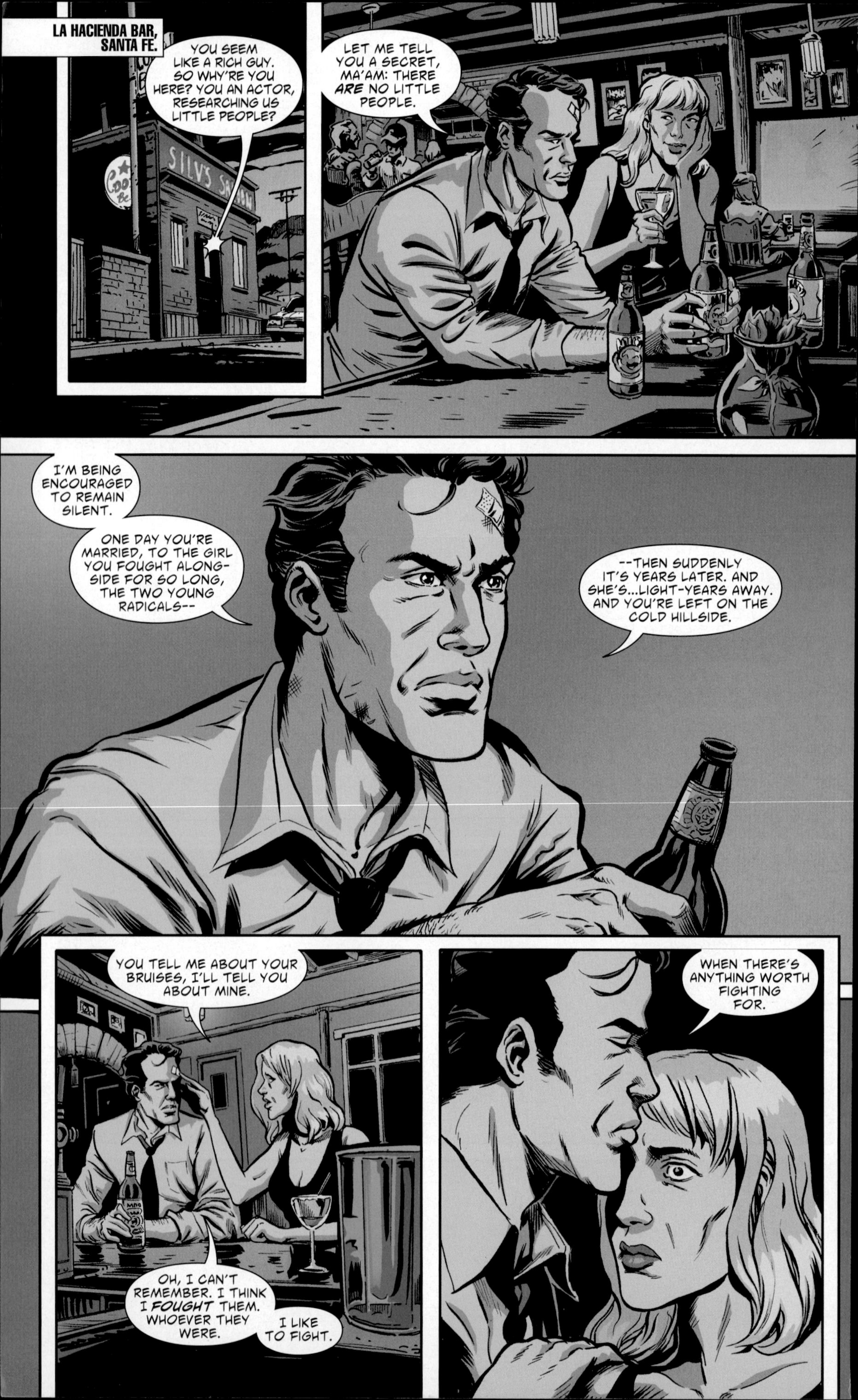
LA HACIENDA BAR, SANTA FE.
YOU SEEM LIKE A RICH GUY. SO WHY'RE YOU HERE? YOU AN ACTOR, RESEARCHING US LITTLE PEOPLE?
LET ME TELL YOU A SECRET, MA'AM: THERE *ARE* NO LITTLE PEOPLE.
I'M BEING ENCOURAGED TO REMAIN SILENT.
ONE DAY YOU'RE MARRIED, TO THE GIRL YOU FOUGHT ALONG-SIDE FOR SO LONG, THE TWO YOUNG RADICALS--
--THEN SUDDENLY IT'S YEARS LATER. AND SHE'S...LIGHT-YEARS AWAY. AND YOU'RE LEFT ON THE COLD HILLSIDE.
YOU TELL ME ABOUT YOUR BRUISES, I'LL TELL YOU ABOUT MINE.
OH, I CAN'T REMEMBER. I THINK I *FOUGHT* THEM. WHOEVER THEY WERE.
I LIKE TO FIGHT.
WHEN THERE'S ANYTHING WORTH FIGHTING FOR.

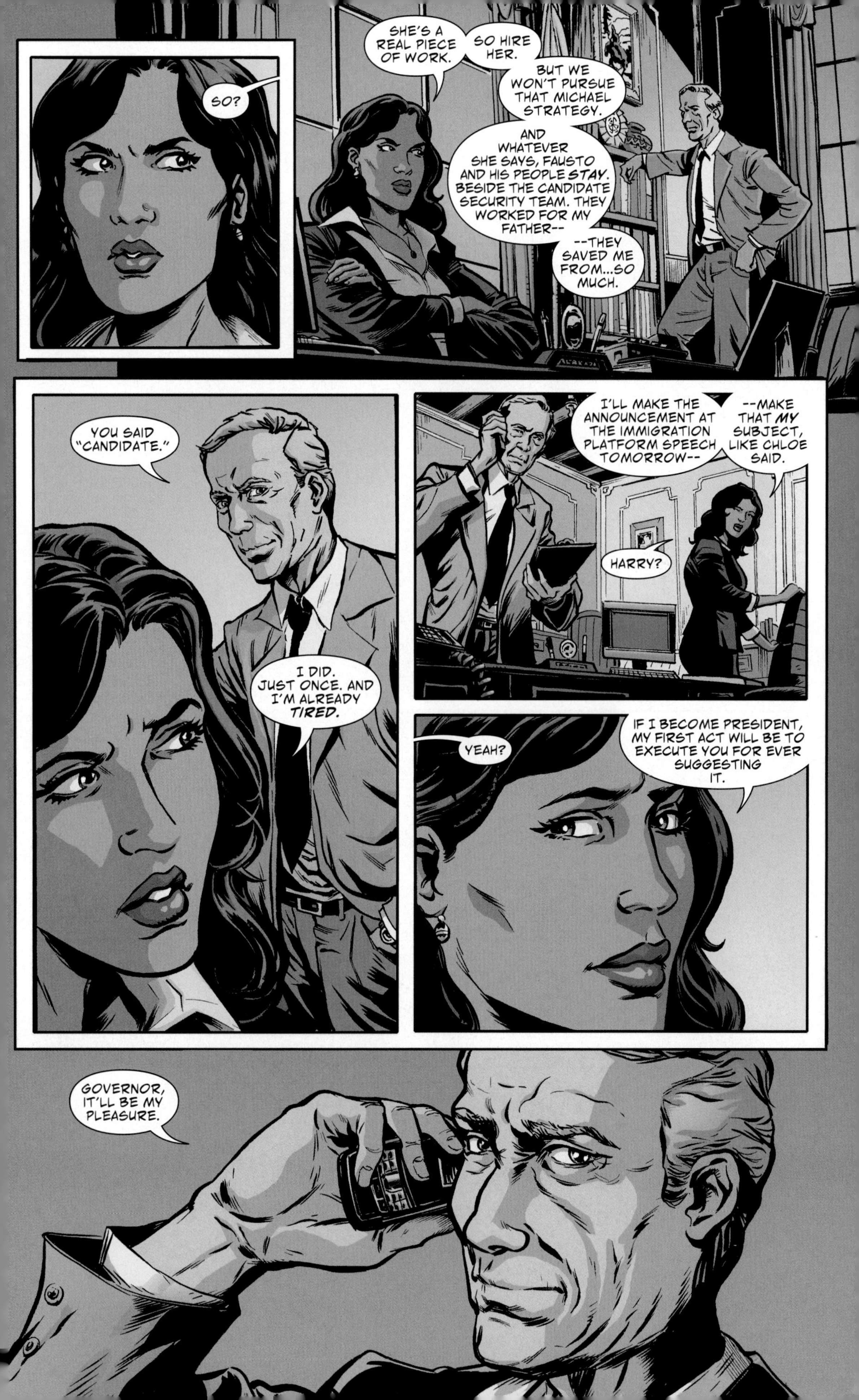
SO?
SHE'S A REAL PIECE OF WORK.
SO HIRE HER.
BUT WE WON'T PURSUE THAT MICHAEL STRATEGY.
AND WHATEVER SHE SAYS, FAUSTO AND HIS PEOPLE STAY. BESIDE THE CANDIDATE SECURITY TEAM. THEY WORKED FOR MY FATHER--
--THEY SAVED ME FROM...SO MUCH.
YOU SAID "CANDIDATE."
I DID. JUST ONCE. AND I'M ALREADY TIRED.
I'LL MAKE THE ANNOUNCEMENT AT THE IMMIGRATION PLATFORM SPEECH TOMORROW--
--MAKE THAT MY SUBJECT, LIKE CHLOE SAID.
HARRY?
YEAH?
IF I BECOME PRESIDENT, MY FIRST ACT WILL BE TO EXECUTE YOU FOR EVER SUGGESTING IT.
GOVERNOR, IT'LL BE MY PLEASURE.

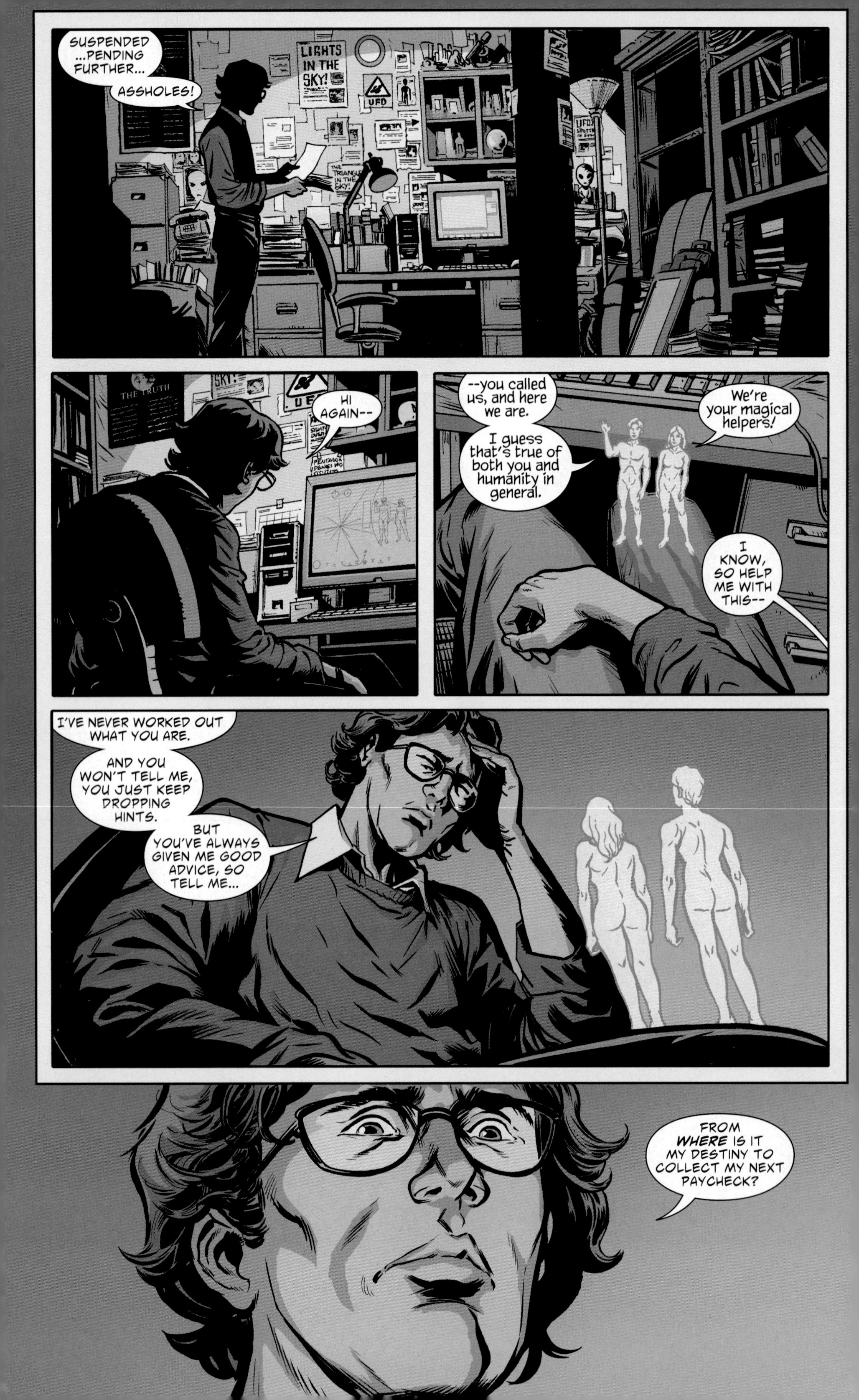
SUSPENDED ...PENDING FURTHER...
ASSHOLES!
LIGHTS IN THE SKY!
UFO
THE TRIANGLE IN THE SKY!
THE TRUTH
HI AGAIN--
--you called us, and here we are.
I guess that's true of both you and humanity in general.
We're your magical helpers!
I KNOW, SO HELP ME WITH THIS--
I'VE NEVER WORKED OUT WHAT YOU ARE.
AND YOU WON'T TELL ME, YOU JUST KEEP DROPPING HINTS.
BUT YOU'VE ALWAYS GIVEN ME GOOD ADVICE, SO TELL ME...
FROM *WHERE* IS IT MY DESTINY TO COLLECT MY NEXT PAYCHECK?

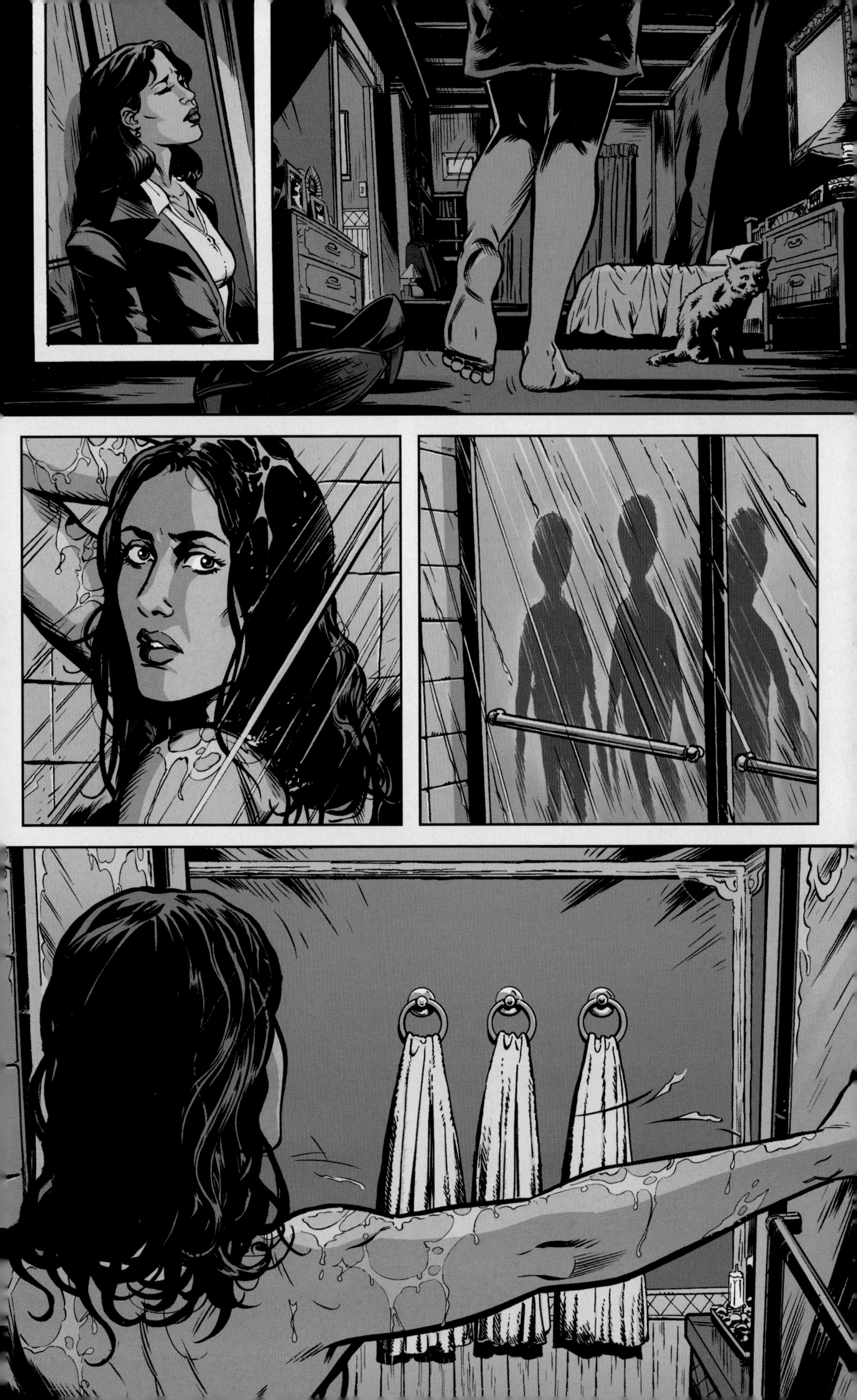

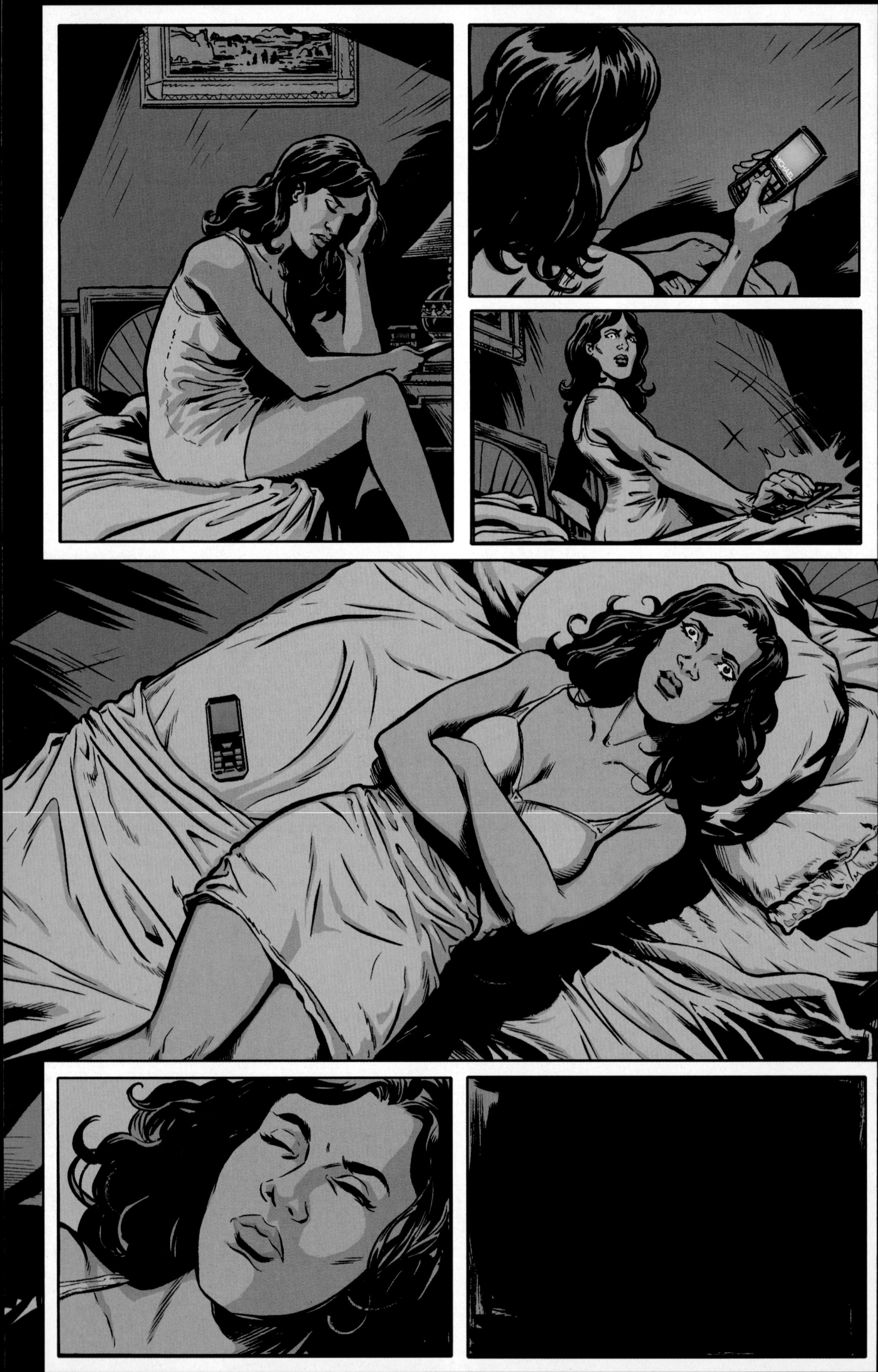
MICHAEL

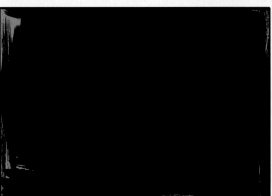

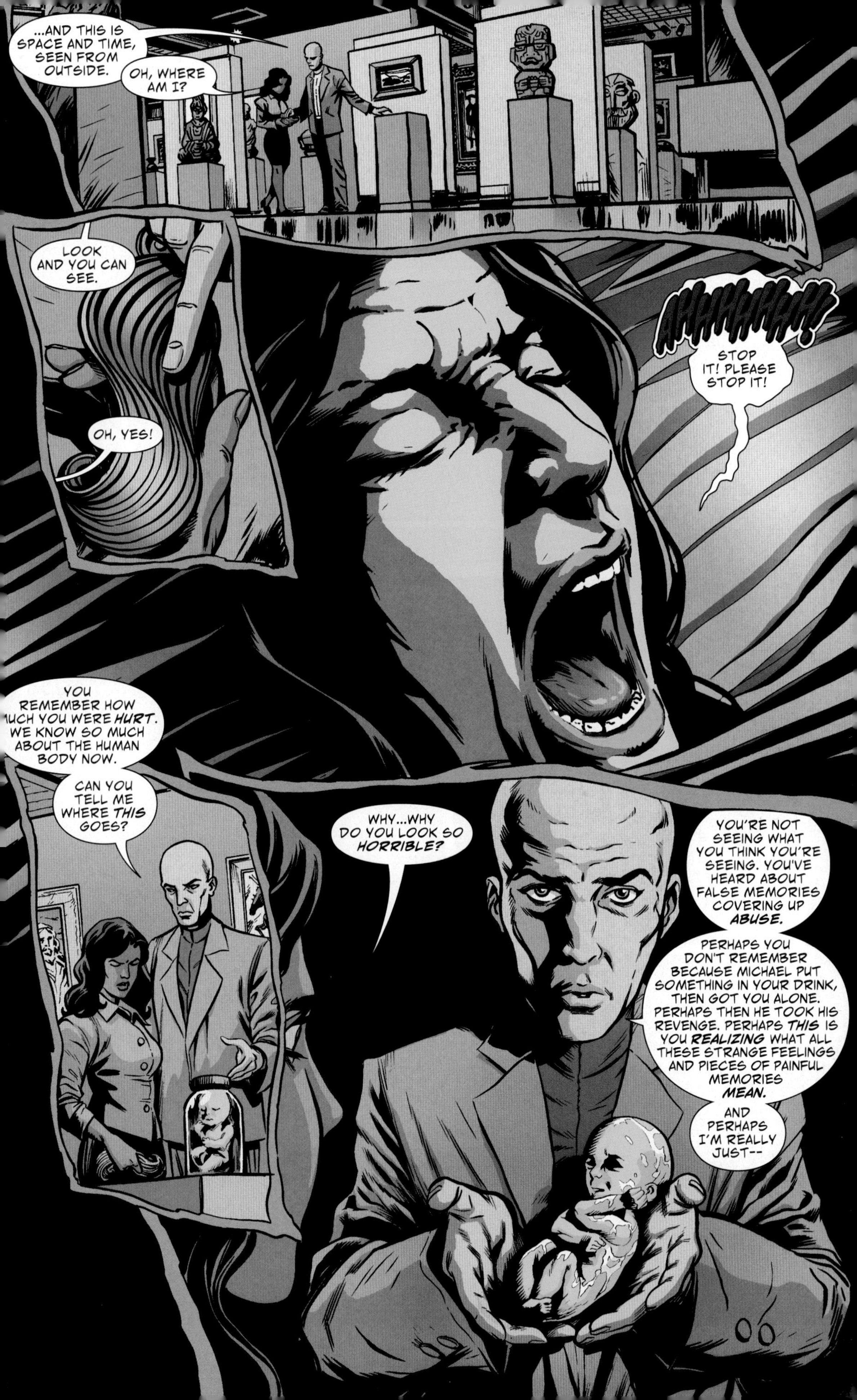
...AND THIS IS SPACE AND TIME, SEEN FROM OUTSIDE.
OH, WHERE AM I?
LOOK AND YOU CAN SEE.
OH, YES!
AHHHHHHHH!
STOP IT! PLEASE STOP IT!
YOU REMEMBER HOW MUCH YOU WERE *HURT*. WE KNOW SO MUCH ABOUT THE HUMAN BODY NOW.
CAN YOU TELL ME WHERE *THIS* GOES?
WHY...WHY DO YOU LOOK SO *HORRIBLE?*
YOU'RE NOT SEEING WHAT YOU THINK YOU'RE SEEING. YOU'VE HEARD ABOUT FALSE MEMORIES COVERING UP *ABUSE.*
PERHAPS YOU DON'T REMEMBER BECAUSE MICHAEL PUT SOMETHING IN YOUR DRINK, THEN GOT YOU ALONE. PERHAPS THEN HE TOOK HIS REVENGE. PERHAPS *THIS* IS YOU *REALIZING* WHAT ALL THESE STRANGE FEELINGS AND PIECES OF PAINFUL MEMORIES *MEAN.*
AND PERHAPS I'M REALLY JUST--

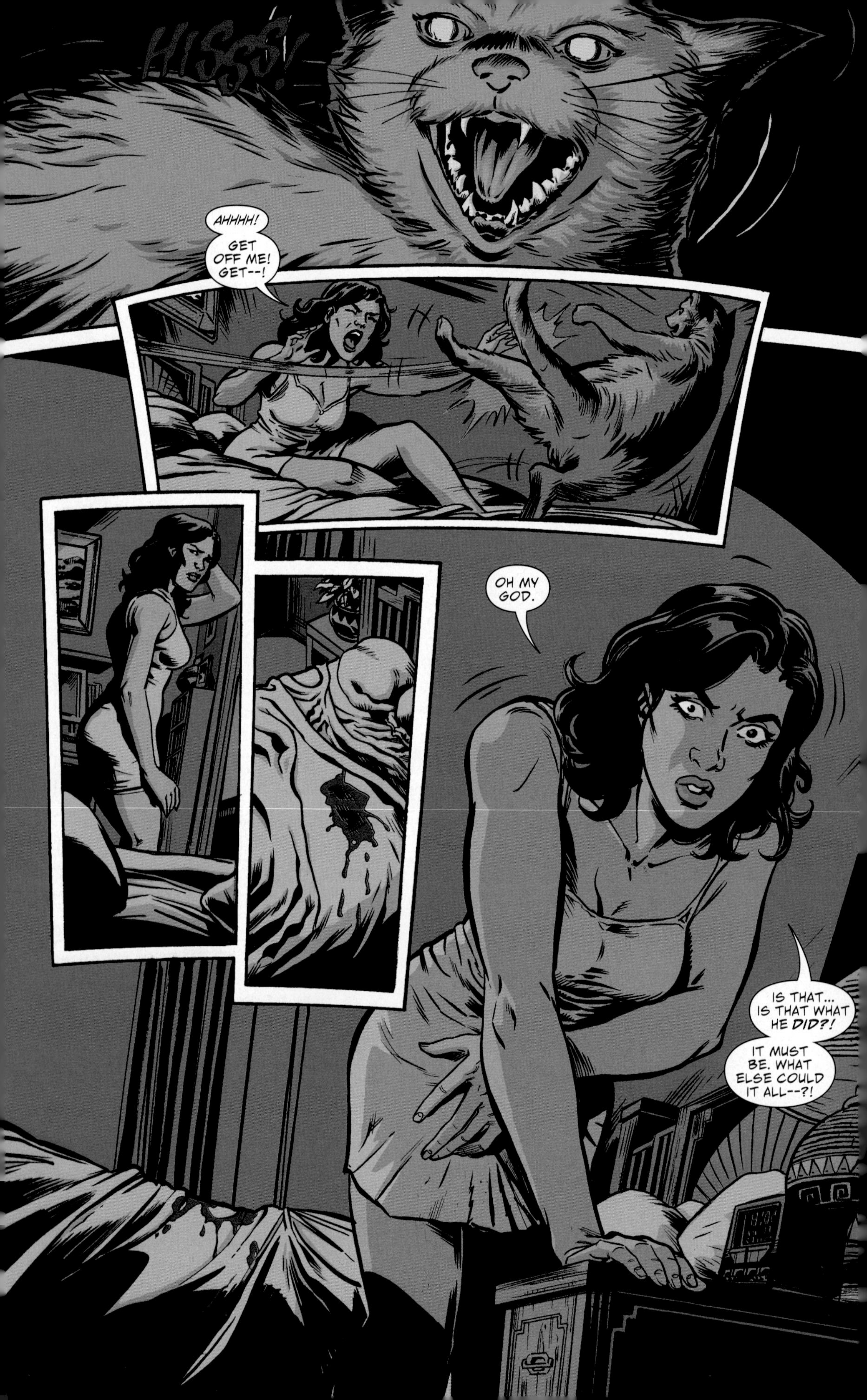
HISSS!
AHHHH!
GET OFF ME! GET--!
OH MY GOD.
IS THAT... IS THAT WHAT HE *DID?!*
IT MUST BE. WHAT ELSE COULD IT ALL--?!

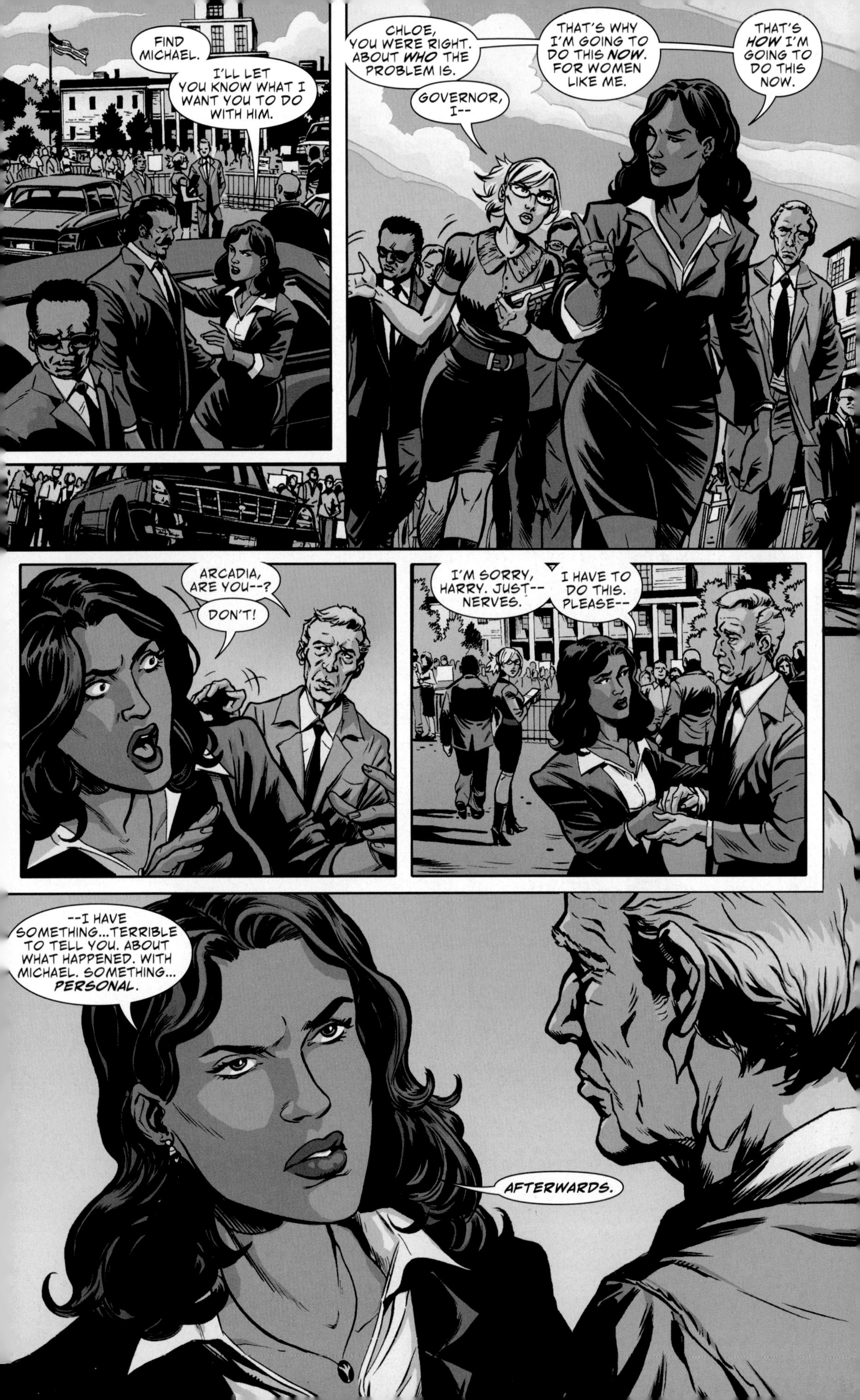
FIND MICHAEL.
I'LL LET YOU KNOW WHAT I WANT YOU TO DO WITH HIM.
CHLOE, YOU WERE RIGHT. ABOUT *WHO* THE PROBLEM IS.
GOVERNOR, I--
THAT'S WHY I'M GOING TO DO THIS *NOW*. FOR WOMEN LIKE ME.
THAT'S *HOW* I'M GOING TO DO THIS NOW.
ARCADIA, ARE YOU--?
DON'T!
I'M SORRY, HARRY. JUST-- NERVES.
I HAVE TO DO THIS. PLEASE--
--I HAVE SOMETHING...TERRIBLE TO TELL YOU. ABOUT WHAT HAPPENED. WITH MICHAEL. SOMETHING... *PERSONAL*.
AFTERWARDS.

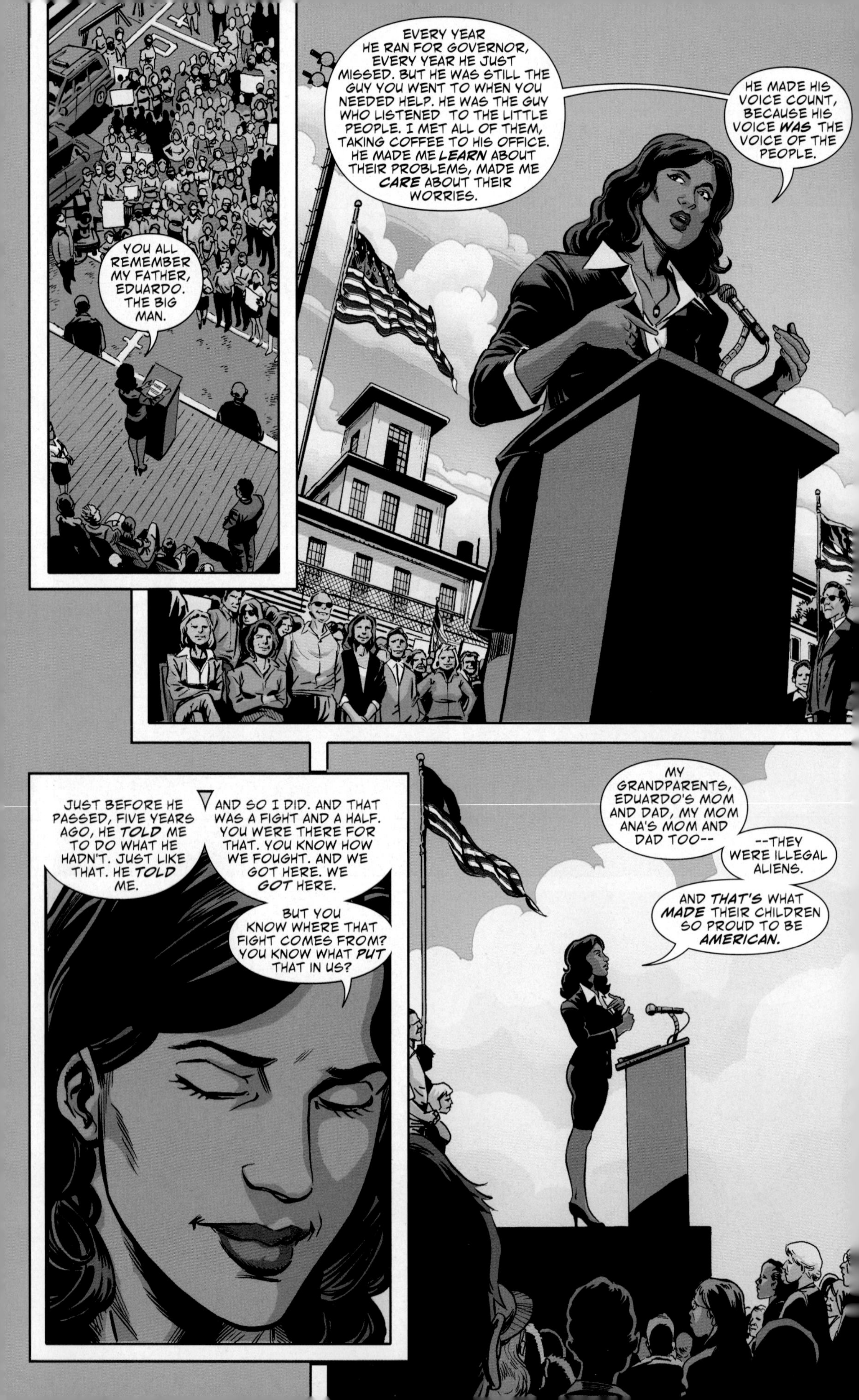
YOU ALL REMEMBER MY FATHER, EDUARDO. THE BIG MAN.
EVERY YEAR HE RAN FOR GOVERNOR, EVERY YEAR HE JUST MISSED. BUT HE WAS STILL THE GUY YOU WENT TO WHEN YOU NEEDED HELP. HE WAS THE GUY WHO LISTENED TO THE LITTLE PEOPLE. I MET ALL OF THEM, TAKING COFFEE TO HIS OFFICE. HE MADE ME LEARN ABOUT THEIR PROBLEMS, MADE ME CARE ABOUT THEIR WORRIES.
HE MADE HIS VOICE COUNT, BECAUSE HIS VOICE WAS THE VOICE OF THE PEOPLE.
JUST BEFORE HE PASSED, FIVE YEARS AGO, HE TOLD ME TO DO WHAT HE HADN'T. JUST LIKE THAT. HE TOLD ME.
AND SO I DID. AND THAT WAS A FIGHT AND A HALF. YOU WERE THERE FOR THAT. YOU KNOW HOW WE FOUGHT. AND WE GOT HERE. WE GOT HERE.
BUT YOU KNOW WHERE THAT FIGHT COMES FROM? YOU KNOW WHAT PUT THAT IN US?
MY GRANDPARENTS, EDUARDO'S MOM AND DAD, MY MOM ANA'S MOM AND DAD TOO--
--THEY WERE ILLEGAL ALIENS.
AND THAT'S WHAT MADE THEIR CHILDREN SO PROUD TO BE AMERICAN.

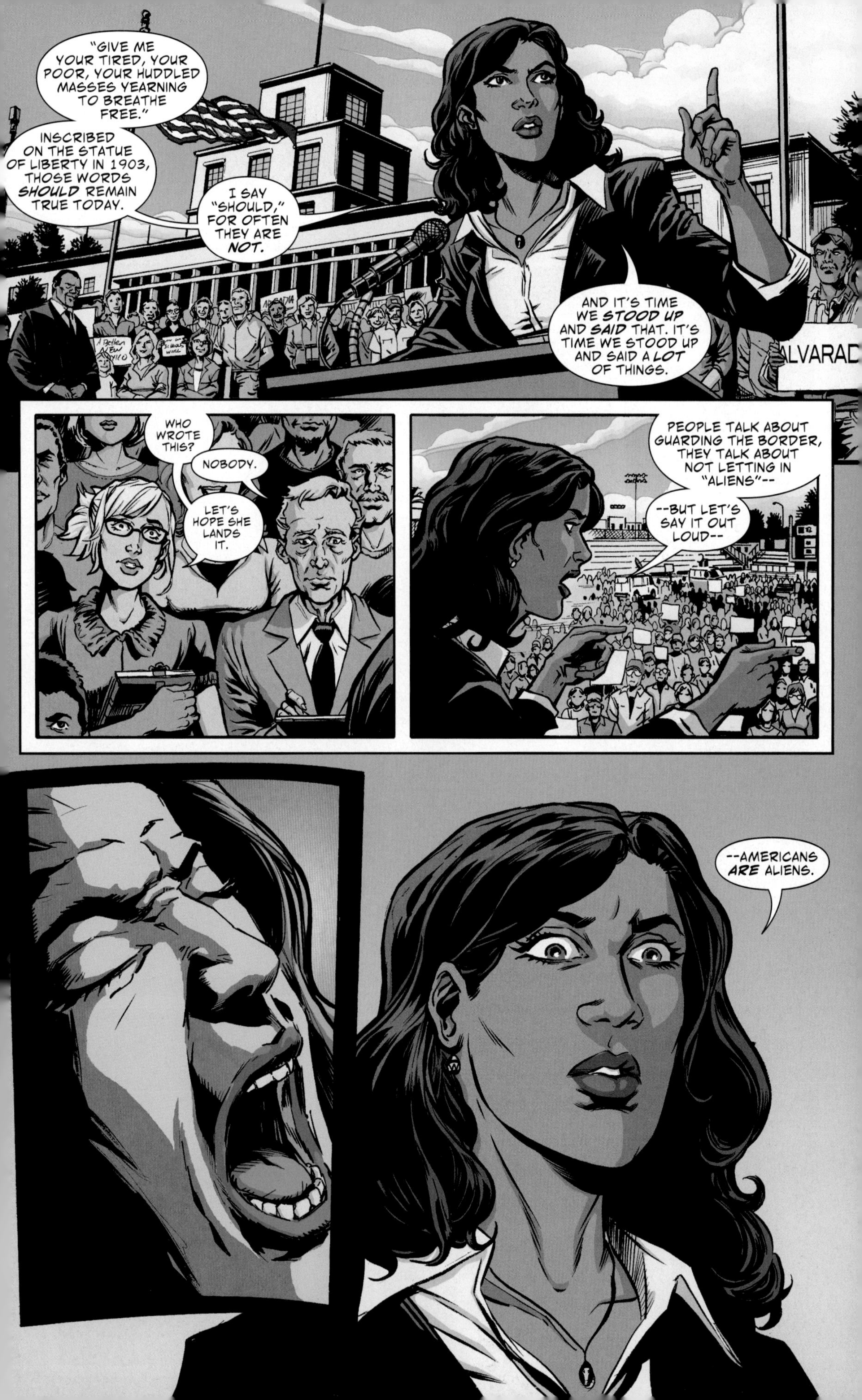
"GIVE ME YOUR TIRED, YOUR POOR, YOUR HUDDLED MASSES YEARNING TO BREATHE FREE."
INSCRIBED ON THE STATUE OF LIBERTY IN 1903, THOSE WORDS SHOULD REMAIN TRUE TODAY.
I SAY "SHOULD," FOR OFTEN THEY ARE NOT.
AND IT'S TIME WE STOOD UP AND SAID THAT. IT'S TIME WE STOOD UP AND SAID A LOT OF THINGS.
ALVARAD
WHO WROTE THIS?
NOBODY.
LET'S HOPE SHE LANDS IT.
PEOPLE TALK ABOUT GUARDING THE BORDER, THEY TALK ABOUT NOT LETTING IN "ALIENS"--
--BUT LET'S SAY IT OUT LOUD--
--AMERICANS ARE ALIENS.

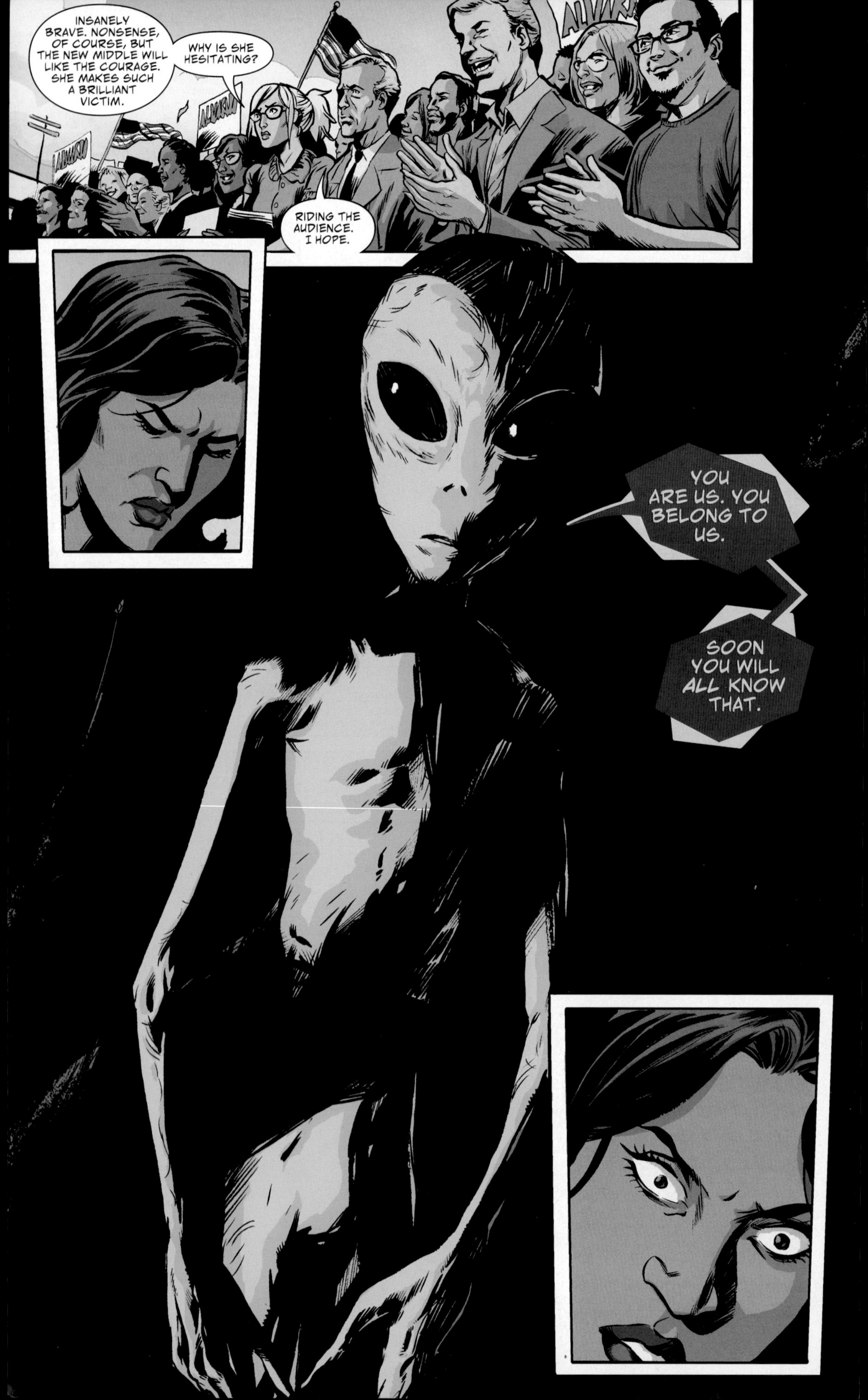
INSANELY BRAVE. NONSENSE, OF COURSE, BUT THE NEW MIDDLE WILL LIKE THE COURAGE. SHE MAKES SUCH A BRILLIANT VICTIM.
WHY IS SHE HESITATING?
RIDING THE AUDIENCE. I HOPE.
YOU ARE US. YOU BELONG TO US.
SOON YOU WILL ALL KNOW THAT.

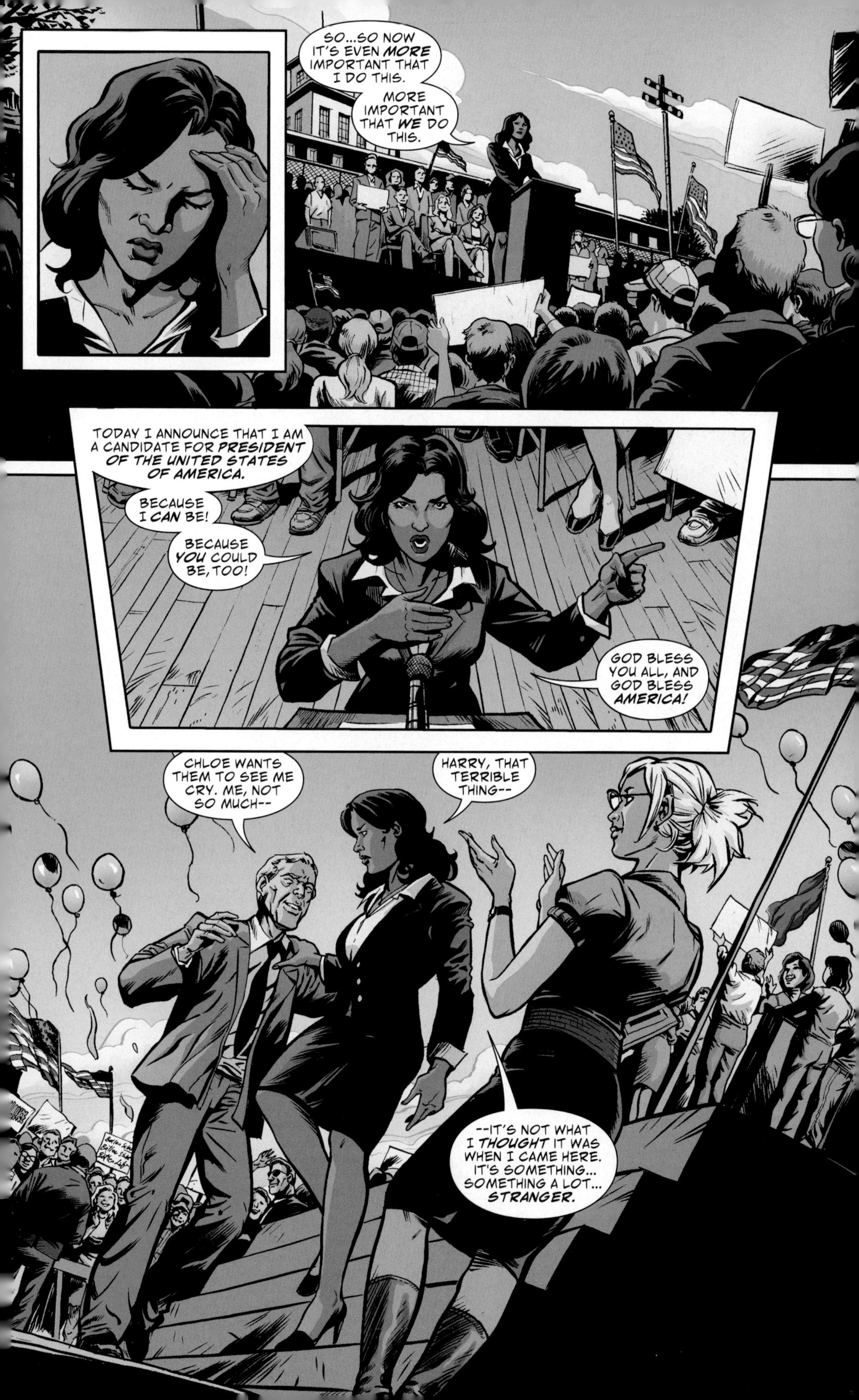
SO...SO NOW IT'S EVEN MORE IMPORTANT THAT I DO THIS.
MORE IMPORTANT THAT WE DO THIS.
TODAY I ANNOUNCE THAT I AM A CANDIDATE FOR PRESIDENT OF THE UNITED STATES OF AMERICA.
BECAUSE I CAN BE!
BECAUSE YOU COULD BE, TOO!
GOD BLESS YOU ALL, AND GOD BLESS AMERICA!
CHLOE WANTS THEM TO SEE ME CRY. ME, NOT SO MUCH--
HARRY, THAT TERRIBLE THING--
--IT'S NOT WHAT I THOUGHT IT WAS WHEN I CAME HERE. IT'S SOMETHING... SOMETHING A LOT... STRANGER.

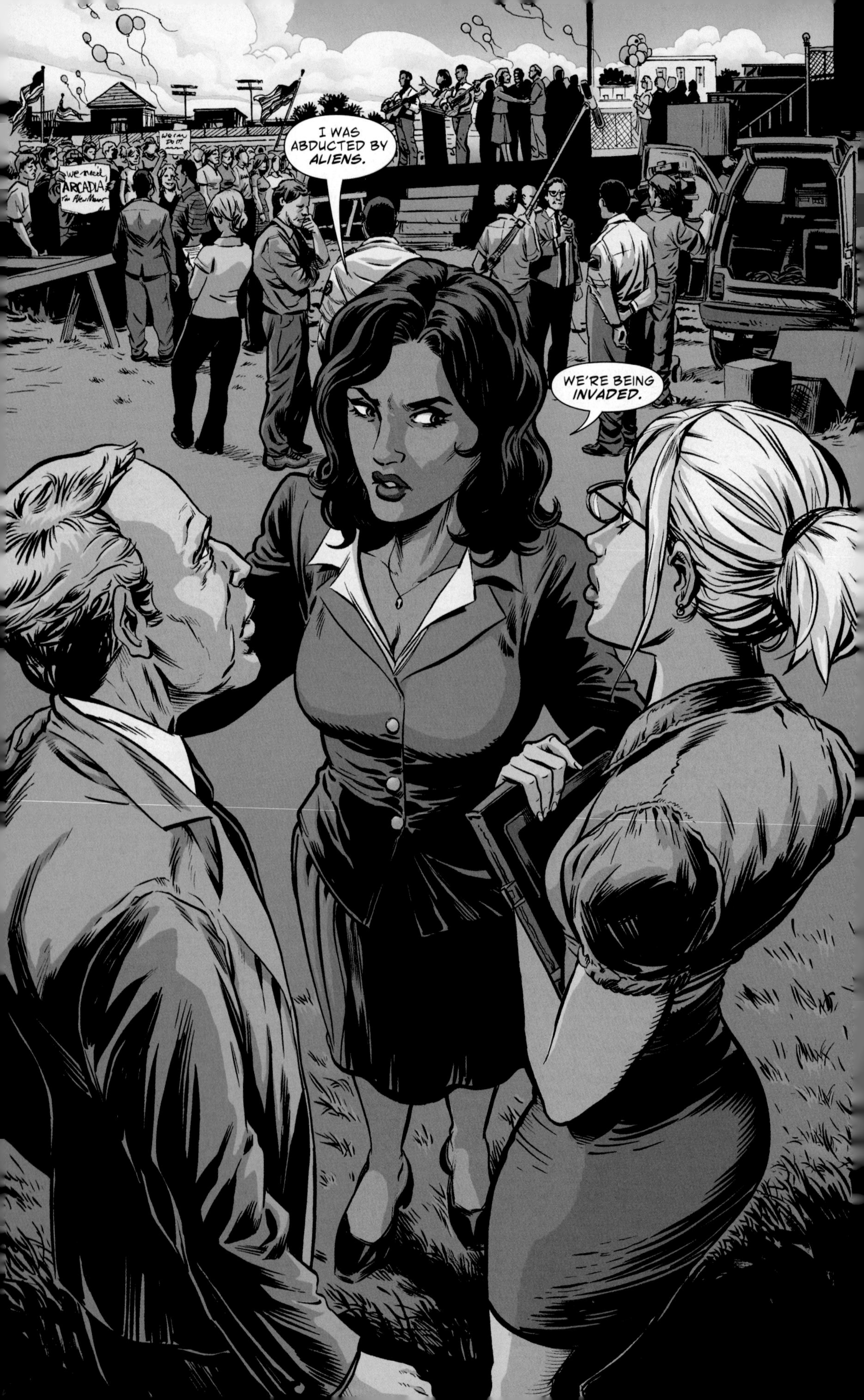
We need ARCADIA
We can DO IT!
I WAS ABDUCTED BY ALIENS.
WE'RE BEING INVADED.

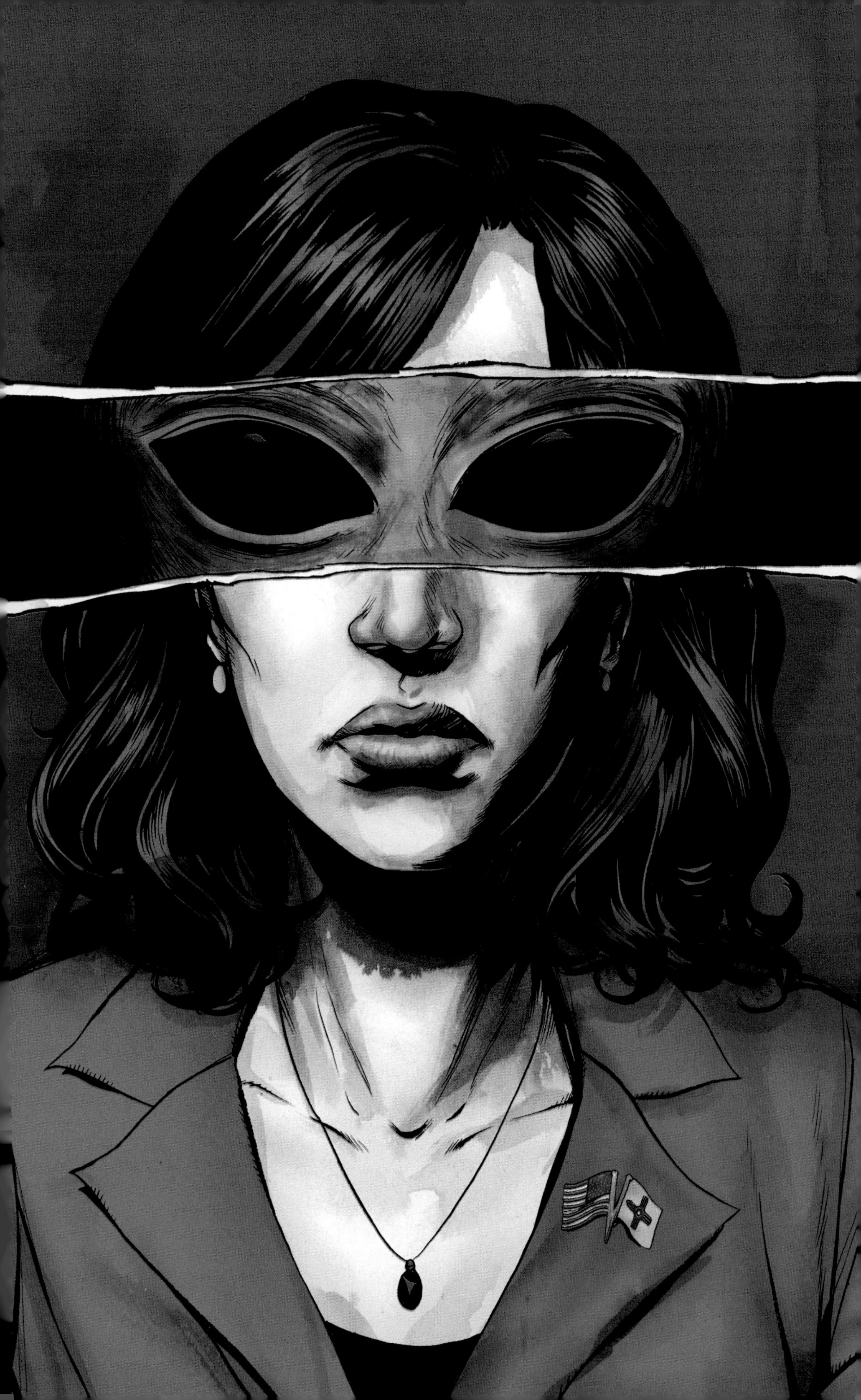

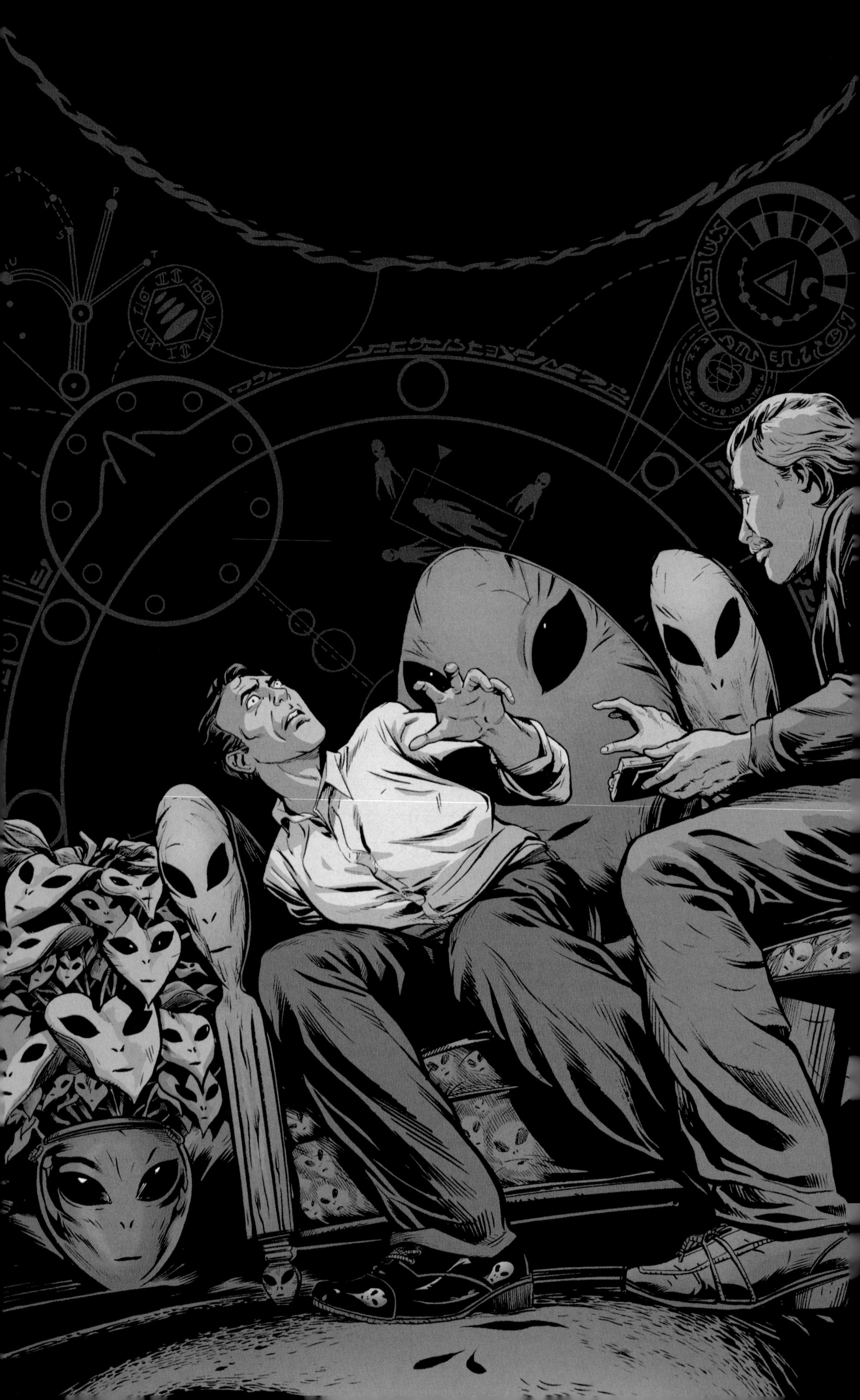

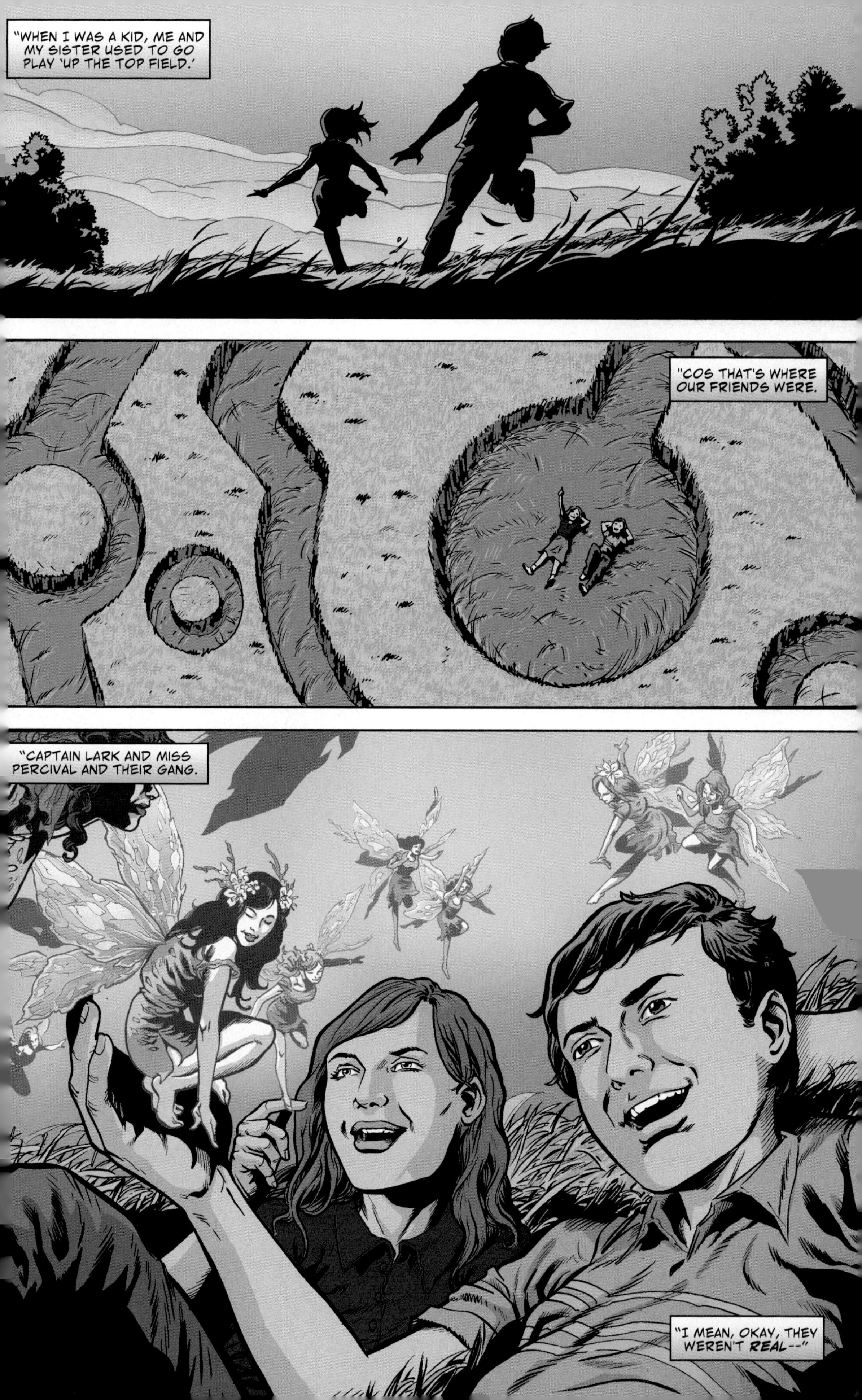
"WHEN I WAS A KID, ME AND MY SISTER USED TO GO PLAY 'UP THE TOP FIELD.'
"COS THAT'S WHERE OUR FRIENDS WERE.
"CAPTAIN LARK AND MISS PERCIVAL AND THEIR GANG.
"I MEAN, OKAY, THEY WEREN'T *REAL*--"

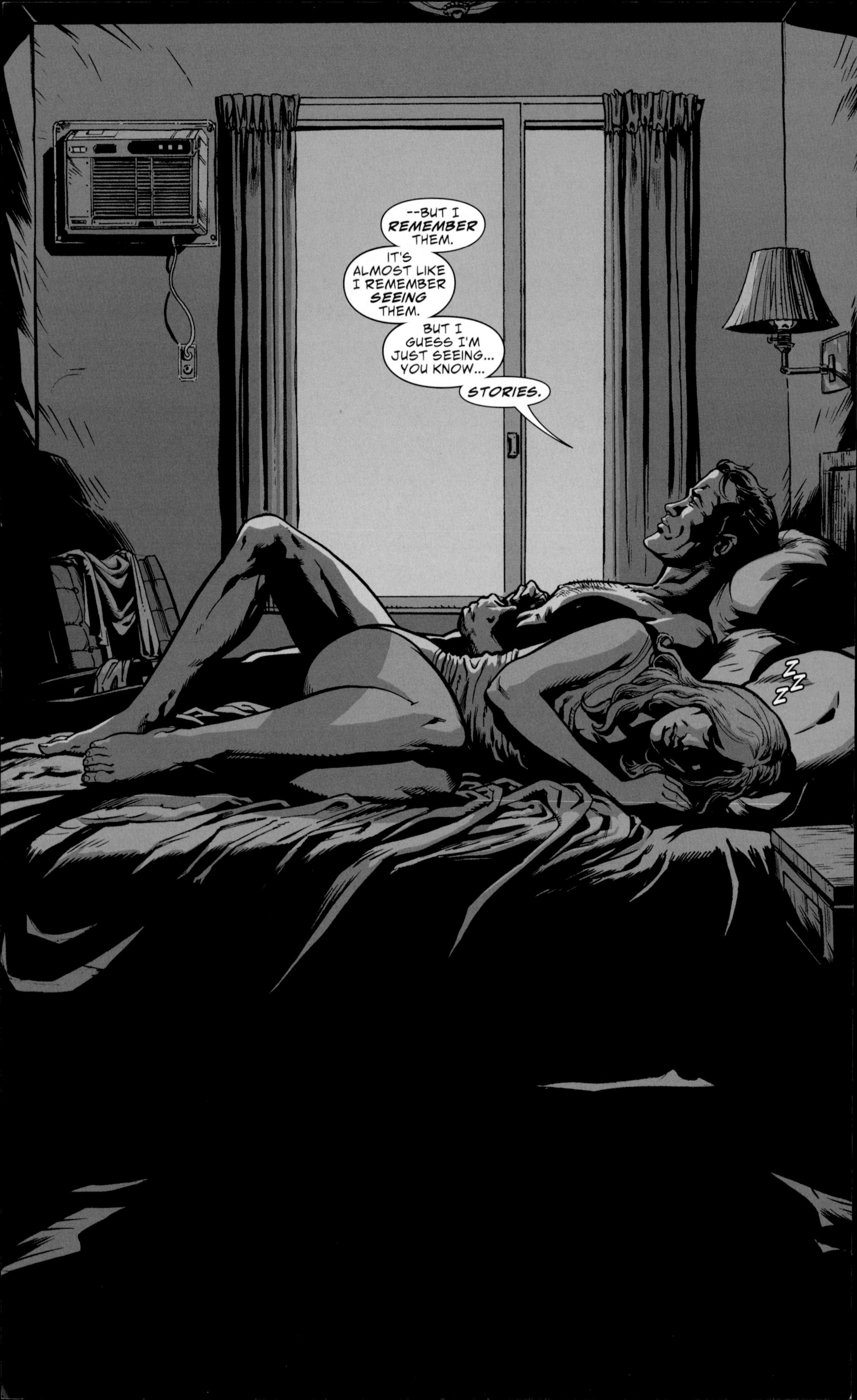
--BUT I REMEMBER THEM.
IT'S ALMOST LIKE I REMEMBER SEEING THEM.
BUT I GUESS I'M JUST SEEING... YOU KNOW...
STORIES.
Z Z Z

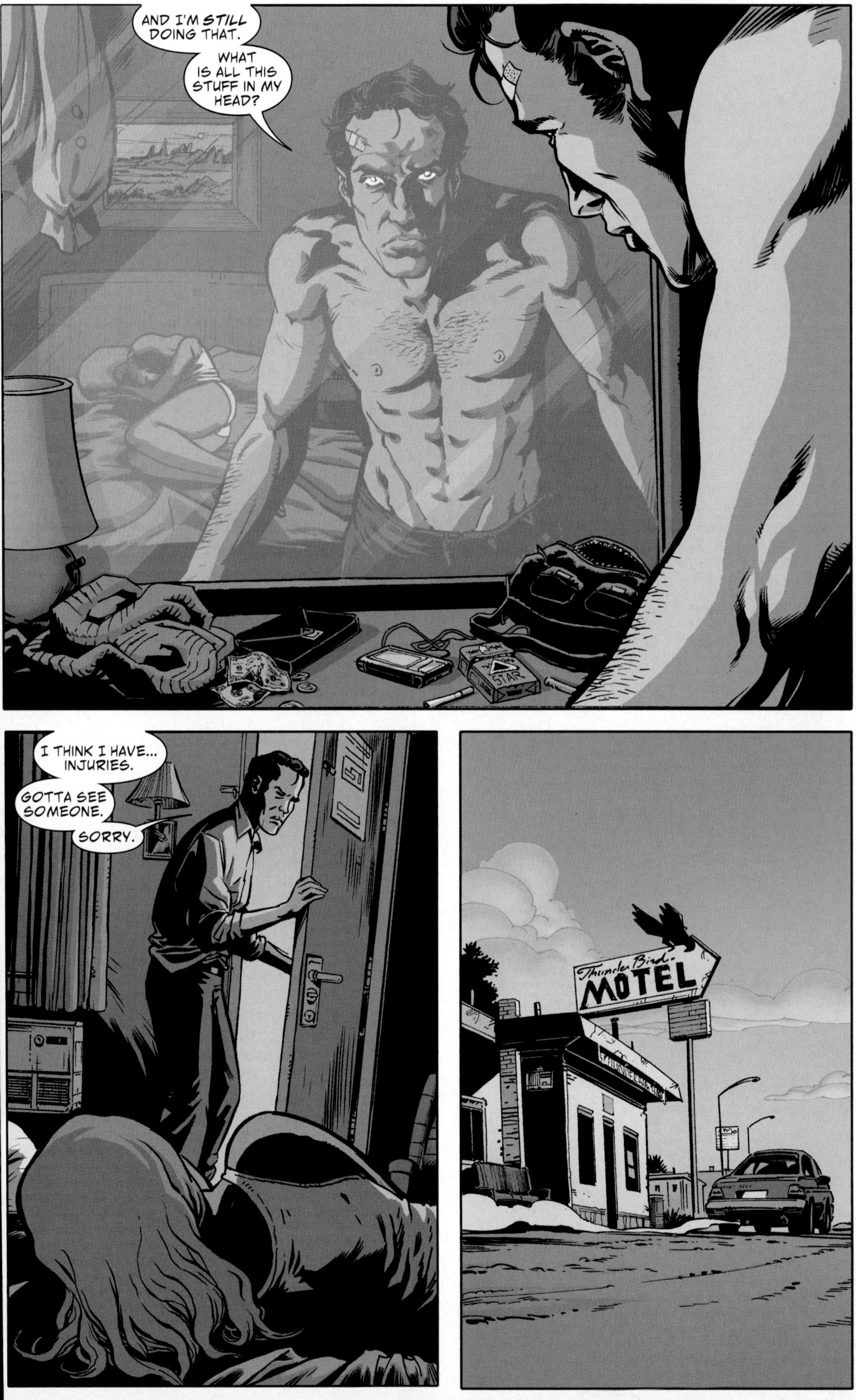
AND I'M *STILL* DOING THAT.
WHAT IS ALL THIS STUFF IN MY HEAD?
I THINK I HAVE... INJURIES.
GOTTA SEE SOMEONE.
SORRY.
Thunder Bird MOTEL

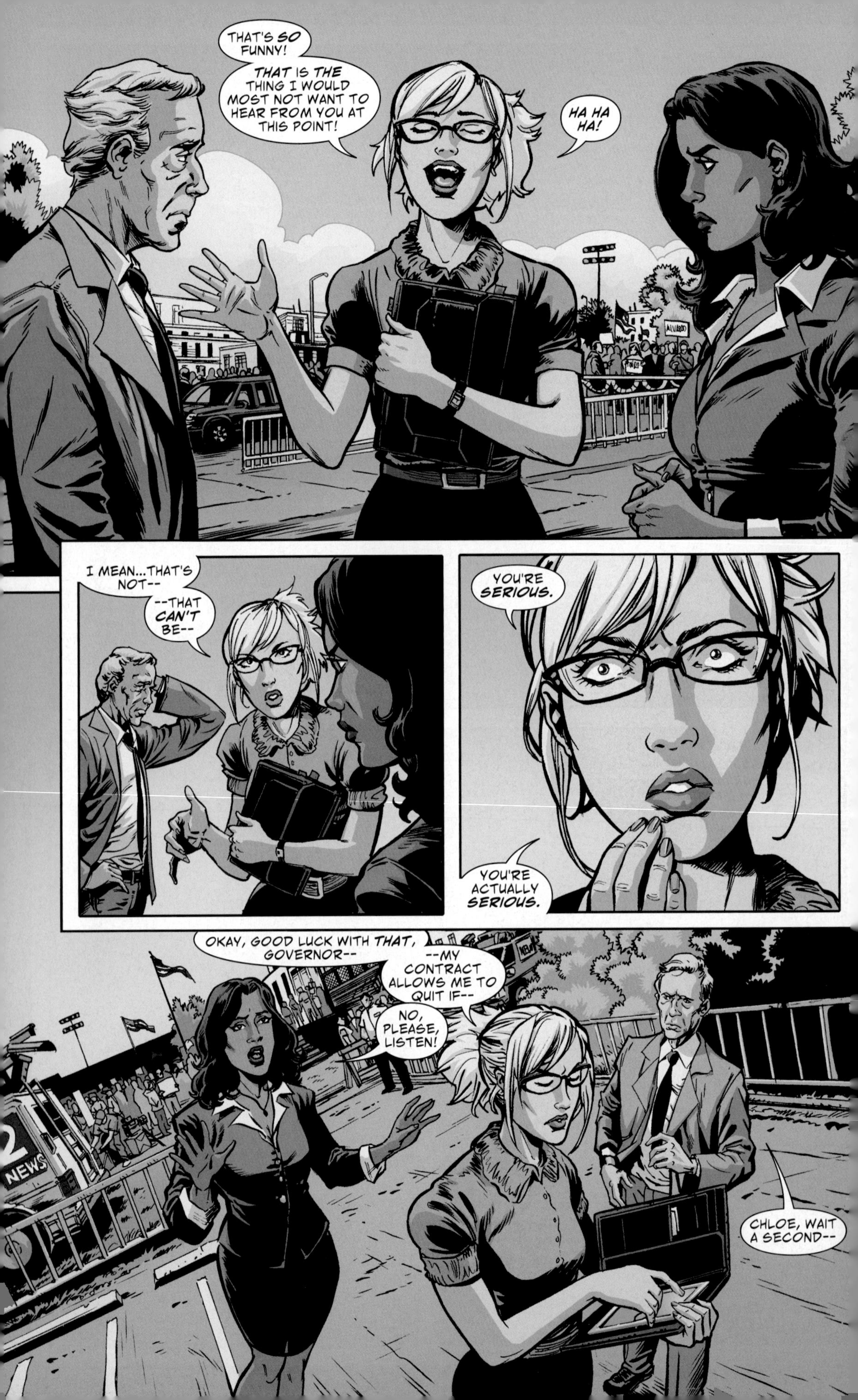

THAT'S SO FUNNY!
THAT IS THE THING I WOULD MOST NOT WANT TO HEAR FROM YOU AT THIS POINT!
HA HA HA!
I MEAN...THAT'S NOT--
--THAT CAN'T BE--
YOU'RE SERIOUS.
YOU'RE ACTUALLY SERIOUS.
OKAY, GOOD LUCK WITH THAT, GOVERNOR--
--MY CONTRACT ALLOWS ME TO QUIT IF--
NO, PLEASE, LISTEN!
CHLOE, WAIT A SECOND--
2 NEWS

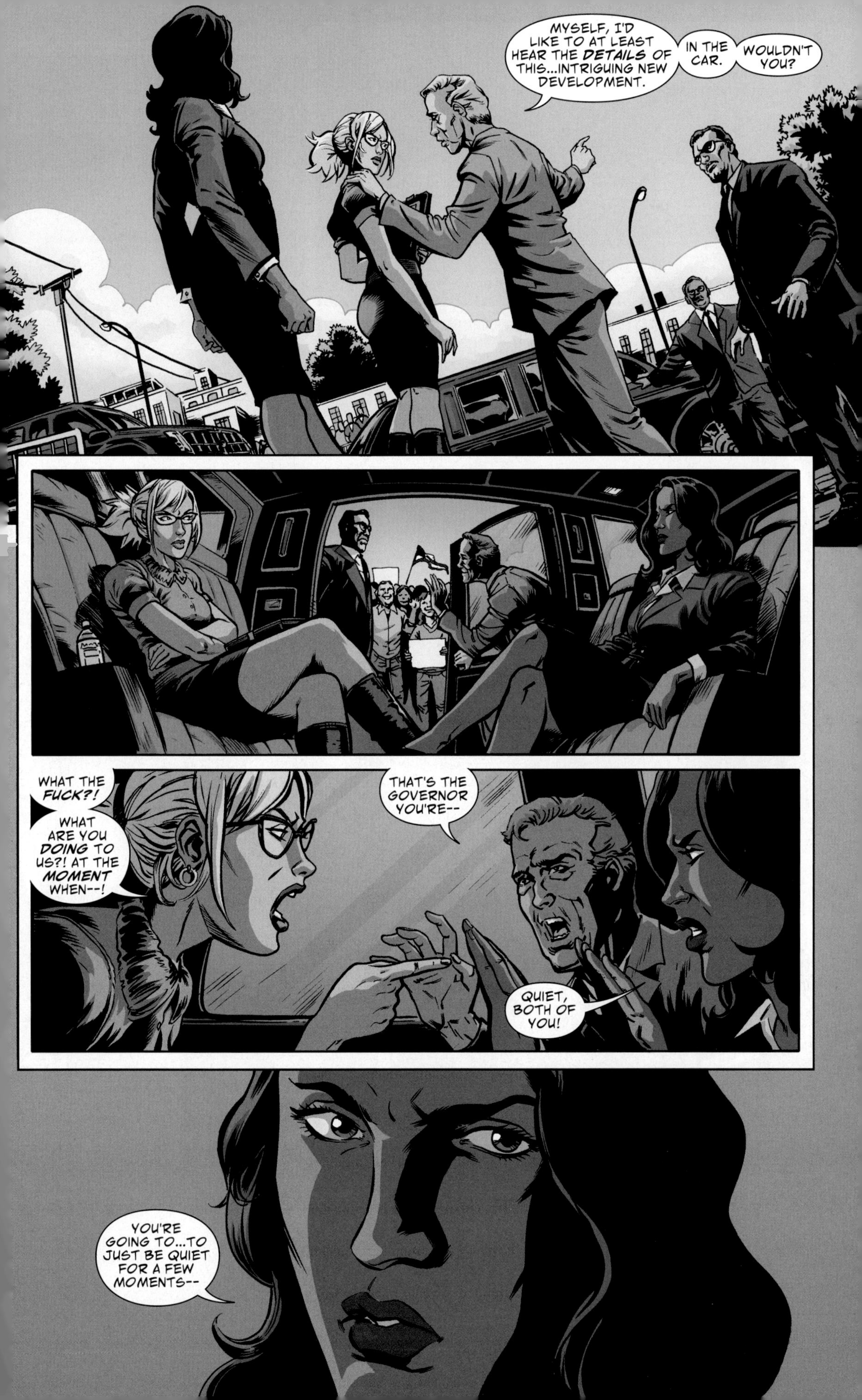
MYSELF, I'D LIKE TO AT LEAST HEAR THE DETAILS OF THIS...INTRIGUING NEW DEVELOPMENT.
IN THE CAR.
WOULDN'T YOU?
WHAT THE FUCK?!
WHAT ARE YOU DOING TO US?! AT THE MOMENT WHEN--!
THAT'S THE GOVERNOR YOU'RE--
QUIET, BOTH OF YOU!
YOU'RE GOING TO...TO JUST BE QUIET FOR A FEW MOMENTS--

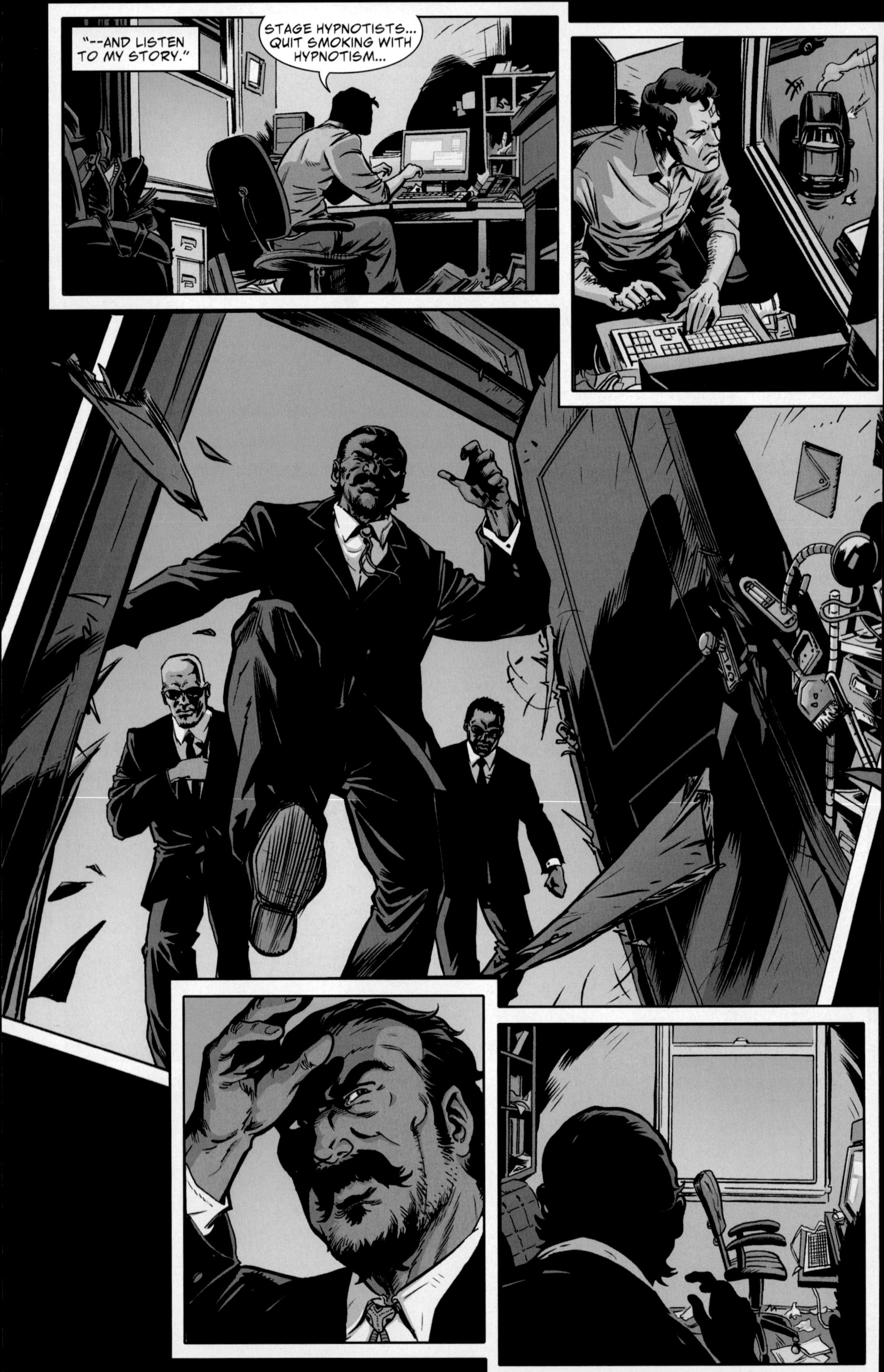
"--AND LISTEN TO MY STORY."
STAGE HYPNOTISTS... QUIT SMOKING WITH HYPNOTISM...

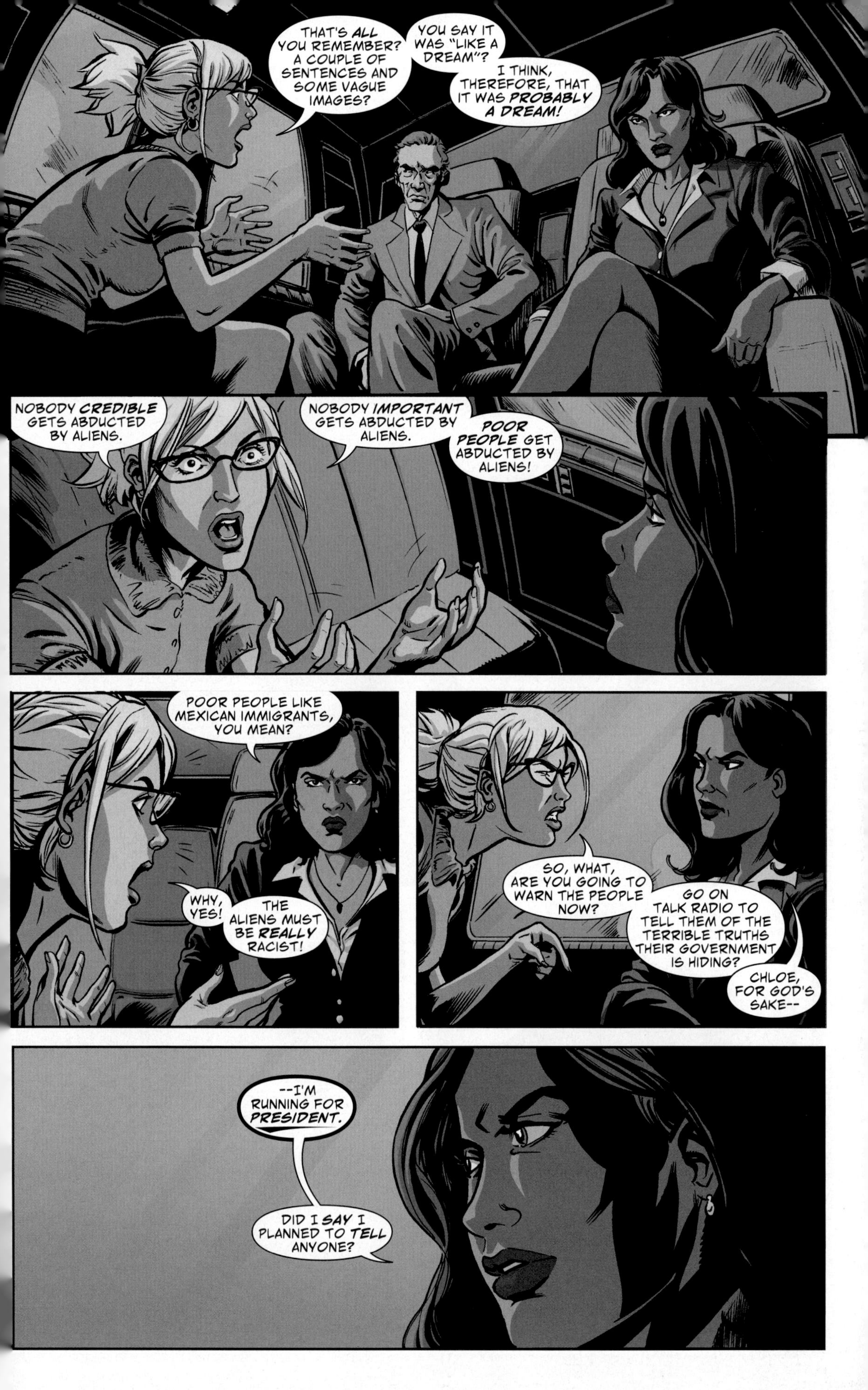
THAT'S ALL YOU REMEMBER? A COUPLE OF SENTENCES AND SOME VAGUE IMAGES?
YOU SAY IT WAS "LIKE A DREAM"?
I THINK, THEREFORE, THAT IT WAS PROBABLY A DREAM!
NOBODY CREDIBLE GETS ABDUCTED BY ALIENS.
NOBODY IMPORTANT GETS ABDUCTED BY ALIENS.
POOR PEOPLE GET ABDUCTED BY ALIENS!
POOR PEOPLE LIKE MEXICAN IMMIGRANTS, YOU MEAN?
WHY, YES!
THE ALIENS MUST BE REALLY RACIST!
SO, WHAT, ARE YOU GOING TO WARN THE PEOPLE NOW?
GO ON TALK RADIO TO TELL THEM OF THE TERRIBLE TRUTHS THEIR GOVERNMENT IS HIDING?
CHLOE, FOR GOD'S SAKE--
--I'M RUNNING FOR PRESIDENT.
DID I SAY I PLANNED TO TELL ANYONE?

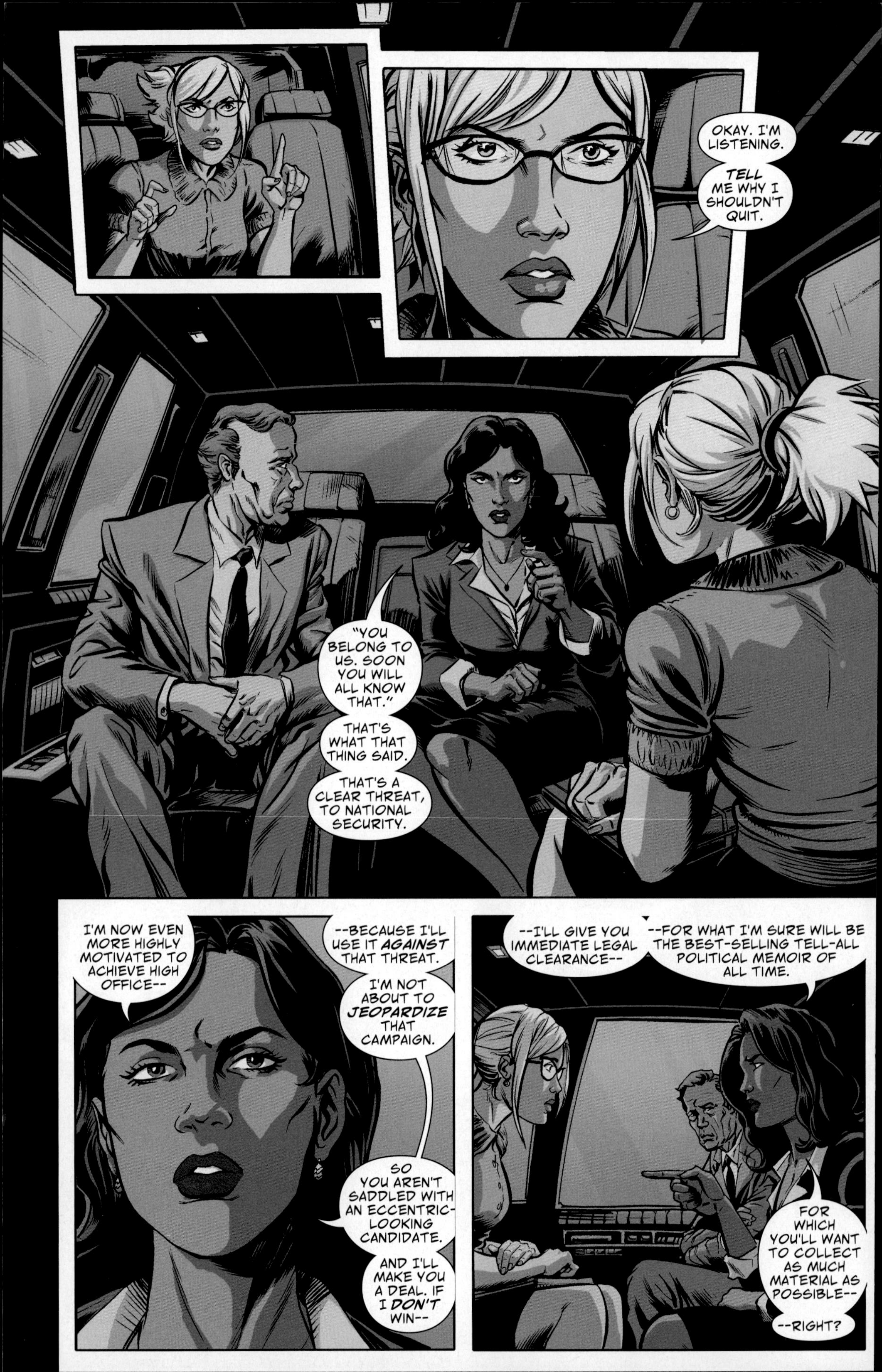
OKAY. I'M LISTENING.
TELL ME WHY I SHOULDN'T QUIT.
"YOU BELONG TO US. SOON YOU WILL ALL KNOW THAT."
THAT'S WHAT THAT THING SAID.
THAT'S A CLEAR THREAT, TO NATIONAL SECURITY.
I'M NOW EVEN MORE HIGHLY MOTIVATED TO ACHIEVE HIGH OFFICE--
--BECAUSE I'LL USE IT AGAINST THAT THREAT.
I'M NOT ABOUT TO JEOPARDIZE THAT CAMPAIGN.
SO YOU AREN'T SADDLED WITH AN ECCENTRIC-LOOKING CANDIDATE.
AND I'LL MAKE YOU A DEAL. IF I DON'T WIN--
--I'LL GIVE YOU IMMEDIATE LEGAL CLEARANCE--
--FOR WHAT I'M SURE WILL BE THE BEST-SELLING TELL-ALL POLITICAL MEMOIR OF ALL TIME.
FOR WHICH YOU'LL WANT TO COLLECT AS MUCH MATERIAL AS POSSIBLE--
--RIGHT?

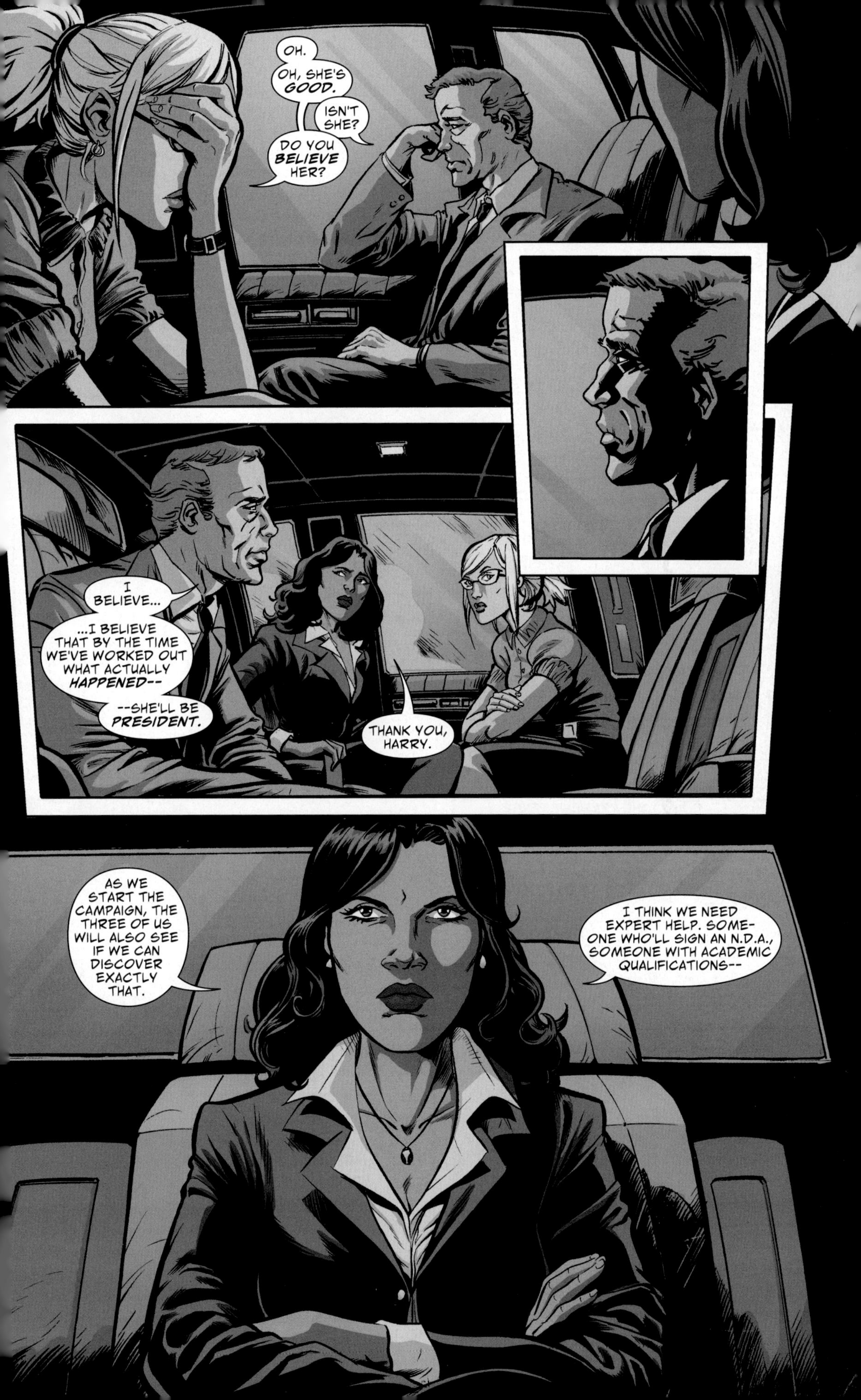
OH.
OH, SHE'S GOOD.
ISN'T SHE?
DO YOU BELIEVE HER?
I BELIEVE...
...I BELIEVE THAT BY THE TIME WE'VE WORKED OUT WHAT ACTUALLY HAPPENED--
--SHE'LL BE PRESIDENT.
THANK YOU, HARRY.
AS WE START THE CAMPAIGN, THE THREE OF US WILL ALSO SEE IF WE CAN DISCOVER EXACTLY THAT.
I THINK WE NEED EXPERT HELP. SOMEONE WHO'LL SIGN AN N.D.A., SOMEONE WITH ACADEMIC QUALIFICATIONS--

"--SOMEONE SANE."

YOU'RE SAYING I'M GOING TO GET A JOB IN *POLITICS*?

Yes--

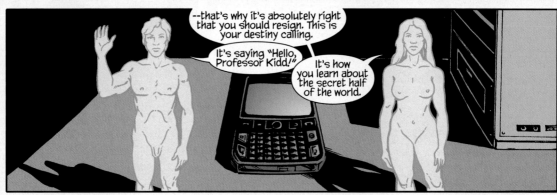

--that's why it's absolutely right that you should resign. This is your destiny calling.

It's saying "Hello, Professor Kidd!"

It's how you learn about the secret half of the world.

THE PRESENT TENSE. LIKE TIME IS A... BOOK TO YOU.

YOU WANT ME TO RESIGN. LET GO MY SECURITY. JUST LIKE THAT.

BECAUSE SOMETHING IMPOSSIBLE *TOLD* ME TO.

THAT'S ME ALL OVER.

Now you answer that.

And greet the representative of your next president.

BzZZ

THAT'S IT IN A NUTSHELL--

--IT WOULD BE A JOB ON STAFF. BUT WE CAN'T TELL YOU MORE UNTIL YOU SIGN THE AGREEMENT.

I'M E-MAILING YOU SALARY DETAILS NOW.

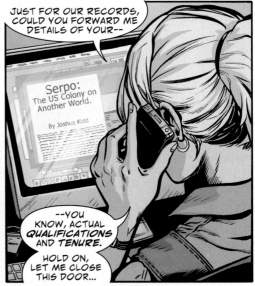

JUST FOR OUR RECORDS, COULD YOU FORWARD ME DETAILS OF YOUR--

Serpo:
The US Colony on Another World.

By Joshua Kidd

--YOU KNOW, ACTUAL *QUALIFICATIONS* AND *TENURE.*

HOLD ON, LET ME CLOSE THIS DOOR...

SERIOUS QUESTION: DO YOU BELIEVE IN UFOS?

OKAY, HOW TO REPHRASE THAT IN ORDER TO GET A--

--COMPREHENSIBLE ANSWER?

DO...*YOU*... BELIEVE...IN... UFOS?

YEAH. RIGHT.

THAT'S WHAT I WAS *AFRAID* OF.

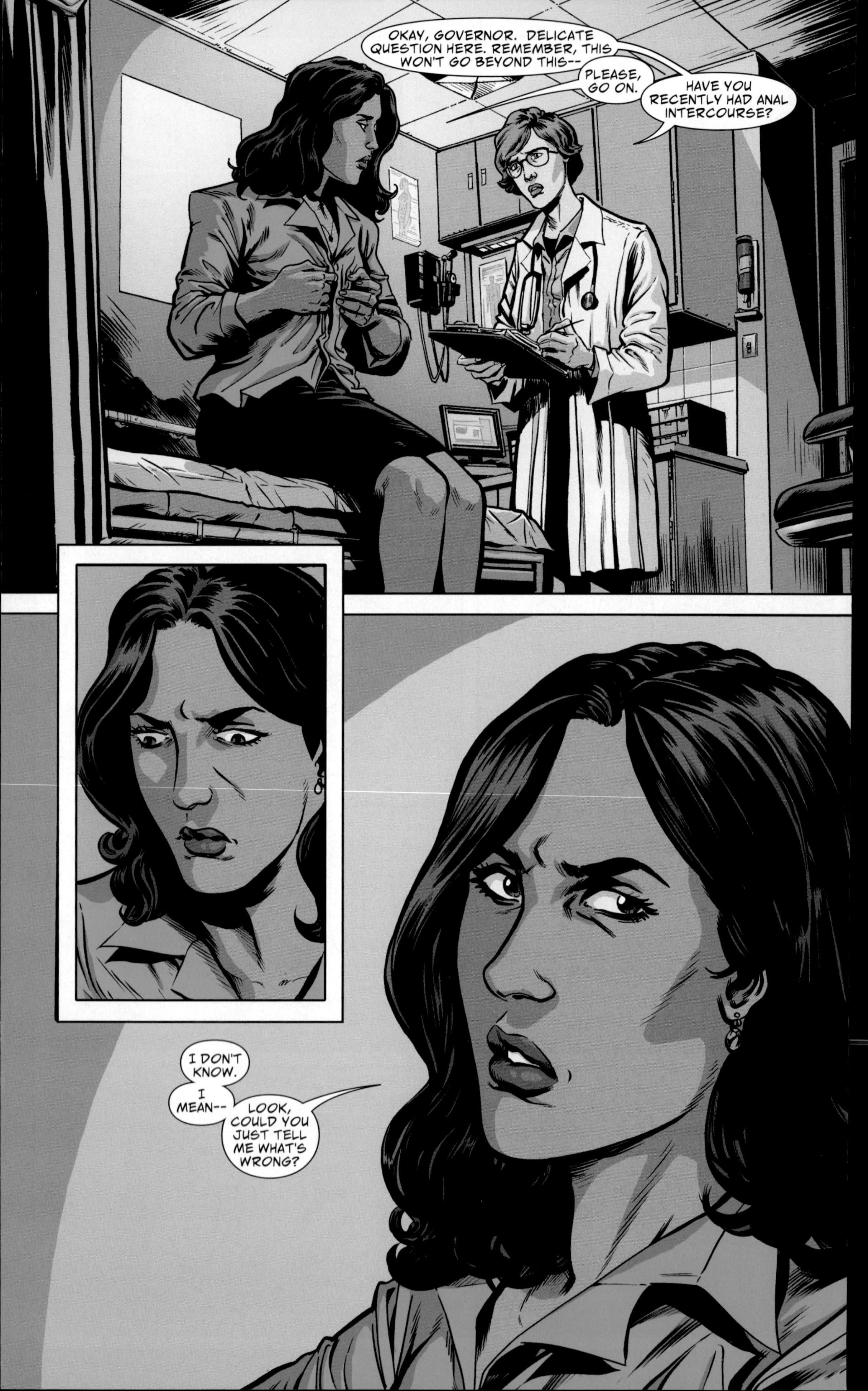
OKAY, GOVERNOR. DELICATE QUESTION HERE. REMEMBER, THIS WON'T GO BEYOND THIS--
PLEASE, GO ON.
HAVE YOU RECENTLY HAD ANAL INTERCOURSE?
I DON'T KNOW.
I MEAN--
LOOK, COULD YOU JUST TELL ME WHAT'S WRONG?

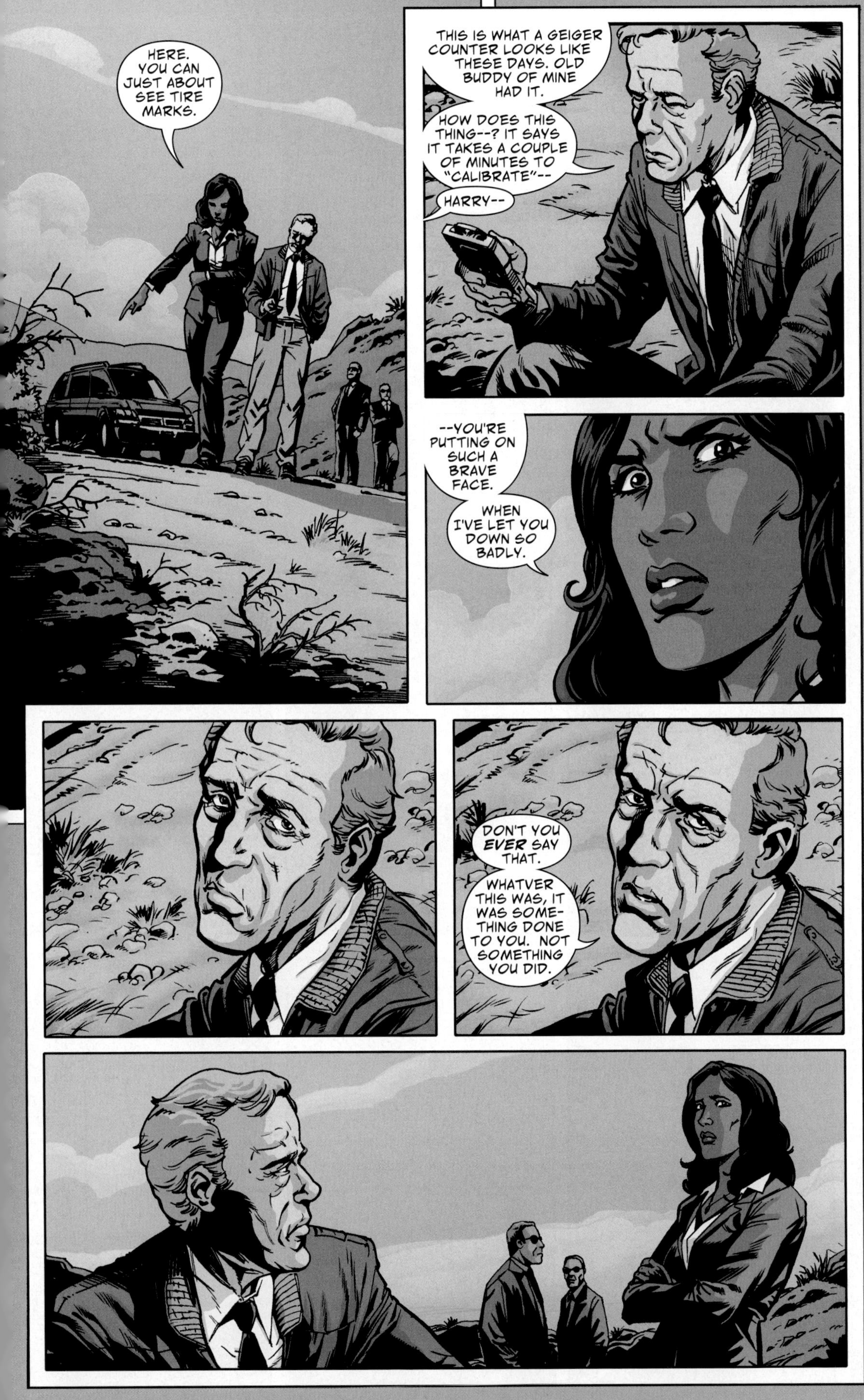
HERE. YOU CAN JUST ABOUT SEE TIRE MARKS.
THIS IS WHAT A GEIGER COUNTER LOOKS LIKE THESE DAYS. OLD BUDDY OF MINE HAD IT.
HOW DOES THIS THING--? IT SAYS IT TAKES A COUPLE OF MINUTES TO "CALIBRATE"--
HARRY--
--YOU'RE PUTTING ON SUCH A BRAVE FACE.
WHEN I'VE LET YOU DOWN SO BADLY.
DON'T YOU EVER SAY THAT.
WHATVER THIS WAS, IT WAS SOME-THING DONE TO YOU. NOT SOMETHING YOU DID.

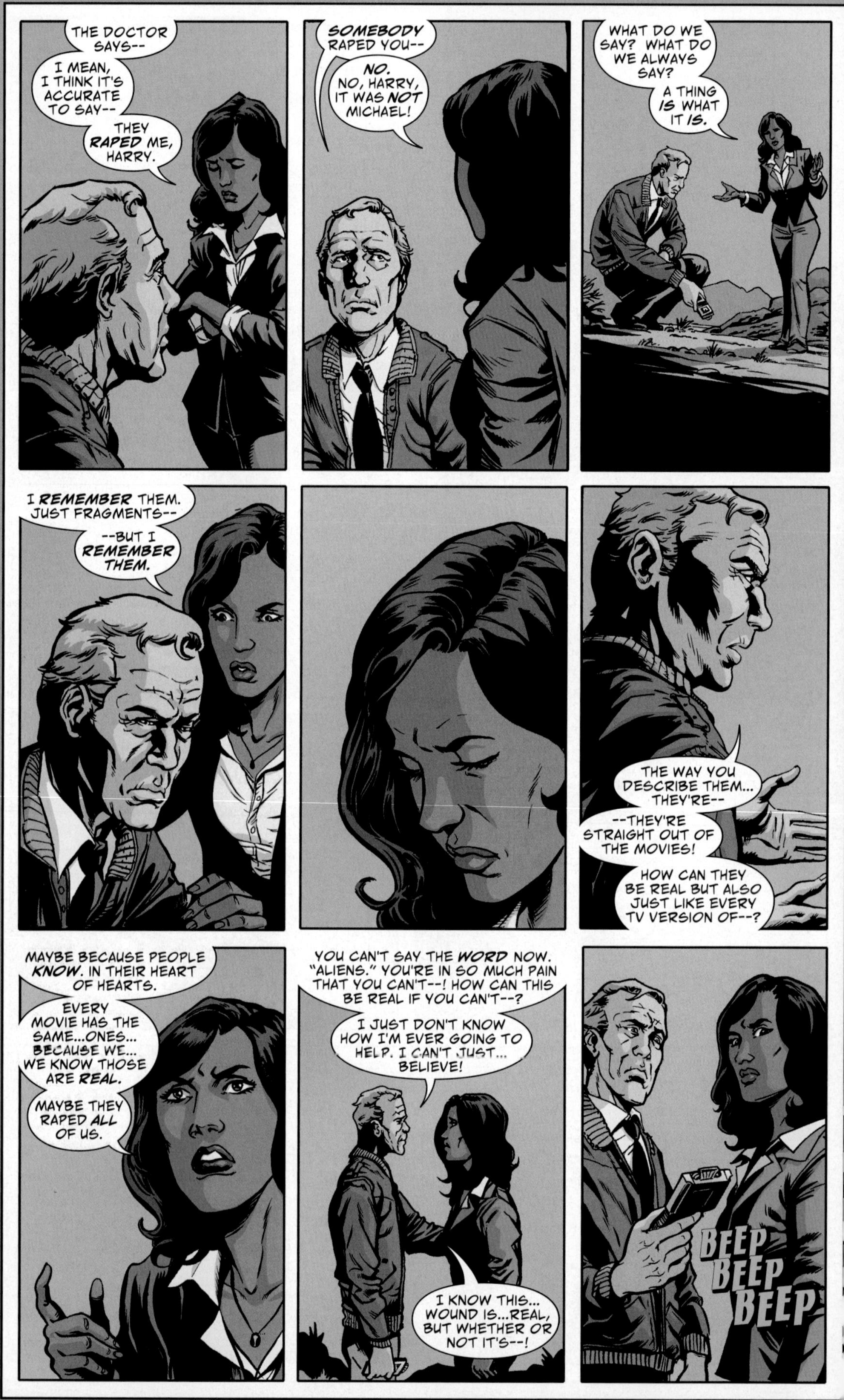
THE DOCTOR SAYS--
I MEAN, I THINK IT'S ACCURATE TO SAY--
THEY *RAPED* ME, HARRY.
SOMEBODY RAPED YOU--
NO. NO, HARRY, IT WAS *NOT* MICHAEL!
WHAT DO WE SAY? WHAT DO WE ALWAYS SAY?
A THING *IS* WHAT IT *IS*.
I *REMEMBER* THEM. JUST FRAGMENTS--
--BUT I *REMEMBER THEM.*
THE WAY YOU DESCRIBE THEM... THEY'RE--
--THEY'RE STRAIGHT OUT OF THE MOVIES!
HOW CAN THEY BE REAL BUT ALSO JUST LIKE EVERY TV VERSION OF--?
MAYBE BECAUSE PEOPLE *KNOW*. IN THEIR HEART OF HEARTS.
EVERY MOVIE HAS THE SAME...ONES... BECAUSE WE... WE KNOW THOSE ARE *REAL.*
MAYBE THEY RAPED *ALL* OF US.
YOU CAN'T SAY THE *WORD* NOW. "ALIENS." YOU'RE IN SO MUCH PAIN THAT YOU CAN'T--! HOW CAN THIS BE REAL IF YOU CAN'T--?
I JUST DON'T KNOW HOW I'M EVER GOING TO HELP. I CAN'T JUST... BELIEVE!
I KNOW THIS... WOUND IS...REAL, BUT WHETHER OR NOT IT'S--!
BEEP BEEP BEEP

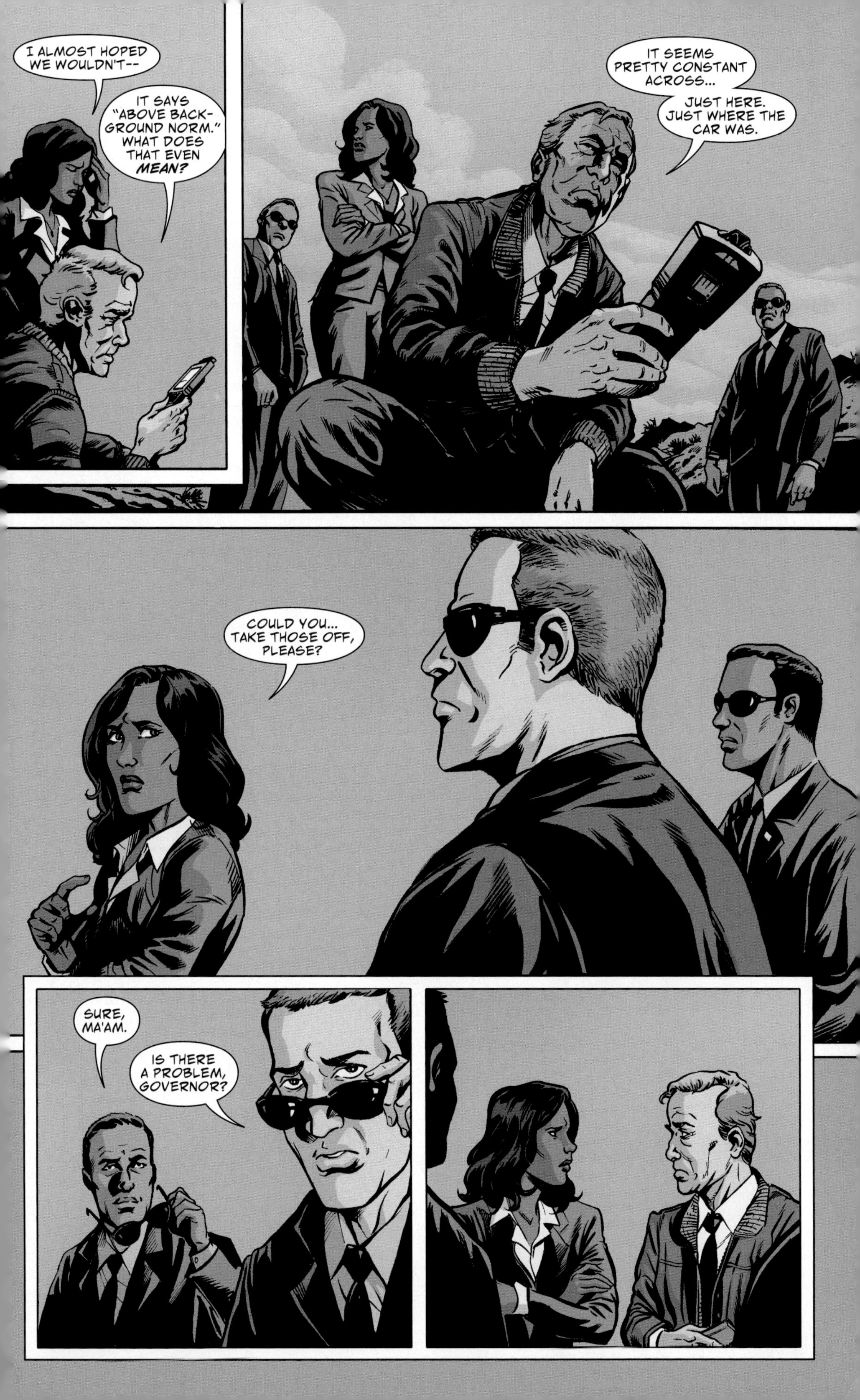
I ALMOST HOPED WE WOULDN'T--
IT SAYS "ABOVE BACK-GROUND NORM." WHAT DOES THAT EVEN *MEAN?*
IT SEEMS PRETTY CONSTANT ACROSS...
JUST HERE. JUST WHERE THE CAR WAS.
COULD YOU... TAKE THOSE OFF, PLEASE?
SURE, MA'AM.
IS THERE A PROBLEM, GOVERNOR?

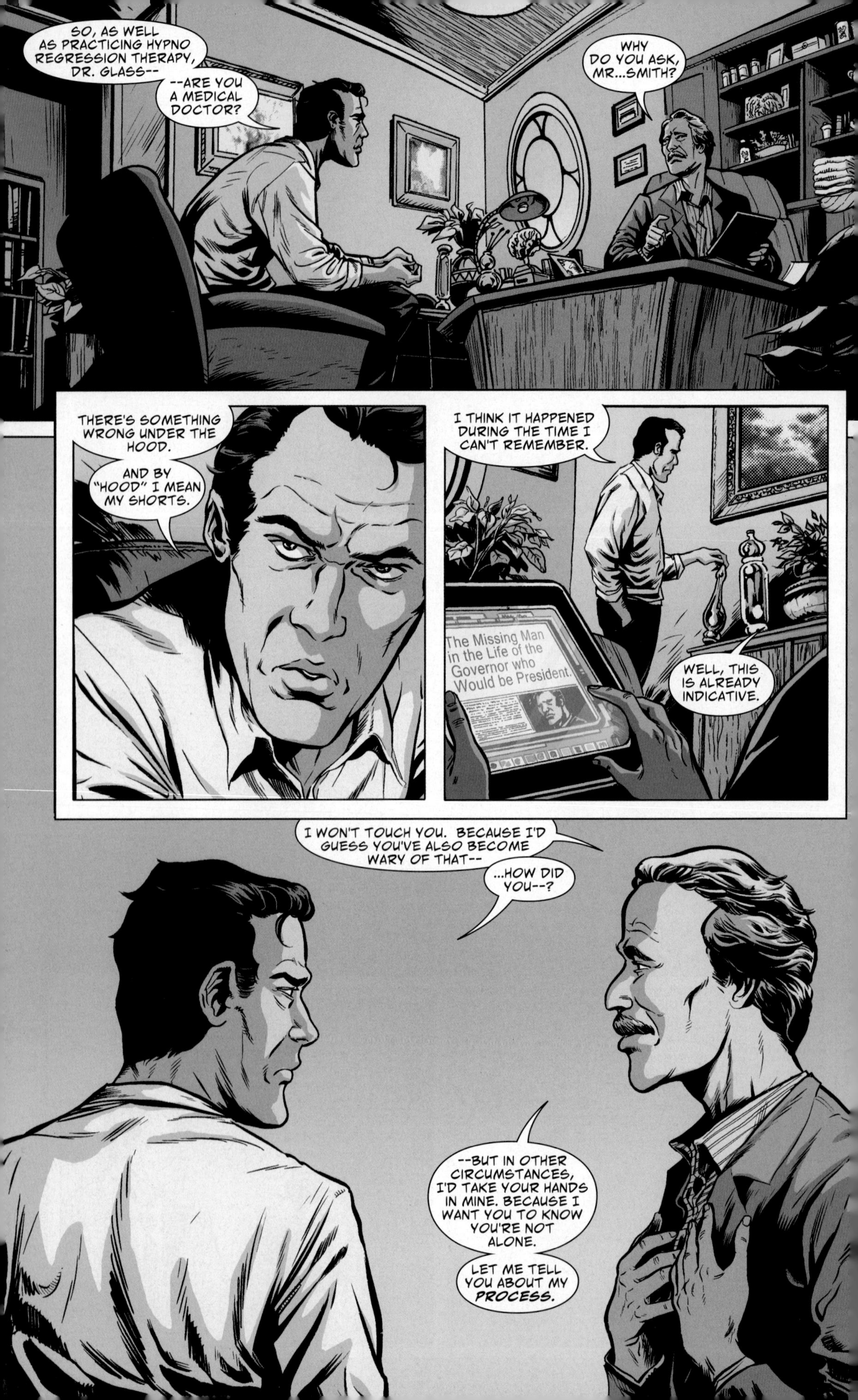
SO, AS WELL AS PRACTICING HYPNO REGRESSION THERAPY, DR. GLASS--
--ARE YOU A MEDICAL DOCTOR?
WHY DO YOU ASK, MR...SMITH?
THERE'S SOMETHING WRONG UNDER THE HOOD.
AND BY "HOOD" I MEAN MY SHORTS.
I THINK IT HAPPENED DURING THE TIME I CAN'T REMEMBER.
The Missing Man in the Life of the Governor who Would be President.
WELL, THIS IS ALREADY INDICATIVE.
I WON'T TOUCH YOU. BECAUSE I'D GUESS YOU'VE ALSO BECOME WARY OF THAT--
...HOW DID YOU--?
--BUT IN OTHER CIRCUMSTANCES, I'D TAKE YOUR HANDS IN MINE. BECAUSE I WANT YOU TO KNOW YOU'RE NOT ALONE.
LET ME TELL YOU ABOUT MY *PROCESS.*

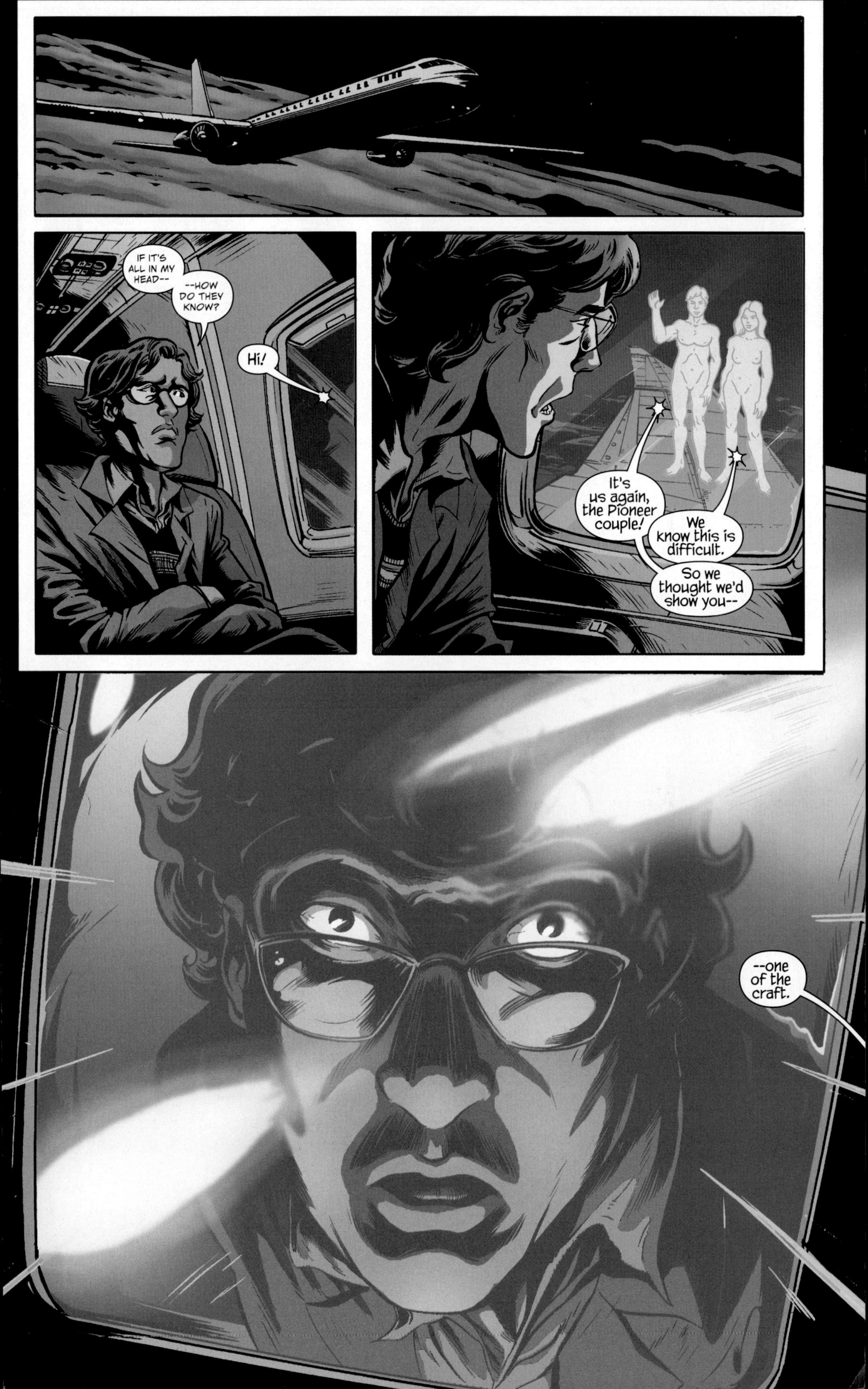
IF IT'S ALL IN MY HEAD--
--HOW DO THEY KNOW?
Hi!
It's us again, the Pioneer couple!
We know this is difficult.
So we thought we'd show you--
--one of the craft.

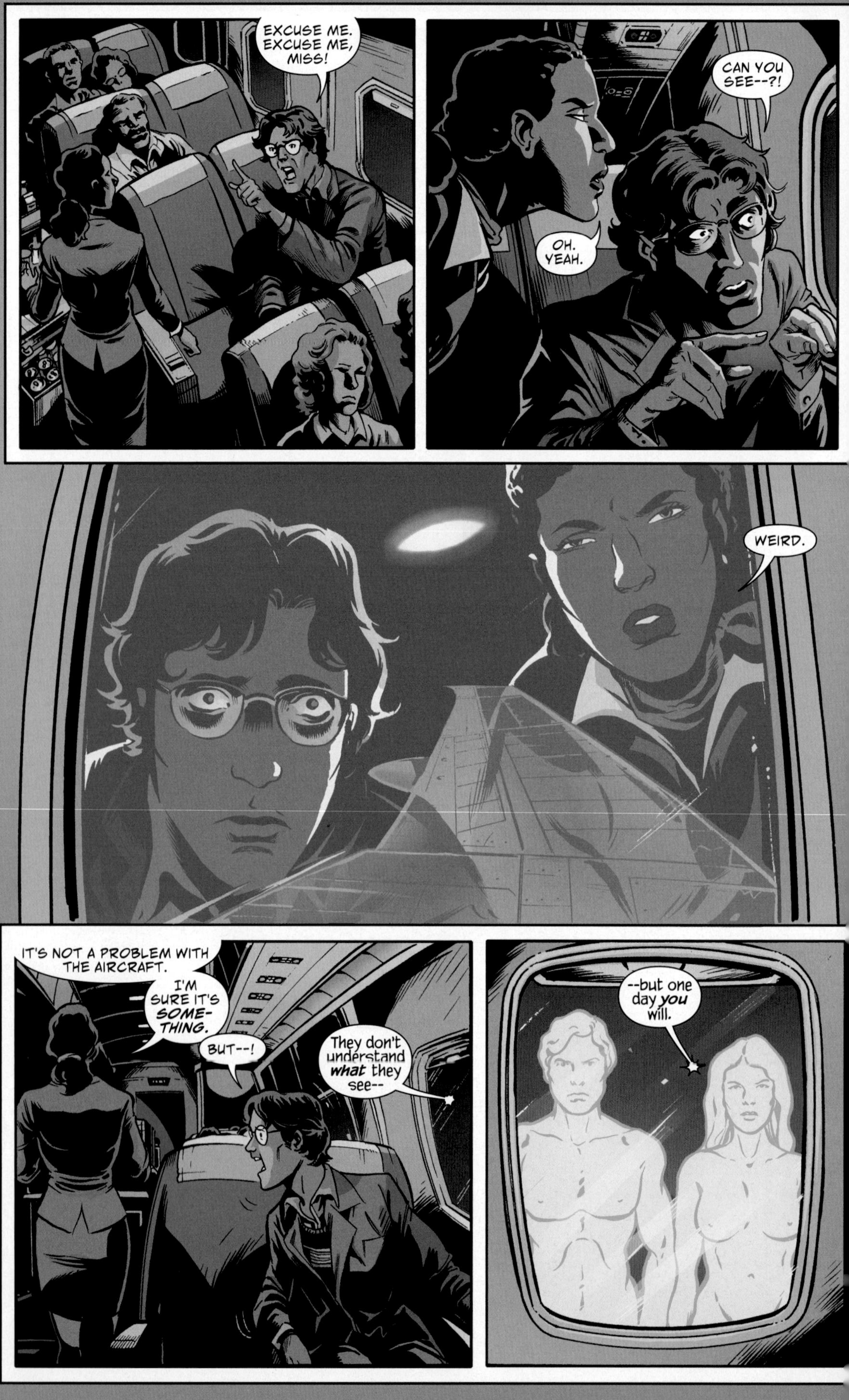
EXCUSE ME. EXCUSE ME, MISS!
CAN YOU SEE--?!
OH. YEAH.
WEIRD.
IT'S NOT A PROBLEM WITH THE AIRCRAFT.
I'M SURE IT'S SOME-THING.
BUT--!
They don't understand what they see--
--but one day you will.

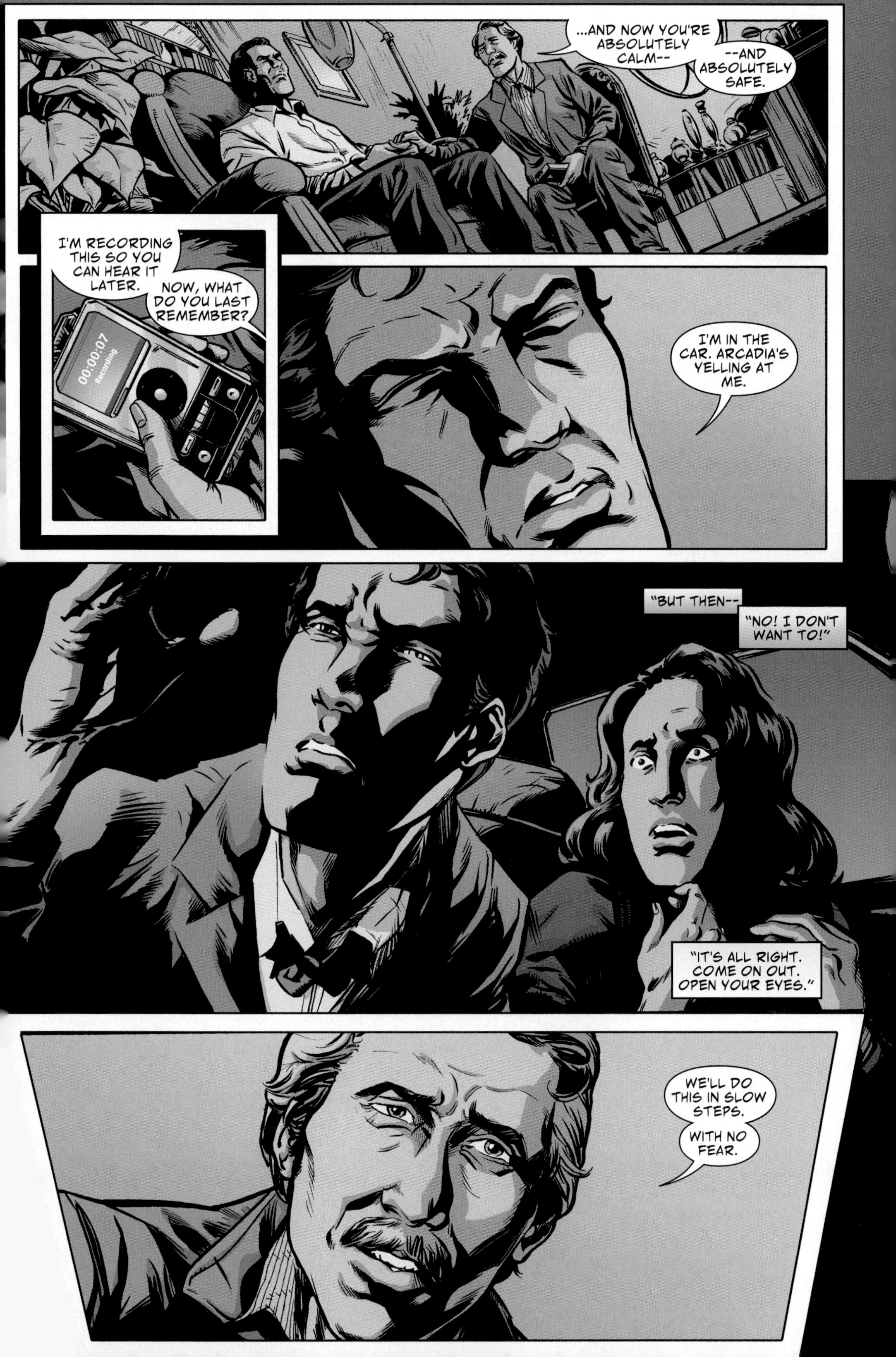
...AND NOW YOU'RE ABSOLUTELY CALM--
--AND ABSOLUTELY SAFE.
I'M RECORDING THIS SO YOU CAN HEAR IT LATER.
NOW, WHAT DO YOU LAST REMEMBER?
00:00:07
Recording
I'M IN THE CAR. ARCADIA'S YELLING AT ME.
"BUT THEN--
"NO! I DON'T WANT TO!"
"IT'S ALL RIGHT. COME ON OUT. OPEN YOUR EYES."
WE'LL DO THIS IN SLOW STEPS.
WITH NO FEAR.

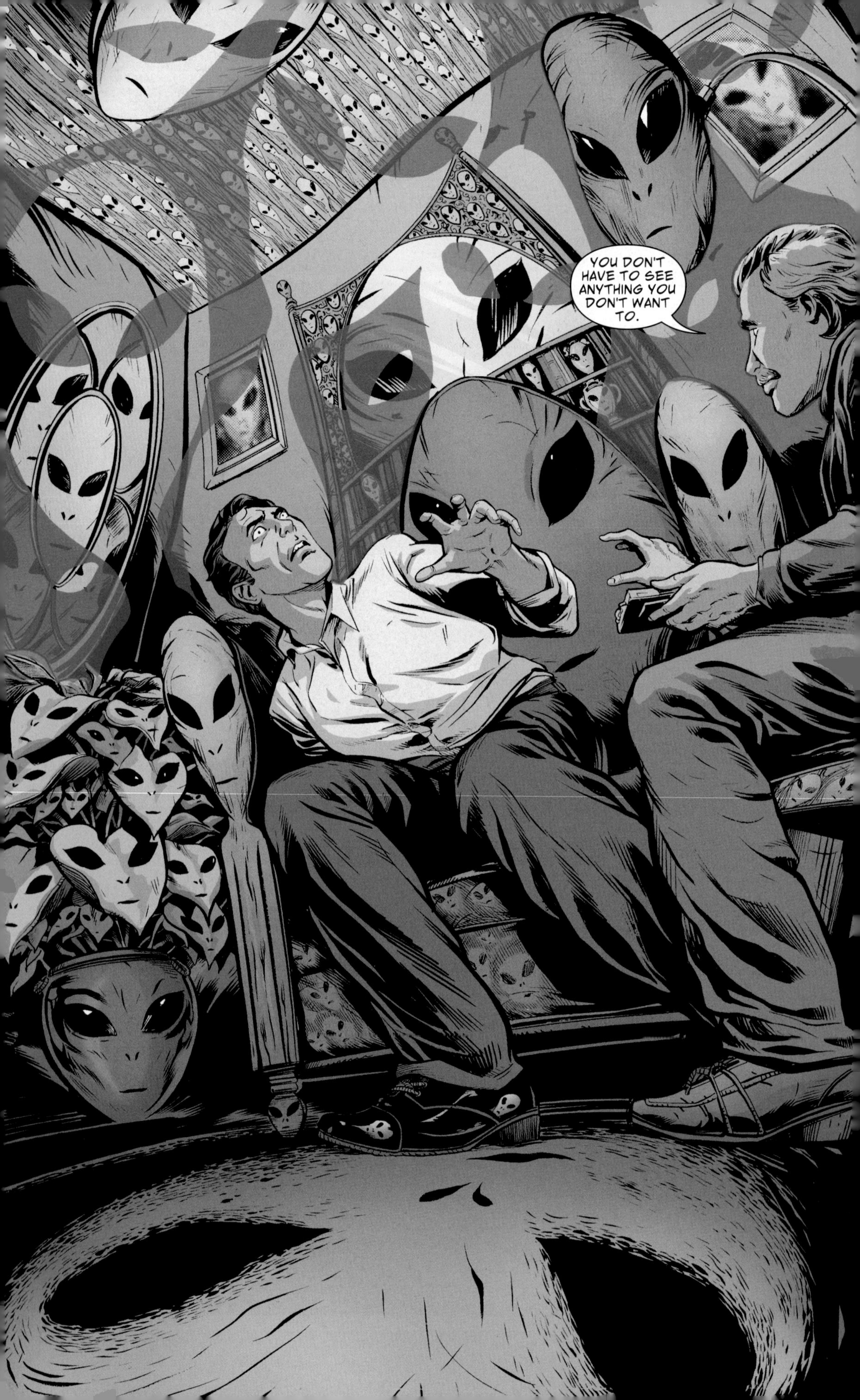
YOU DON'T HAVE TO SEE ANYTHING YOU DON'T WANT TO.

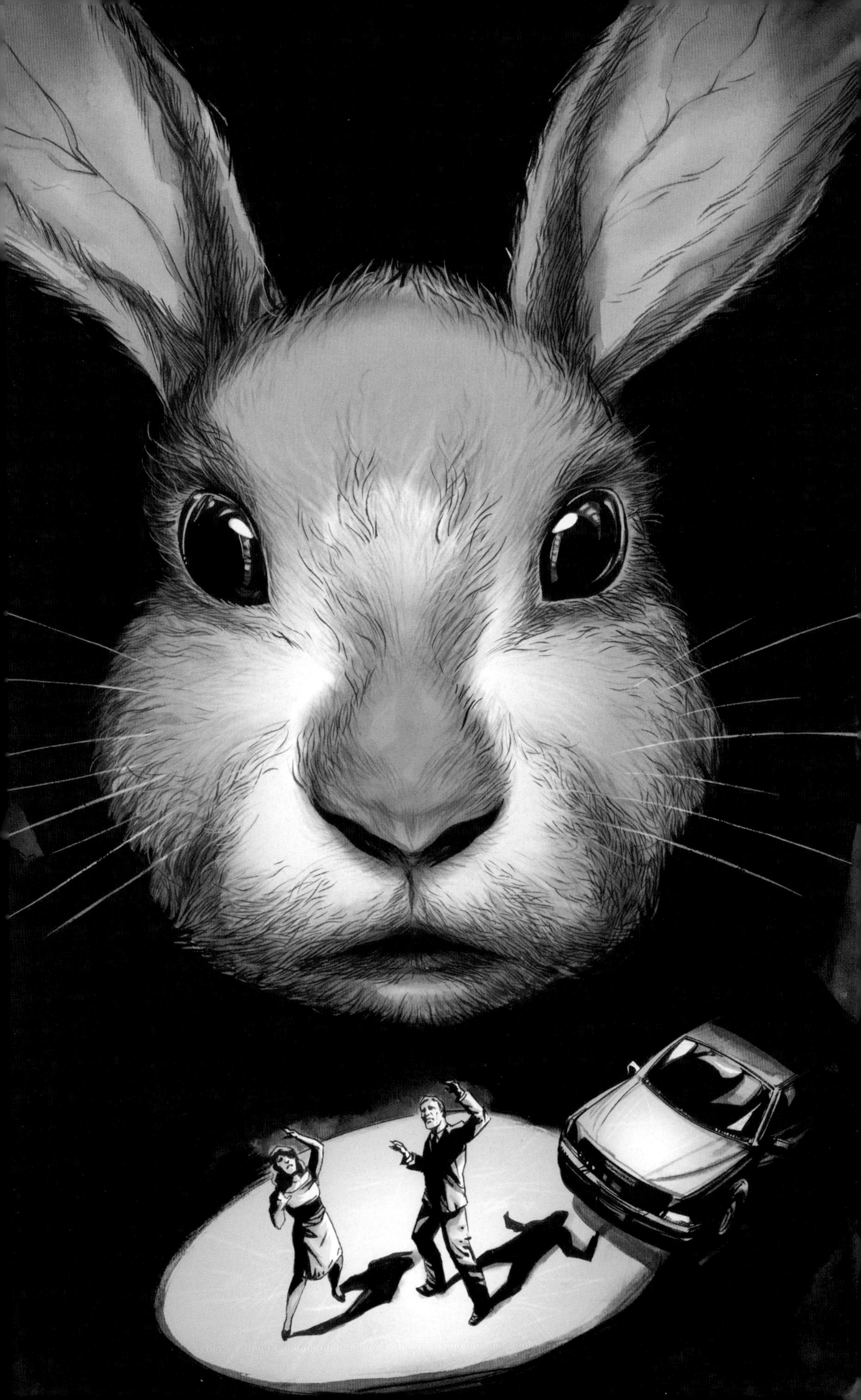

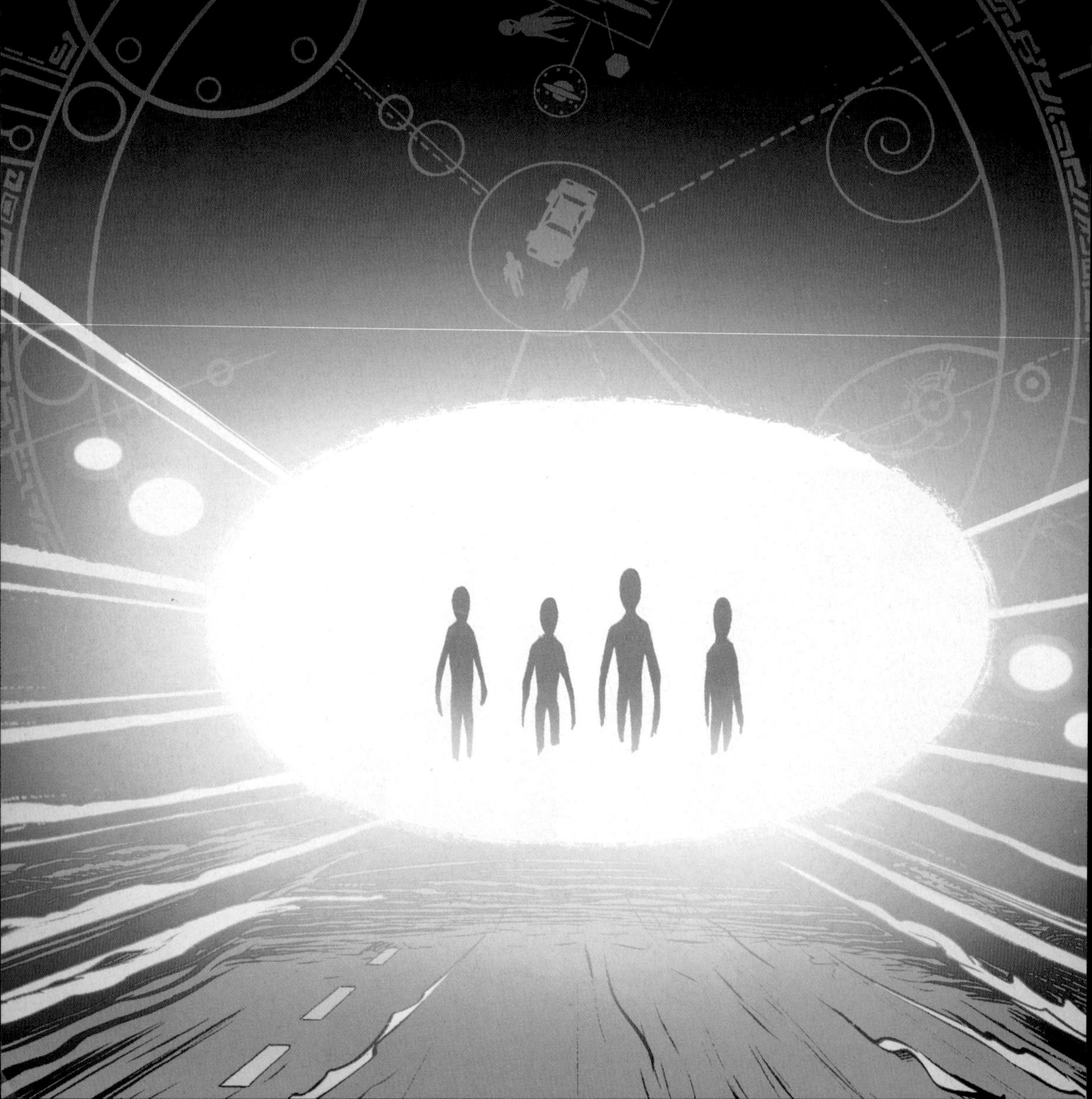

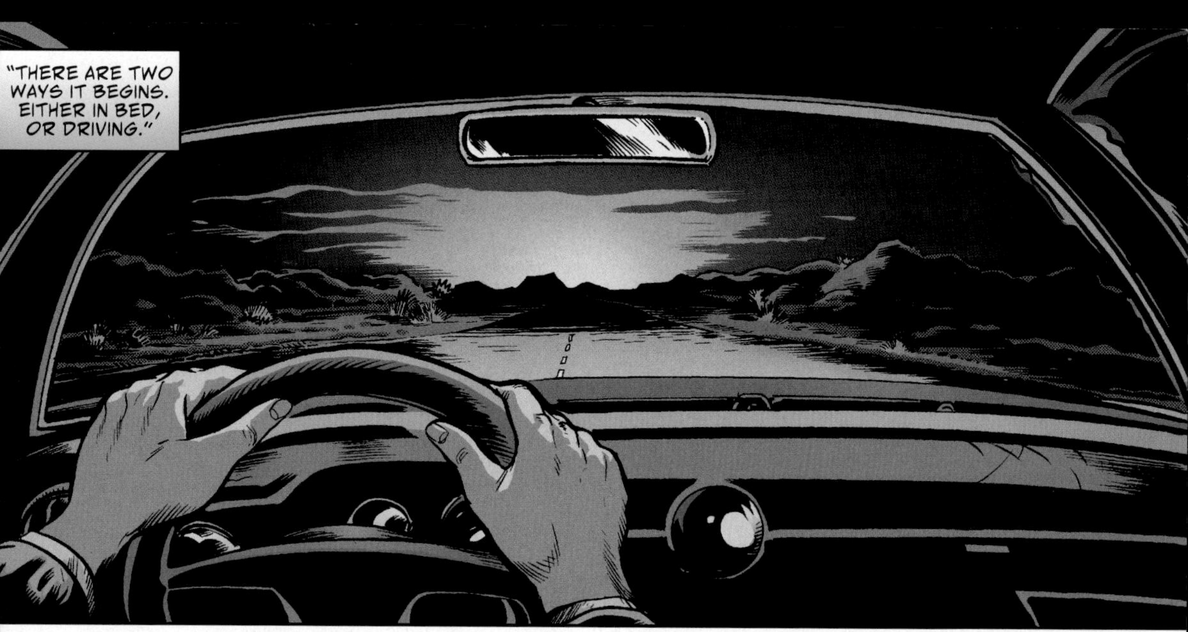
"THERE ARE TWO WAYS IT BEGINS. EITHER IN BED, OR DRIVING."

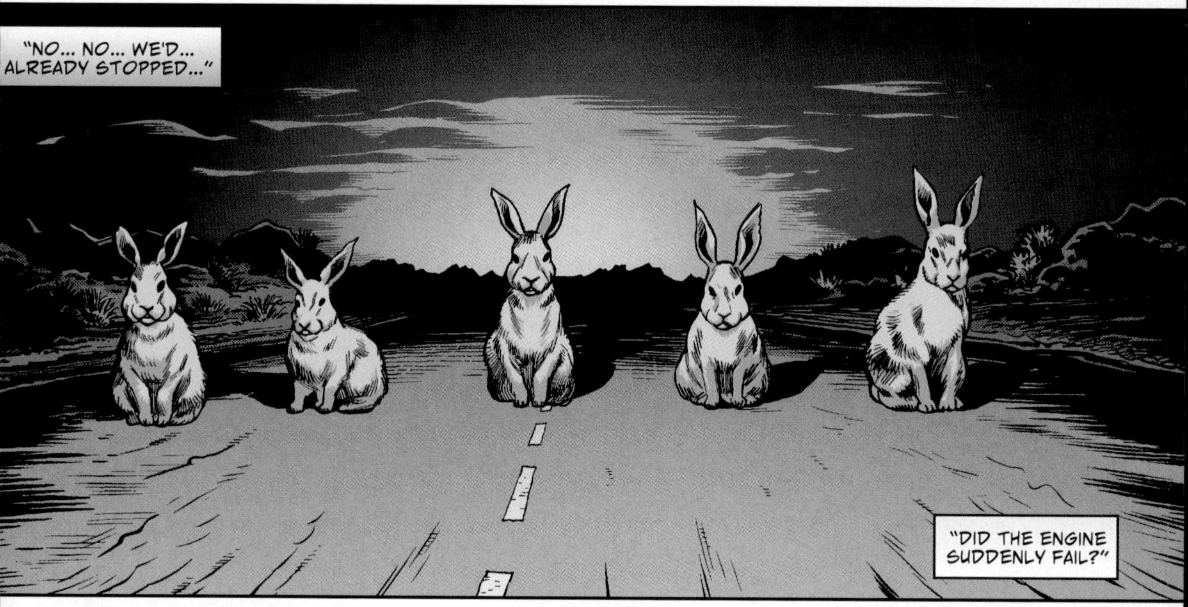
"NO... NO... WE'D... ALREADY STOPPED..."
"DID THE ENGINE SUDDENLY FAIL?"

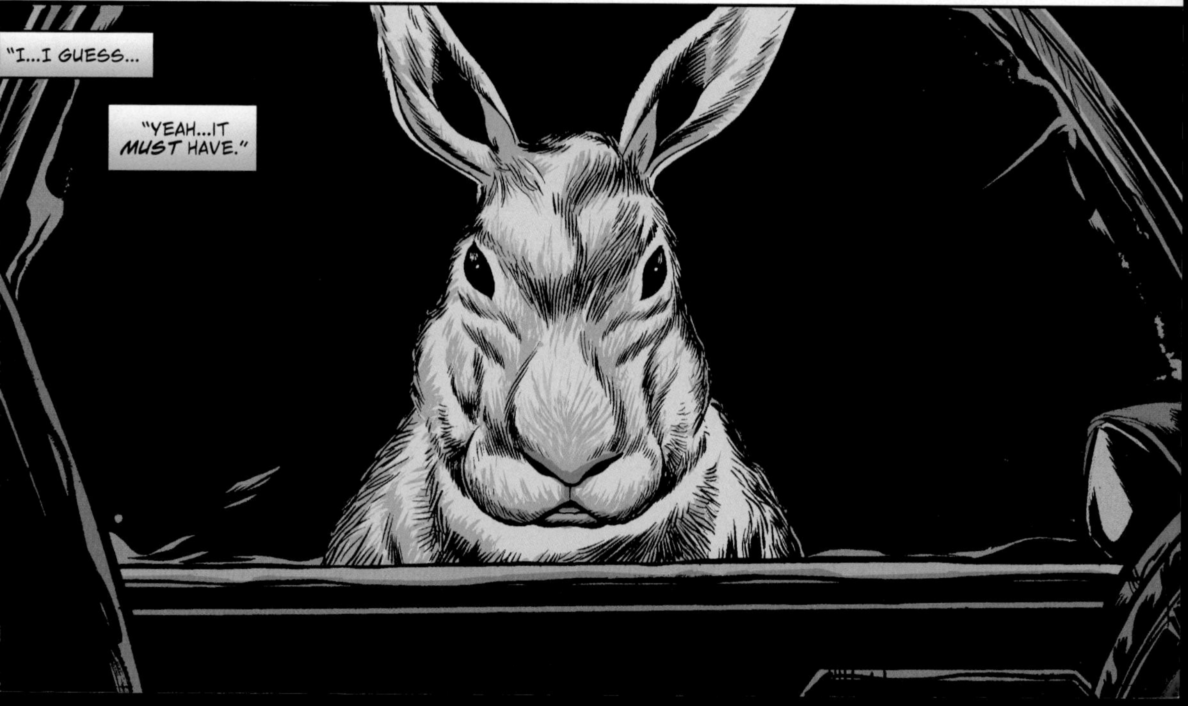
"I...I GUESS...
"YEAH...IT *MUST* HAVE."

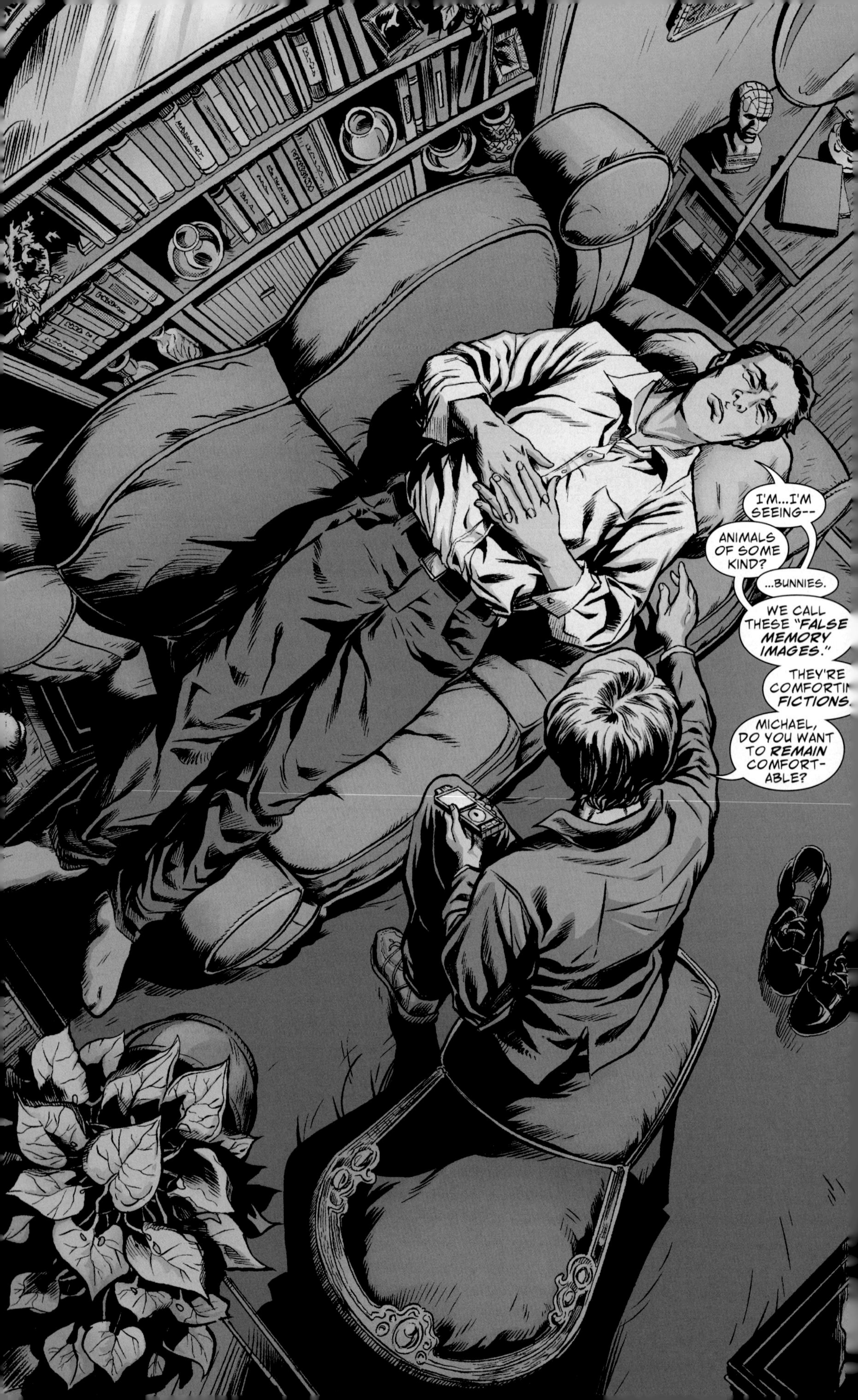
I'M...I'M SEEING--
ANIMALS OF SOME KIND?
...BUNNIES.
WE CALL THESE "FALSE MEMORY IMAGES."
THEY'RE COMFORTIN FICTIONS.
MICHAEL, DO YOU WANT TO REMAIN COMFORT-ABLE?

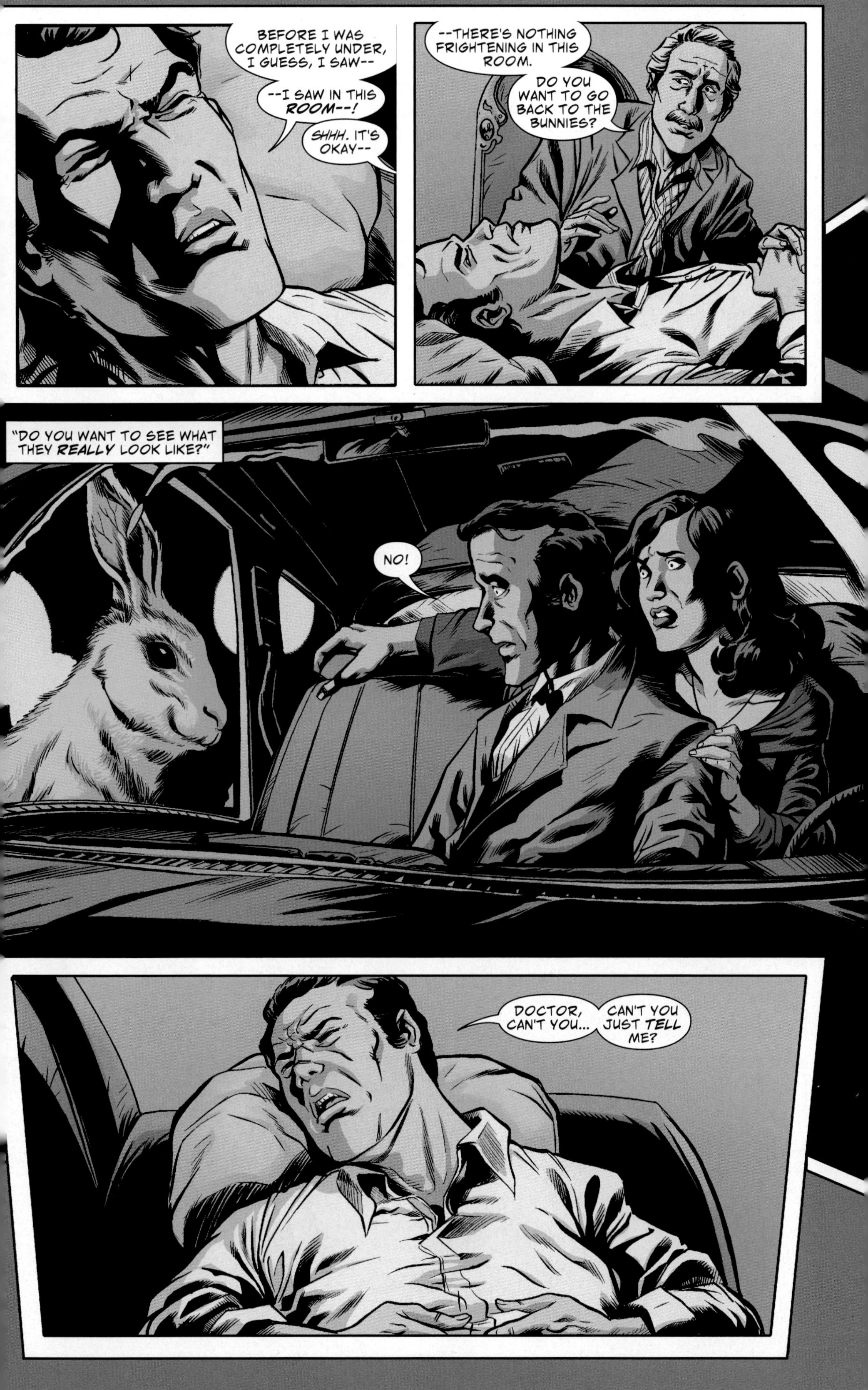
BEFORE I WAS COMPLETELY UNDER, I GUESS, I SAW--
--I SAW IN THIS ROOM--!
SHHH. IT'S OKAY--
--THERE'S NOTHING FRIGHTENING IN THIS ROOM.
DO YOU WANT TO GO BACK TO THE BUNNIES?
"DO YOU WANT TO SEE WHAT THEY REALLY LOOK LIKE?"
NO!
DOCTOR, CAN'T YOU...
CAN'T YOU JUST TELL ME?

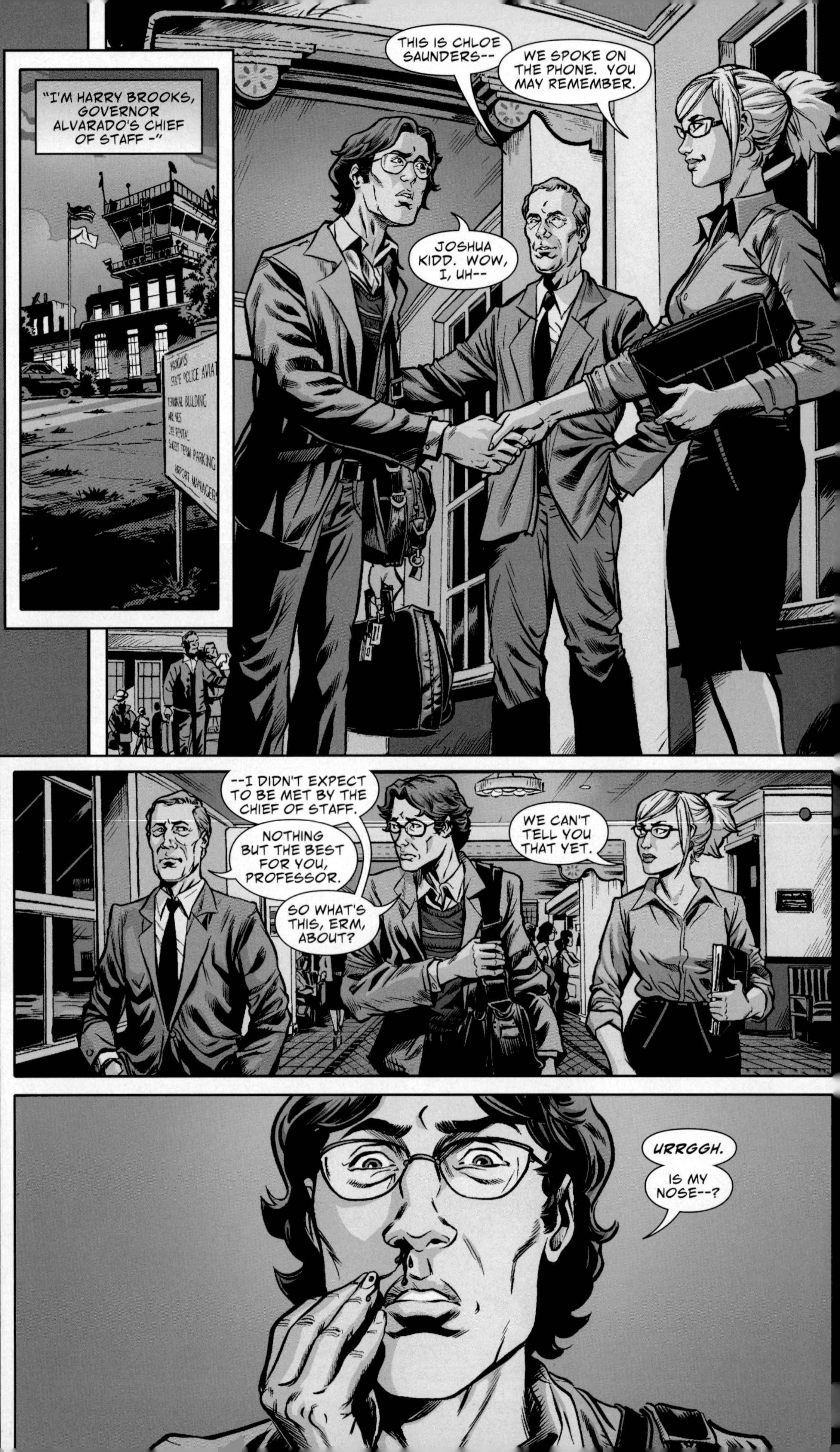
"I'M HARRY BROOKS, GOVERNOR ALVARADO'S CHIEF OF STAFF -"
THIS IS CHLOE SAUNDERS--
WE SPOKE ON THE PHONE. YOU MAY REMEMBER.
JOSHUA KIDD. WOW, I, UH--
--I DIDN'T EXPECT TO BE MET BY THE CHIEF OF STAFF.
NOTHING BUT THE BEST FOR YOU, PROFESSOR.
SO WHAT'S THIS, ERM, ABOUT?
WE CAN'T TELL YOU THAT YET.
URRGGH.
IS MY NOSE--?

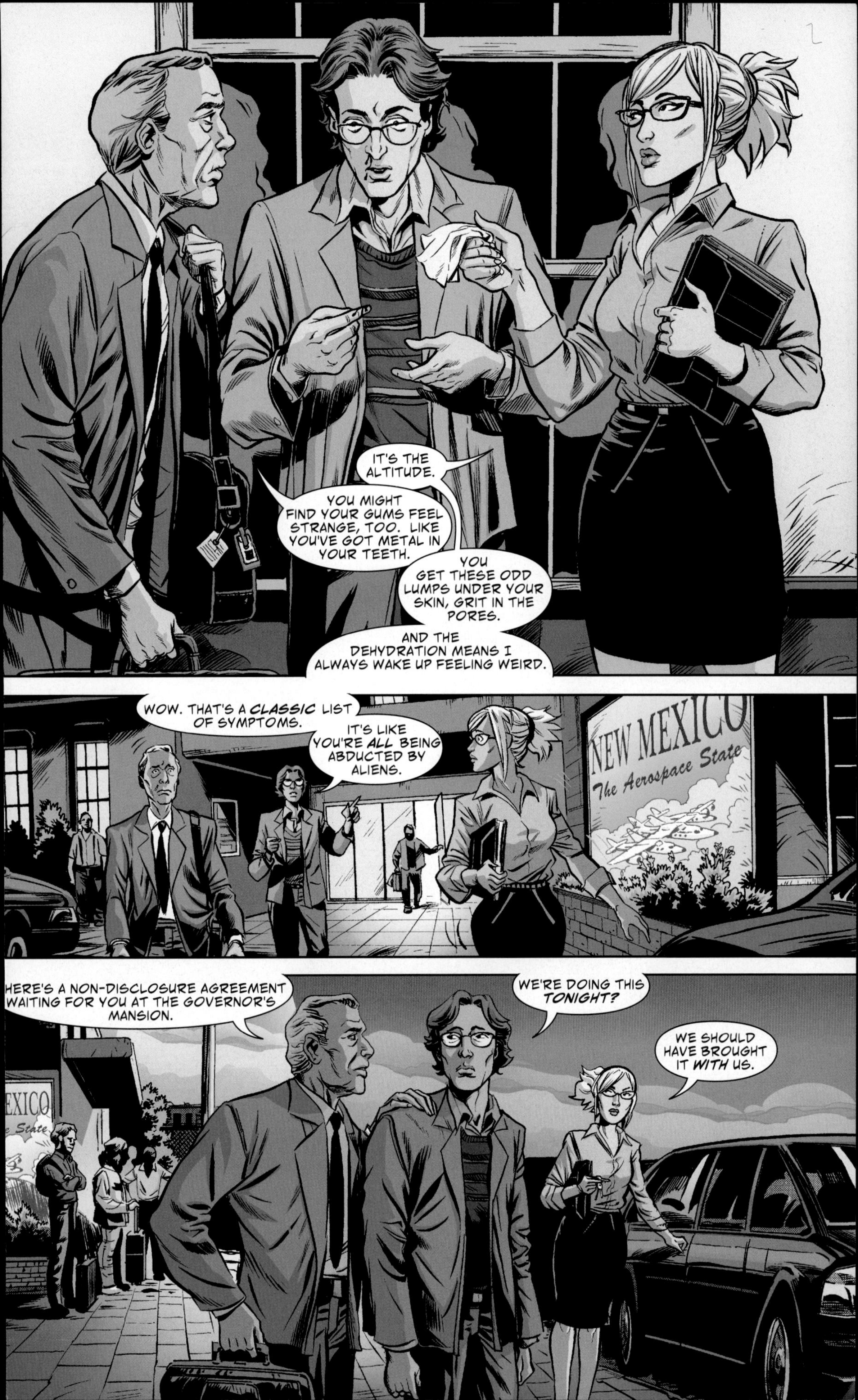
IT'S THE ALTITUDE.
YOU MIGHT FIND YOUR GUMS FEEL STRANGE, TOO. LIKE YOU'VE GOT METAL IN YOUR TEETH.
YOU GET THESE ODD LUMPS UNDER YOUR SKIN, GRIT IN THE PORES.
AND THE DEHYDRATION MEANS I ALWAYS WAKE UP FEELING WEIRD.
WOW. THAT'S A *CLASSIC* LIST OF SYMPTOMS.
IT'S LIKE YOU'RE *ALL* BEING ABDUCTED BY ALIENS.
NEW MEXICO
The Aerospace State
THERE'S A NON-DISCLOSURE AGREEMENT WAITING FOR YOU AT THE GOVERNOR'S MANSION.
WE'RE DOING THIS *TONIGHT?*
WE SHOULD HAVE BROUGHT IT *WITH* US.

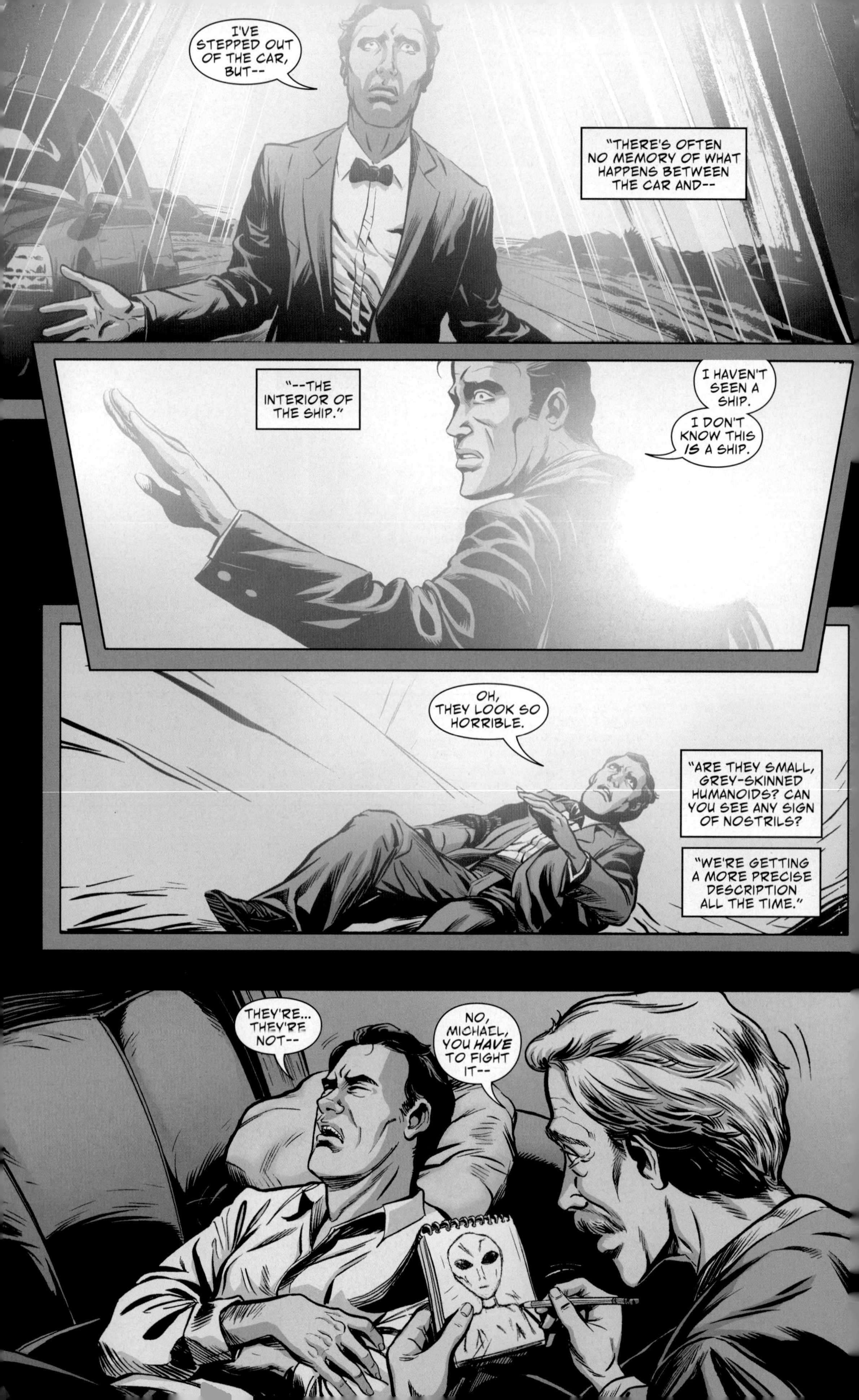
I'VE STEPPED OUT OF THE CAR, BUT--
"THERE'S OFTEN NO MEMORY OF WHAT HAPPENS BETWEEN THE CAR AND--
"--THE INTERIOR OF THE SHIP."
I HAVEN'T SEEN A SHIP.
I DON'T KNOW THIS *IS* A SHIP.
OH, THEY LOOK SO HORRIBLE.
"ARE THEY SMALL, GREY-SKINNED HUMANOIDS? CAN YOU SEE ANY SIGN OF NOSTRILS?
"WE'RE GETTING A MORE PRECISE DESCRIPTION ALL THE TIME."
THEY'RE... THEY'RE NOT--
NO, MICHAEL, YOU *HAVE* TO FIGHT IT--

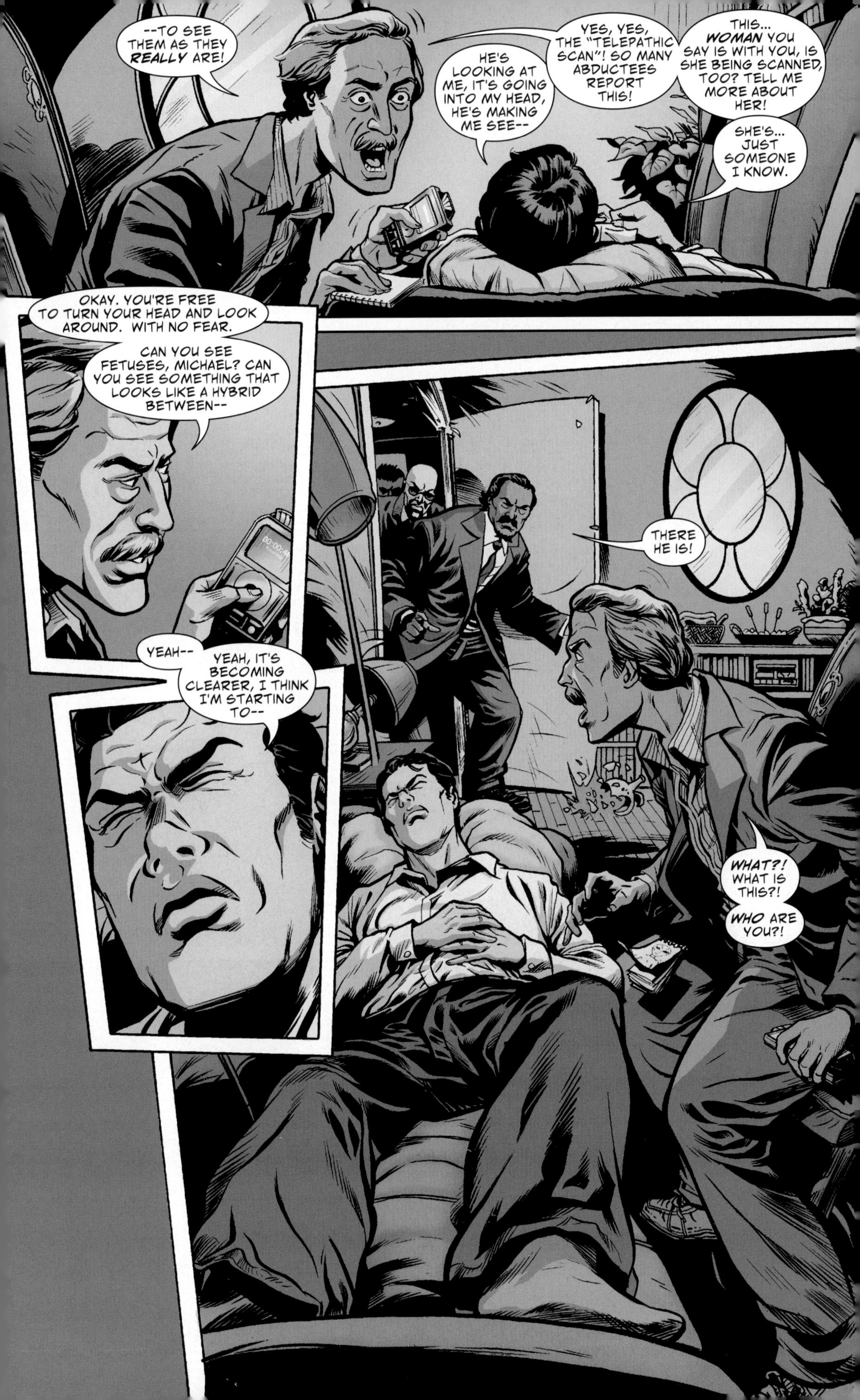
--TO SEE THEM AS THEY REALLY ARE!
HE'S LOOKING AT ME, IT'S GOING INTO MY HEAD, HE'S MAKING ME SEE--
YES, YES, THE "TELEPATHIC SCAN"! SO MANY ABDUCTEES REPORT THIS!
THIS... WOMAN YOU SAY IS WITH YOU, IS SHE BEING SCANNED, TOO? TELL ME MORE ABOUT HER!
SHE'S... JUST SOMEONE I KNOW.
OKAY. YOU'RE FREE TO TURN YOUR HEAD AND LOOK AROUND. WITH NO FEAR.
CAN YOU SEE FETUSES, MICHAEL? CAN YOU SEE SOMETHING THAT LOOKS LIKE A HYBRID BETWEEN--
YEAH--
YEAH, IT'S BECOMING CLEARER, I THINK I'M STARTING TO--
THERE HE IS!
WHAT?! WHAT IS THIS?!
WHO ARE YOU?!

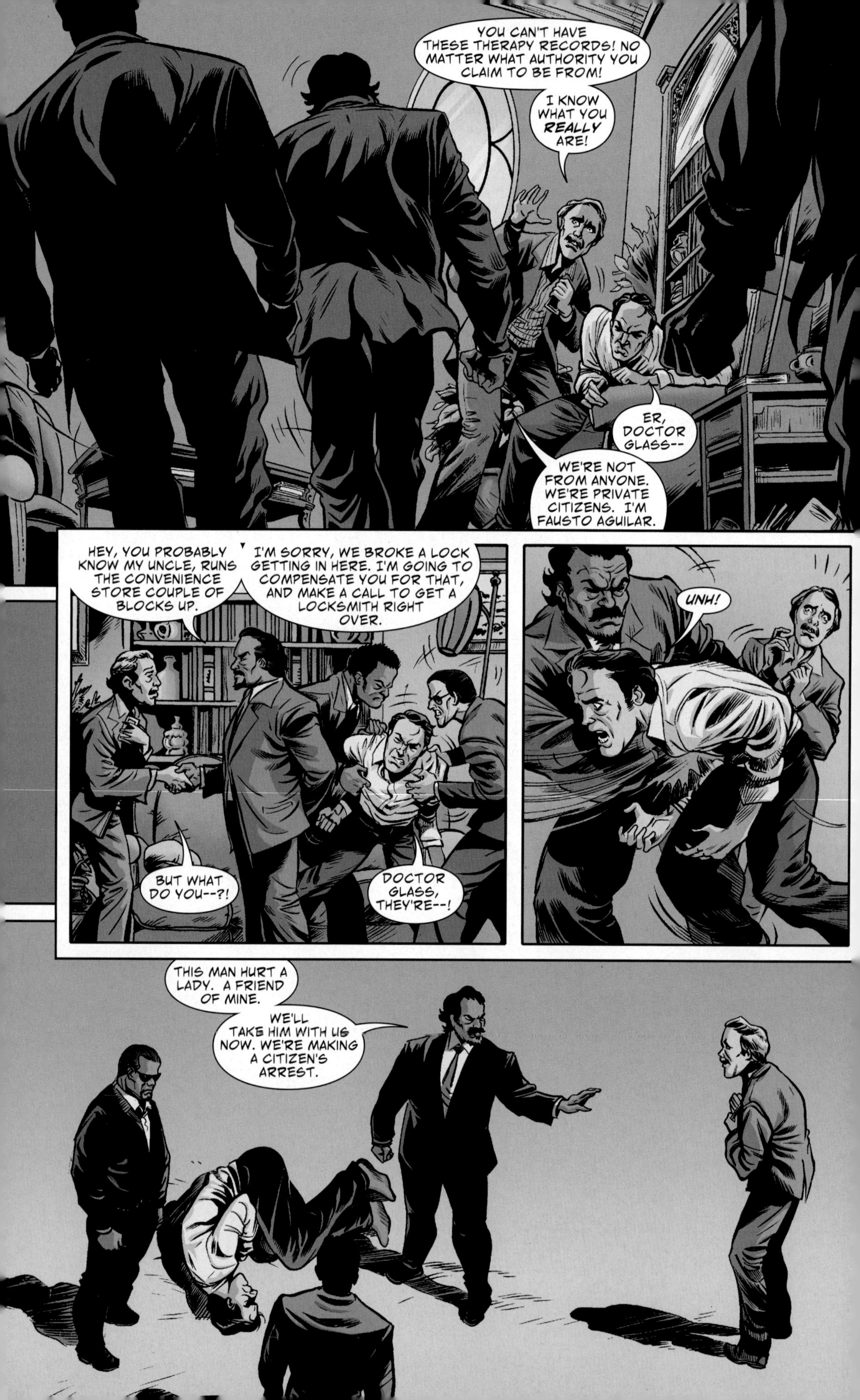
YOU CAN'T HAVE THESE THERAPY RECORDS! NO MATTER WHAT AUTHORITY YOU CLAIM TO BE FROM!
I KNOW WHAT YOU REALLY ARE!
ER, DOCTOR GLASS--
WE'RE NOT FROM ANYONE. WE'RE PRIVATE CITIZENS. I'M FAUSTO AGUILAR.
HEY, YOU PROBABLY KNOW MY UNCLE, RUNS THE CONVENIENCE STORE COUPLE OF BLOCKS UP.
I'M SORRY, WE BROKE A LOCK GETTING IN HERE. I'M GOING TO COMPENSATE YOU FOR THAT, AND MAKE A CALL TO GET A LOCKSMITH RIGHT OVER.
BUT WHAT DO YOU--?!
DOCTOR GLASS, THEY'RE--!
UNH!
THIS MAN HURT A LADY. A FRIEND OF MINE.
WE'LL TAKE HIM WITH US NOW. WE'RE MAKING A CITIZEN'S ARREST.

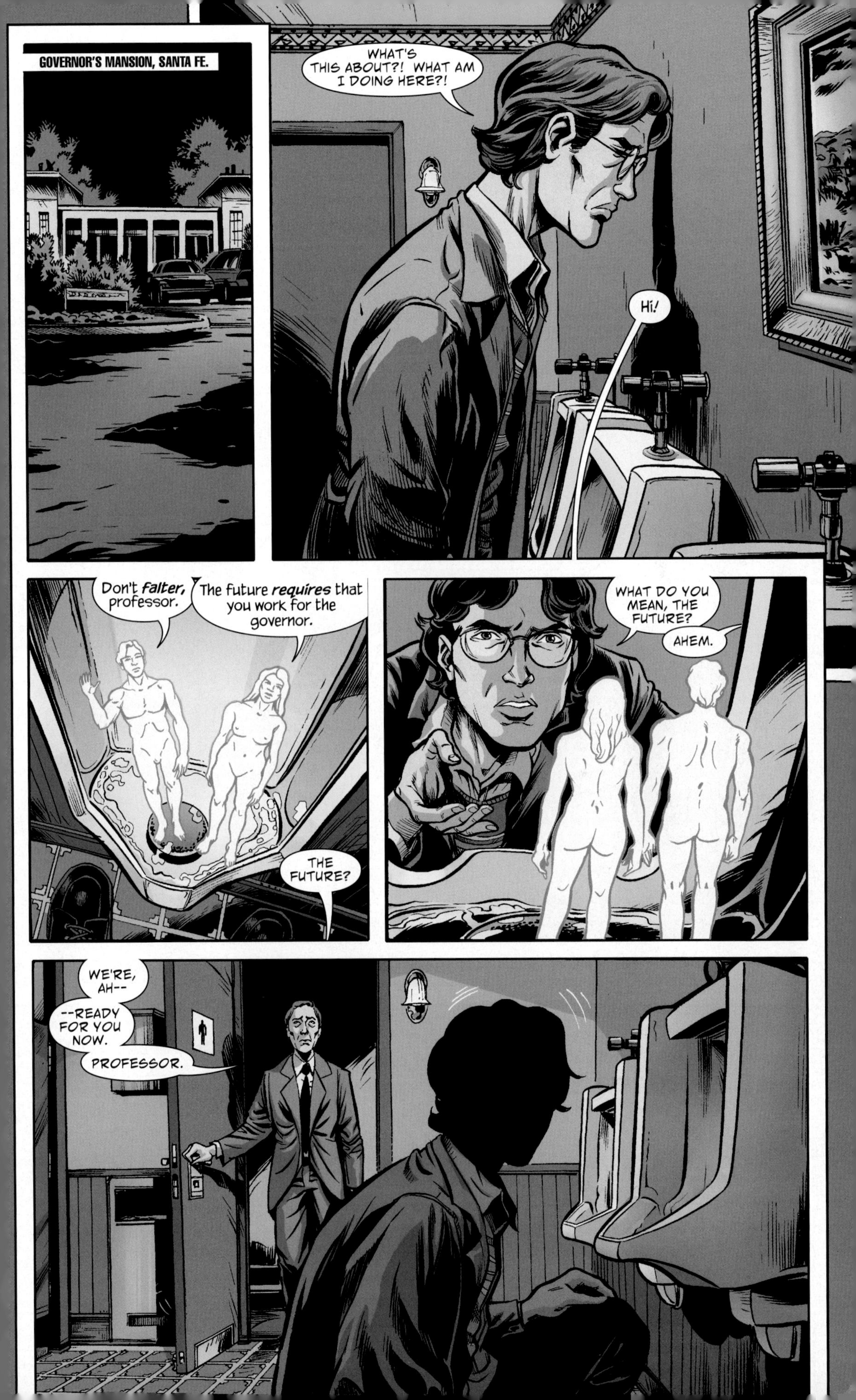
GOVERNOR'S MANSION, SANTA FE.
WHAT'S THIS ABOUT?! WHAT AM I DOING HERE?!
Hi!
Don't *falter,* professor.
The future *requires* that you work for the governor.
THE FUTURE?
WHAT DO YOU MEAN, THE FUTURE?
AHEM.
WE'RE, AH--
--READY FOR YOU NOW.
PROFESSOR.

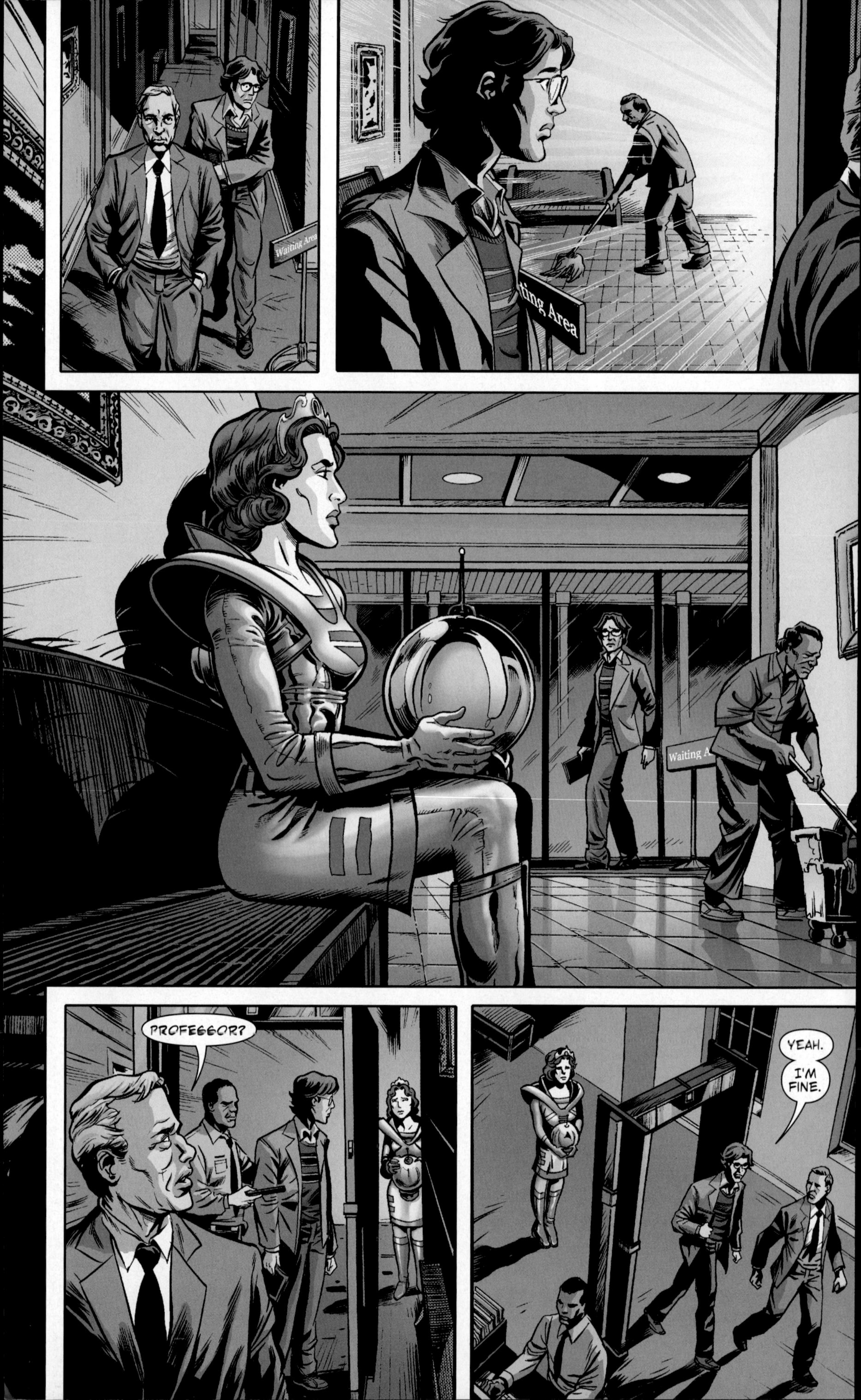
Waiting Area
Waiting Area
Waiting Area
PROFESSOR?
YEAH. I'M FINE.

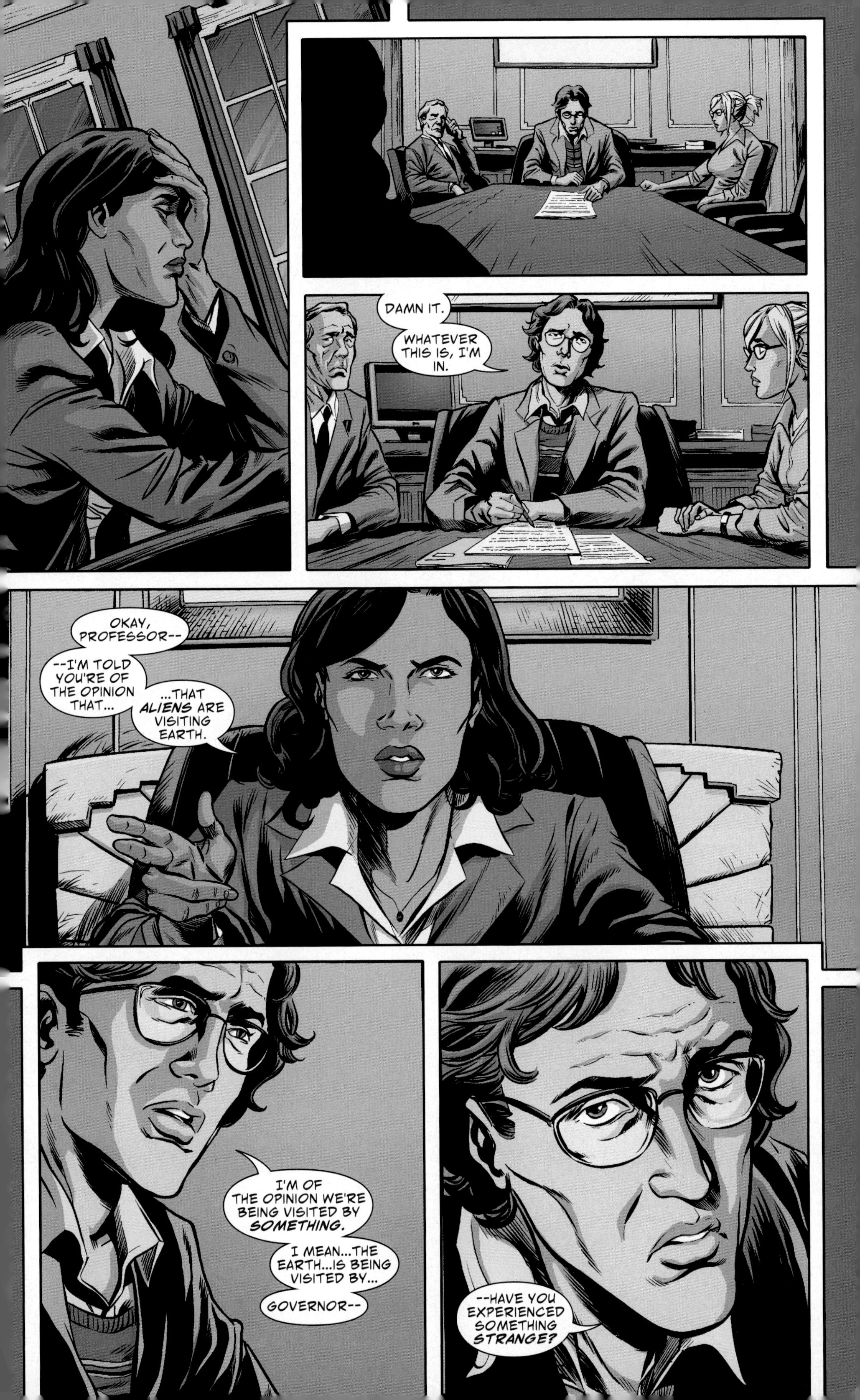
DAMN IT.
WHATEVER THIS IS, I'M IN.
OKAY, PROFESSOR--
--I'M TOLD YOU'RE OF THE OPINION THAT...
...THAT ALIENS ARE VISITING EARTH.
I'M OF THE OPINION WE'RE BEING VISITED BY SOMETHING.
I MEAN...THE EARTH...IS BEING VISITED BY...
GOVERNOR--
--HAVE YOU EXPERIENCED SOMETHING STRANGE?

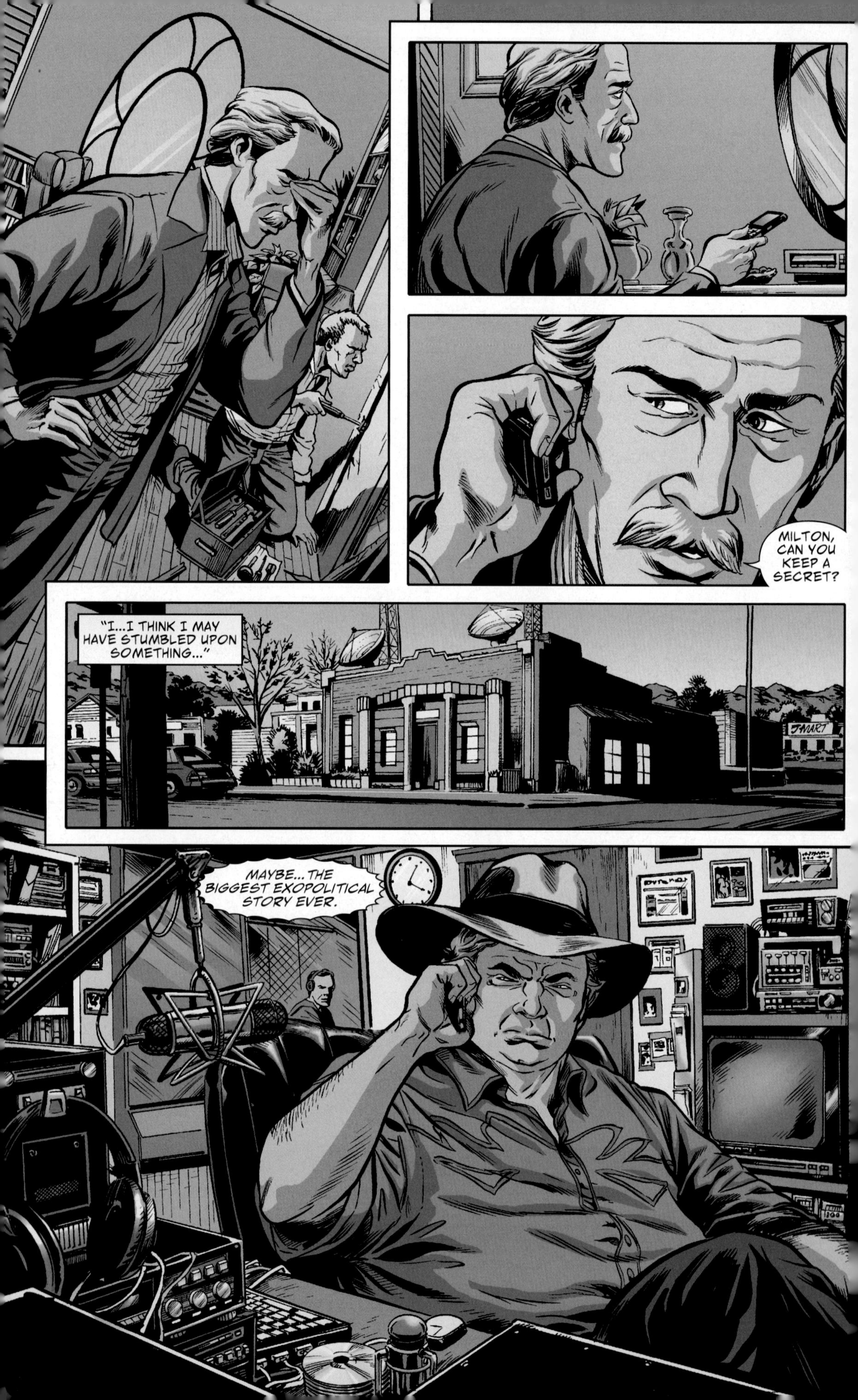
MILTON, CAN YOU KEEP A SECRET?
"I...I THINK I MAY HAVE STUMBLED UPON SOMETHING..."
MAYBE... THE BIGGEST EXOPOLITICAL STORY EVER.

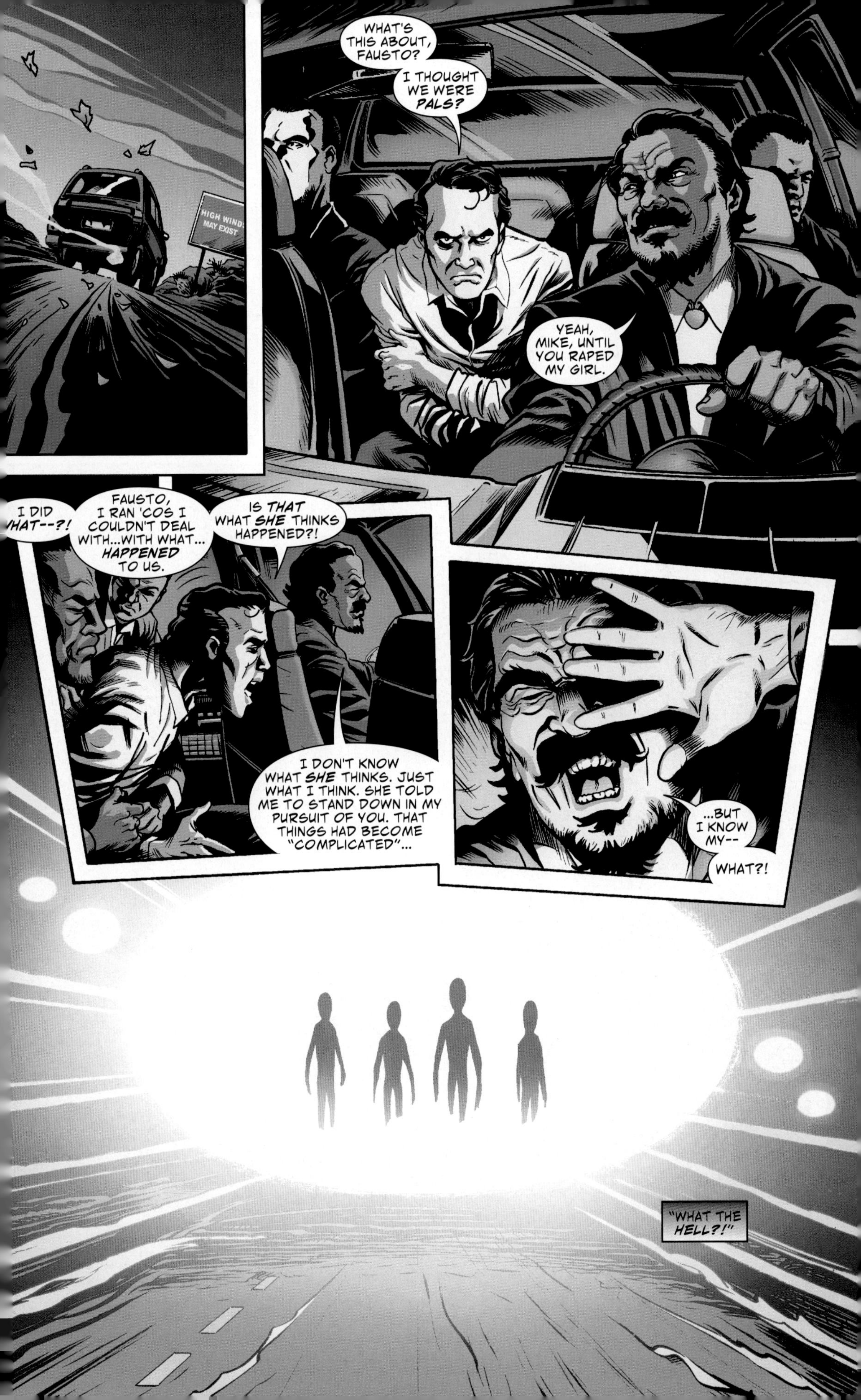
HIGH WINDS MAY EXIST
WHAT'S THIS ABOUT, FAUSTO?
I THOUGHT WE WERE PALS?
YEAH, MIKE, UNTIL YOU RAPED MY GIRL.
I DID WHAT--?!
FAUSTO, I RAN 'COS I COULDN'T DEAL WITH...WITH WHAT... HAPPENED TO US.
IS THAT WHAT SHE THINKS HAPPENED?!
I DON'T KNOW WHAT SHE THINKS. JUST WHAT I THINK. SHE TOLD ME TO STAND DOWN IN MY PURSUIT OF YOU. THAT THINGS HAD BECOME "COMPLICATED"...
...BUT I KNOW MY--
WHAT?!
"WHAT THE HELL?!"

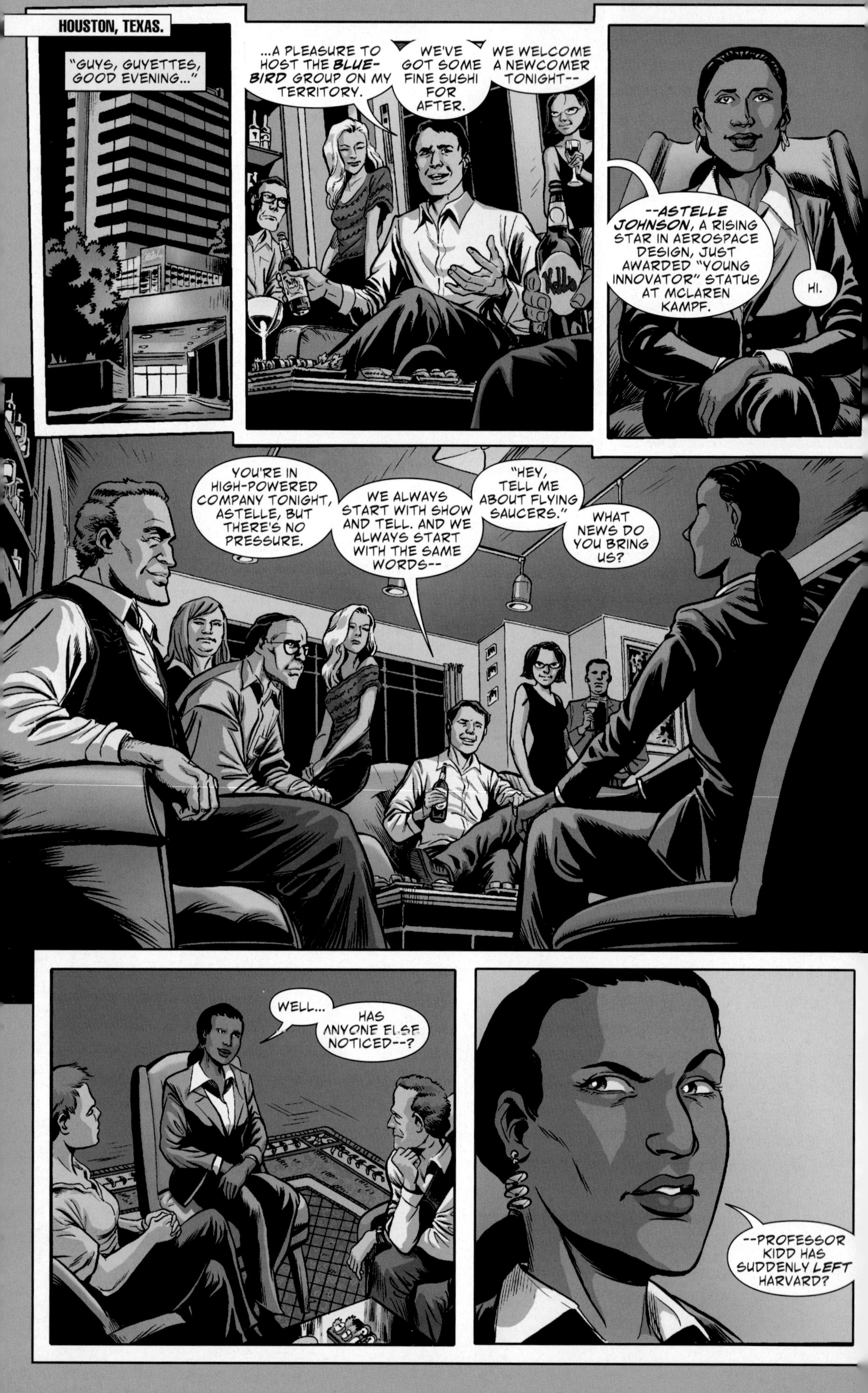
HOUSTON, TEXAS.
"GUYS, GUYETTES, GOOD EVENING..."
...A PLEASURE TO HOST THE BLUEBIRD GROUP ON MY TERRITORY.
WE'VE GOT SOME FINE SUSHI FOR AFTER.
WE WELCOME A NEWCOMER TONIGHT--
--ASTELLE JOHNSON, A RISING STAR IN AEROSPACE DESIGN, JUST AWARDED "YOUNG INNOVATOR" STATUS AT MCLAREN KAMPF.
HI.
YOU'RE IN HIGH-POWERED COMPANY TONIGHT, ASTELLE, BUT THERE'S NO PRESSURE.
WE ALWAYS START WITH SHOW AND TELL. AND WE ALWAYS START WITH THE SAME WORDS--
"HEY, TELL ME ABOUT FLYING SAUCERS."
WHAT NEWS DO YOU BRING US?
WELL...
HAS ANYONE ELSE NOTICED--?
--PROFESSOR KIDD HAS SUDDENLY LEFT HARVARD?

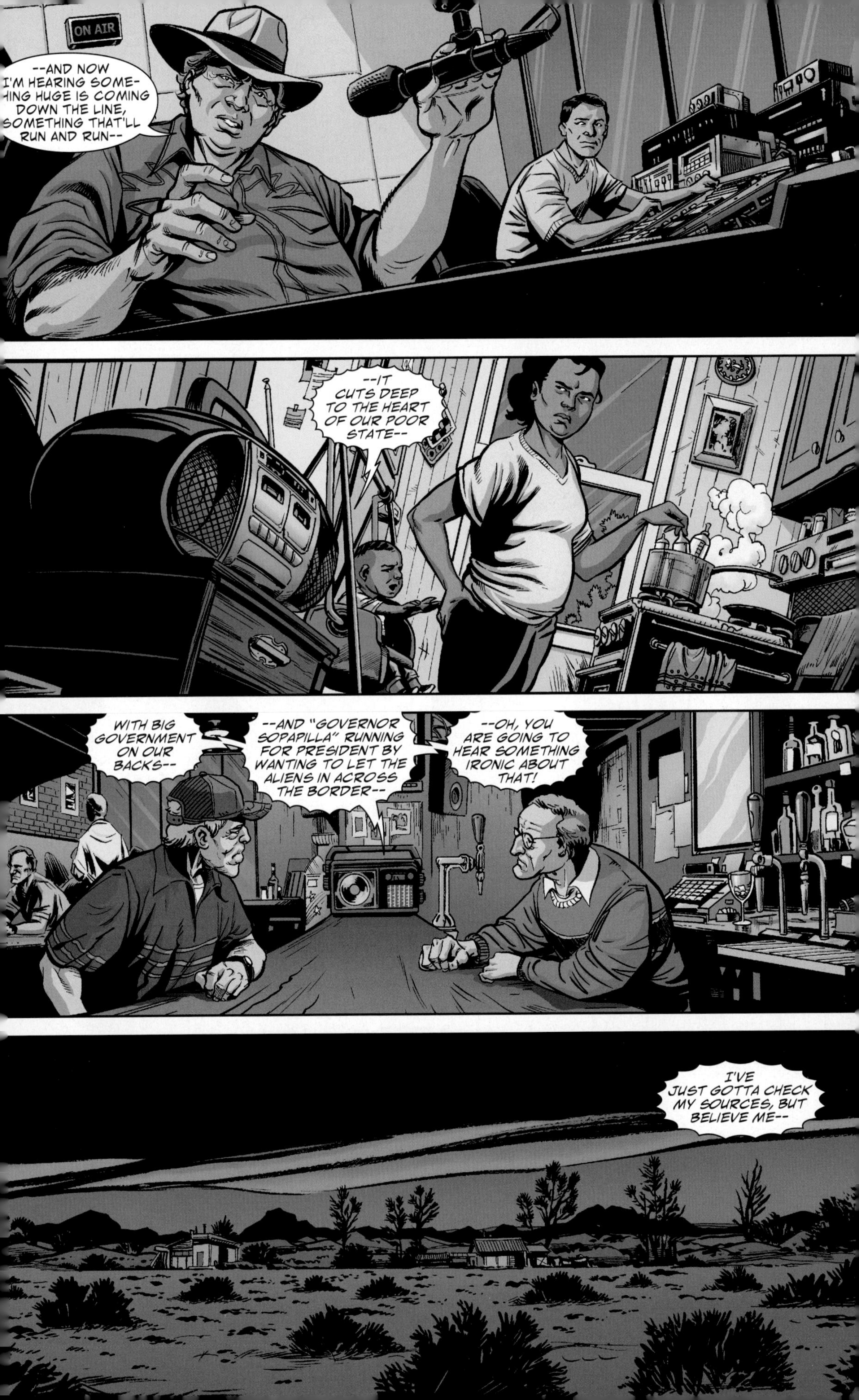
ON AIR
--AND NOW I'M HEARING SOMETHING HUGE IS COMING DOWN THE LINE, SOMETHING THAT'LL RUN AND RUN--
--IT CUTS DEEP TO THE HEART OF OUR POOR STATE--
WITH BIG GOVERNMENT ON OUR BACKS--
--AND "GOVERNOR SOPAPILLA" RUNNING FOR PRESIDENT BY WANTING TO LET THE ALIENS IN ACROSS THE BORDER--
--OH, YOU ARE GOING TO HEAR SOMETHING IRONIC ABOUT THAT!
I'VE JUST GOTTA CHECK MY SOURCES, BUT BELIEVE ME--

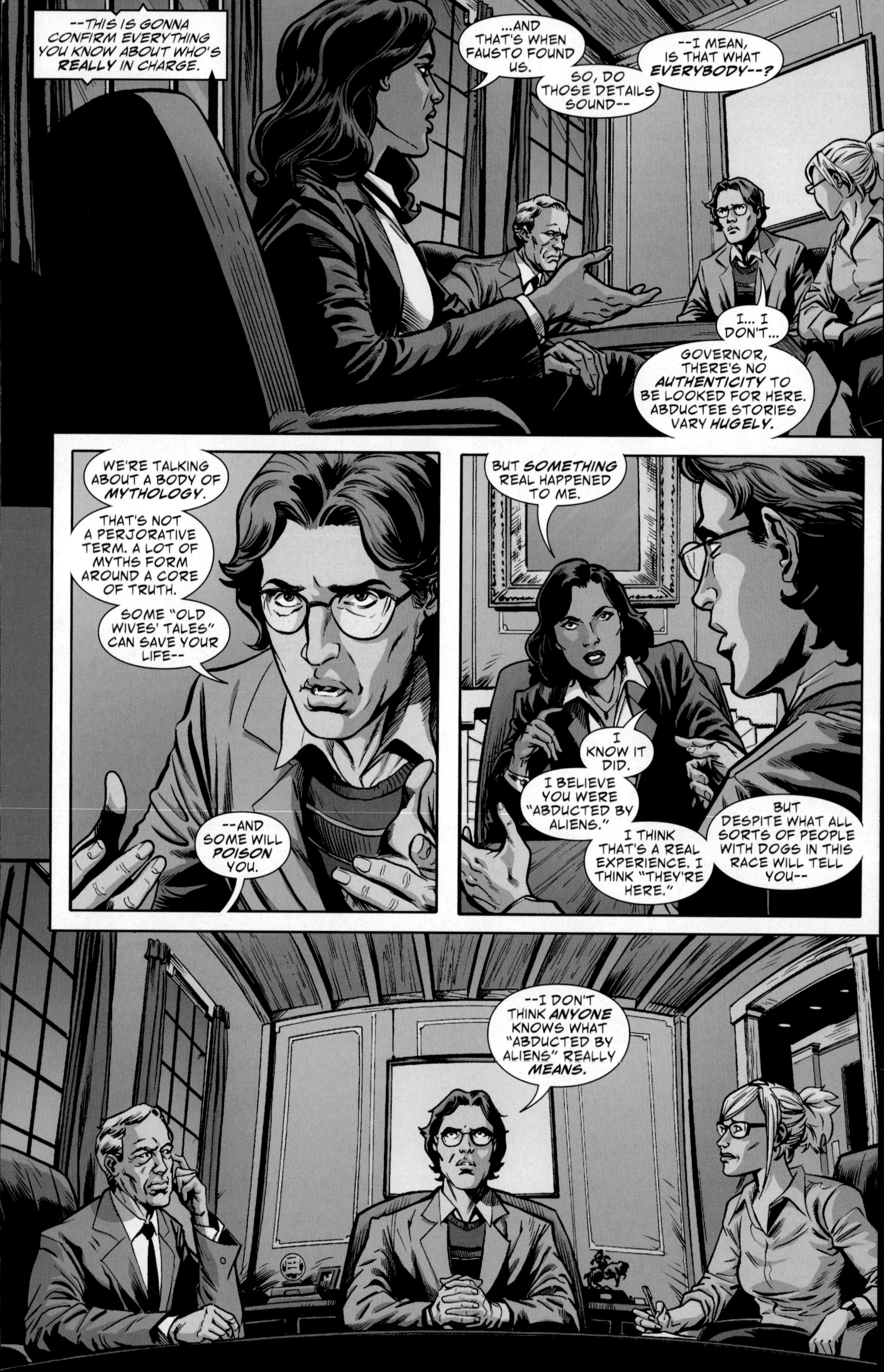
--THIS IS GONNA CONFIRM EVERYTHING YOU KNOW ABOUT WHO'S REALLY IN CHARGE.
...AND THAT'S WHEN FAUSTO FOUND US.
SO, DO THOSE DETAILS SOUND--
--I MEAN, IS THAT WHAT EVERYBODY--?
I... I DON'T...
GOVERNOR, THERE'S NO AUTHENTICITY TO BE LOOKED FOR HERE. ABDUCTEE STORIES VARY HUGELY.
WE'RE TALKING ABOUT A BODY OF MYTHOLOGY.
THAT'S NOT A PERJORATIVE TERM. A LOT OF MYTHS FORM AROUND A CORE OF TRUTH.
SOME "OLD WIVES' TALES" CAN SAVE YOUR LIFE--
--AND SOME WILL POISON YOU.
BUT SOMETHING REAL HAPPENED TO ME.
I KNOW IT DID.
I BELIEVE YOU WERE "ABDUCTED BY ALIENS."
I THINK THAT'S A REAL EXPERIENCE. I THINK "THEY'RE HERE."
BUT DESPITE WHAT ALL SORTS OF PEOPLE WITH DOGS IN THIS RACE WILL TELL YOU--
--I DON'T THINK ANYONE KNOWS WHAT "ABDUCTED BY ALIENS" REALLY MEANS.

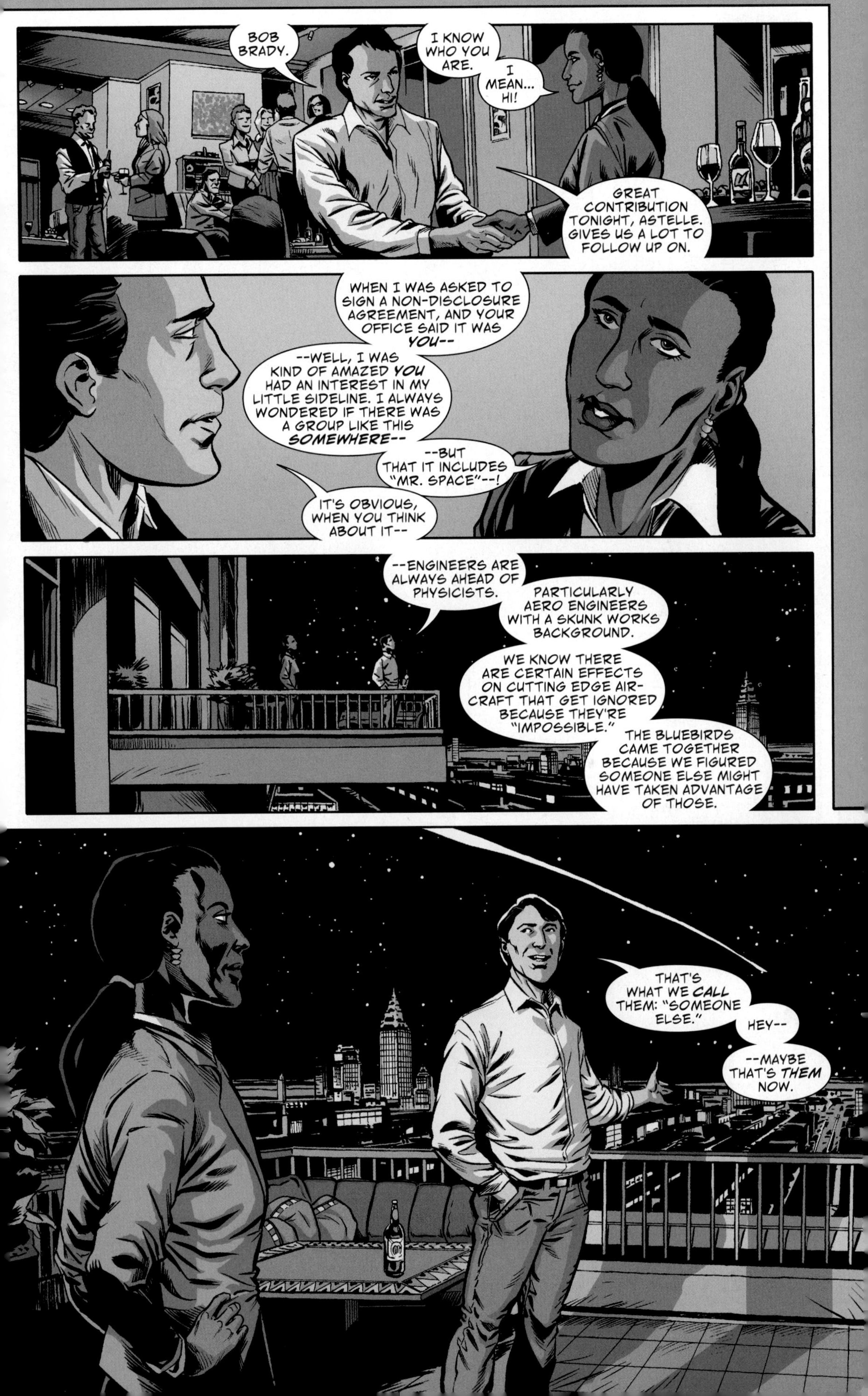
BOB BRADY.
I KNOW WHO YOU ARE.
I MEAN... HI!
GREAT CONTRIBUTION TONIGHT, ASTELLE. GIVES US A LOT TO FOLLOW UP ON.
WHEN I WAS ASKED TO SIGN A NON-DISCLOSURE AGREEMENT, AND YOUR OFFICE SAID IT WAS YOU--
--WELL, I WAS KIND OF AMAZED YOU HAD AN INTEREST IN MY LITTLE SIDELINE. I ALWAYS WONDERED IF THERE WAS A GROUP LIKE THIS SOMEWHERE--
--BUT THAT IT INCLUDES "MR. SPACE"--!
IT'S OBVIOUS, WHEN YOU THINK ABOUT IT--
--ENGINEERS ARE ALWAYS AHEAD OF PHYSICISTS.
PARTICULARLY AERO ENGINEERS WITH A SKUNK WORKS BACKGROUND.
WE KNOW THERE ARE CERTAIN EFFECTS ON CUTTING EDGE AIRCRAFT THAT GET IGNORED BECAUSE THEY'RE "IMPOSSIBLE."
THE BLUEBIRDS CAME TOGETHER BECAUSE WE FIGURED SOMEONE ELSE MIGHT HAVE TAKEN ADVANTAGE OF THOSE.
THAT'S WHAT WE CALL THEM: "SOMEONE ELSE."
HEY--
--MAYBE THAT'S THEM NOW.

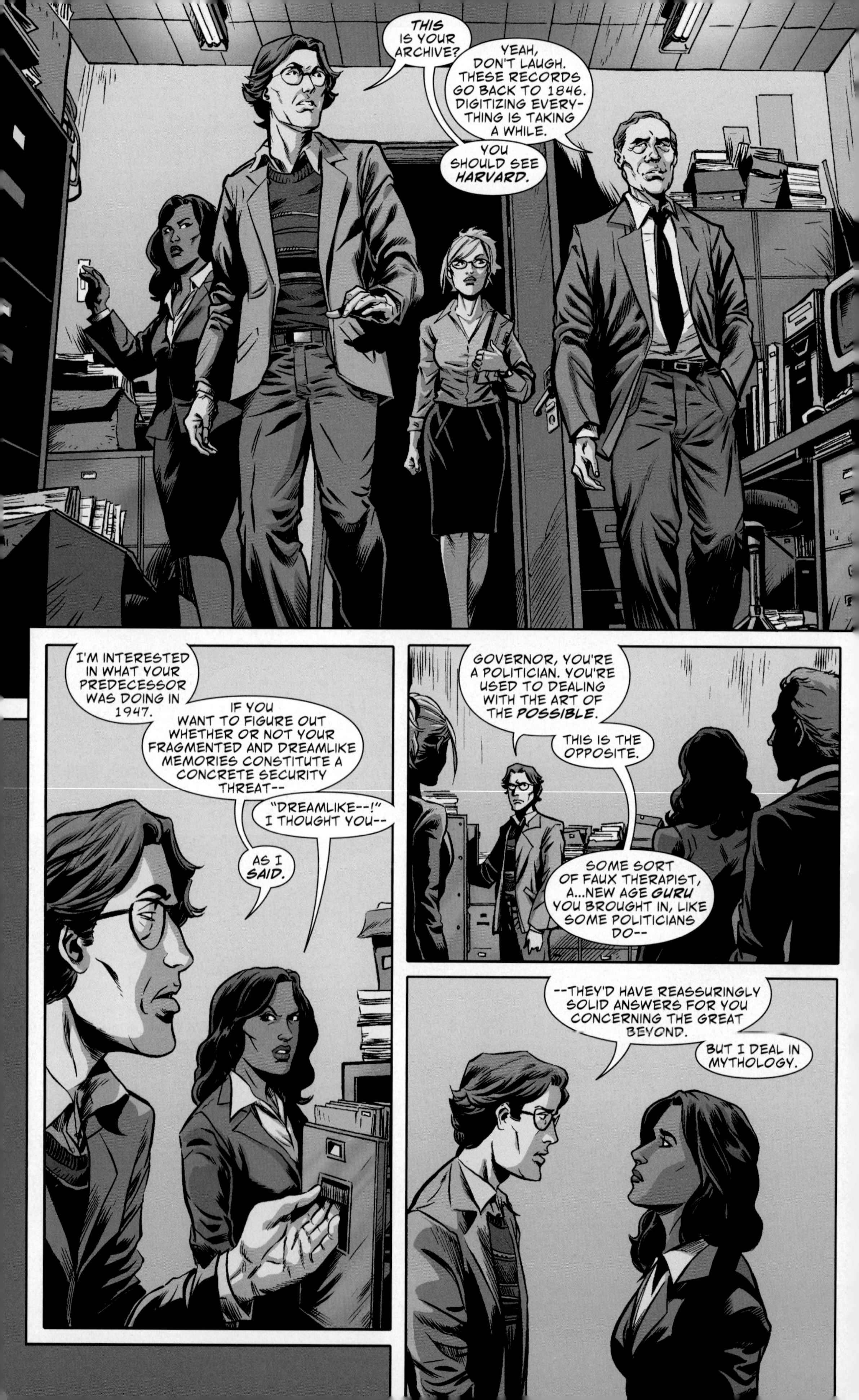

THIS IS YOUR ARCHIVE?
YEAH, DON'T LAUGH. THESE RECORDS GO BACK TO 1846. DIGITIZING EVERYTHING IS TAKING A WHILE.
YOU SHOULD SEE HARVARD.
I'M INTERESTED IN WHAT YOUR PREDECESSOR WAS DOING IN 1947.
IF YOU WANT TO FIGURE OUT WHETHER OR NOT YOUR FRAGMENTED AND DREAMLIKE MEMORIES CONSTITUTE A CONCRETE SECURITY THREAT--
"DREAMLIKE--!" I THOUGHT YOU--
AS I SAID.
GOVERNOR, YOU'RE A POLITICIAN. YOU'RE USED TO DEALING WITH THE ART OF THE POSSIBLE.
THIS IS THE OPPOSITE.
SOME SORT OF FAUX THERAPIST, A...NEW AGE GURU YOU BROUGHT IN, LIKE SOME POLITICIANS DO--
--THEY'D HAVE REASSURINGLY SOLID ANSWERS FOR YOU CONCERNING THE GREAT BEYOND.
BUT I DEAL IN MYTHOLOGY.

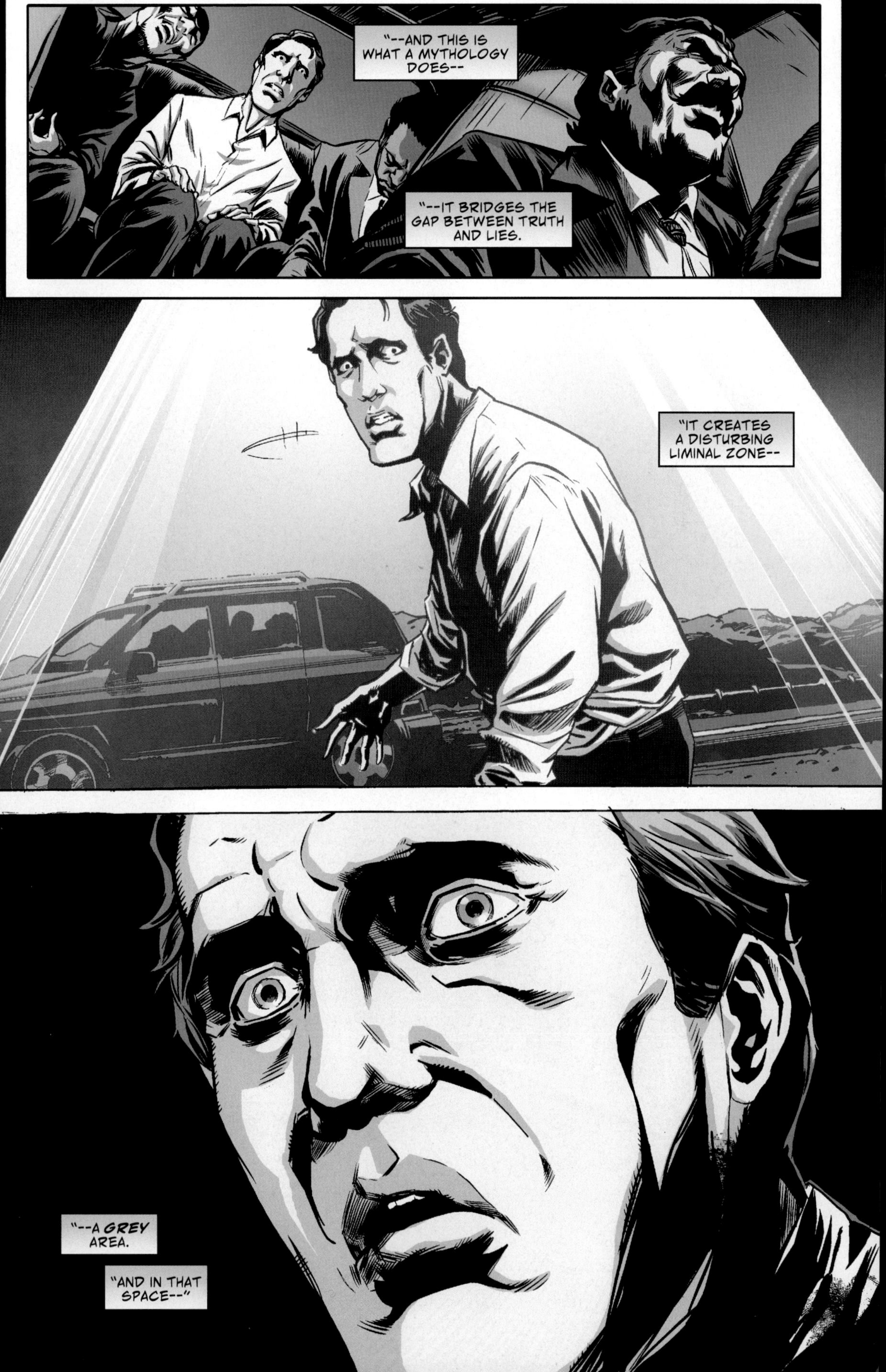
"--AND THIS IS WHAT A MYTHOLOGY DOES--
"--IT BRIDGES THE GAP BETWEEN TRUTH AND LIES.
"IT CREATES A DISTURBING LIMINAL ZONE--
"--A *GREY* AREA.
"AND IN THAT SPACE--"

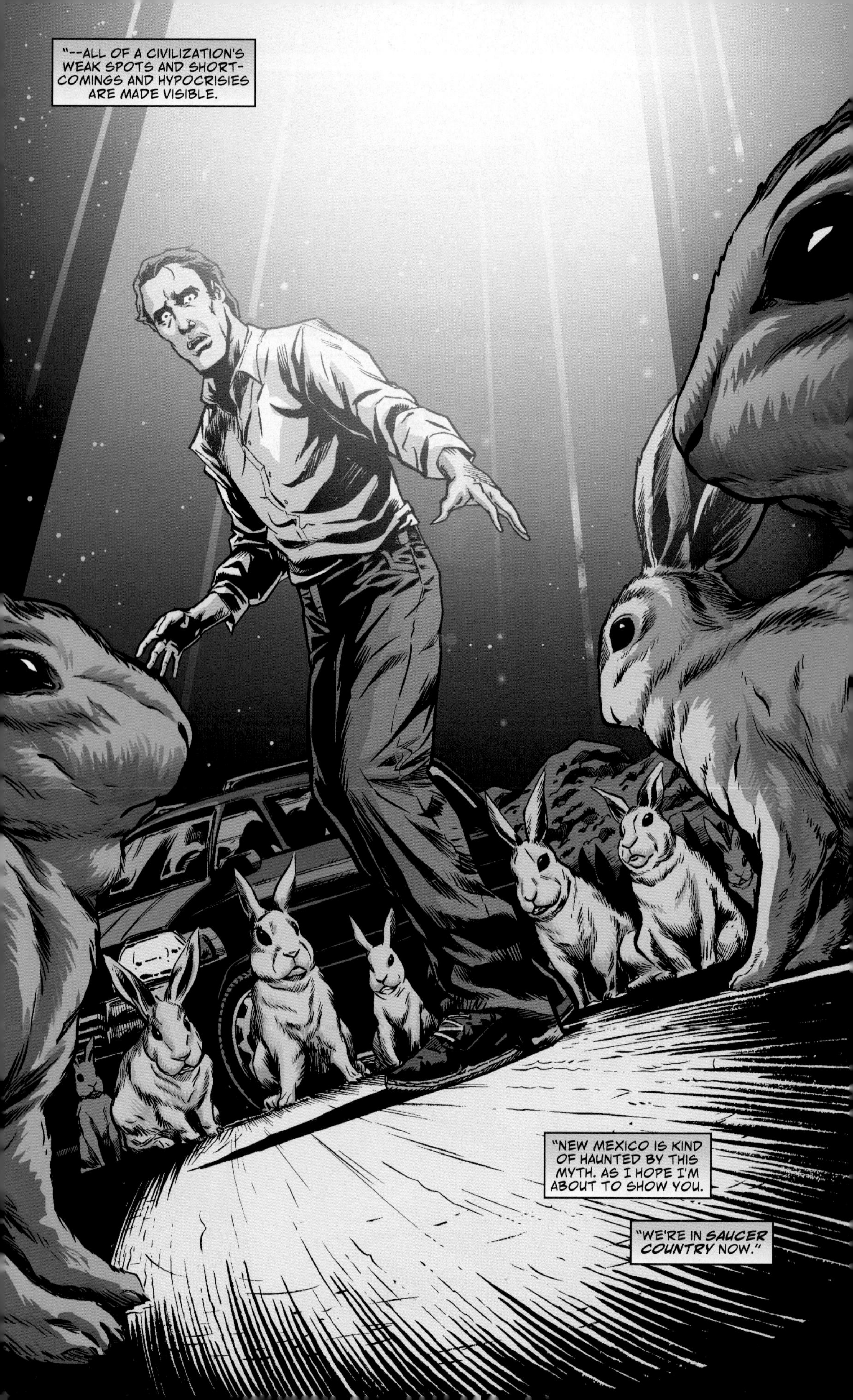
"--ALL OF A CIVILIZATION'S WEAK SPOTS AND SHORT-COMINGS AND HYPOCRISIES ARE MADE VISIBLE.
"NEW MEXICO IS KIND OF HAUNTED BY THIS MYTH. AS I HOPE I'M ABOUT TO SHOW YOU.
"WE'RE IN *SAUCER COUNTRY* NOW."

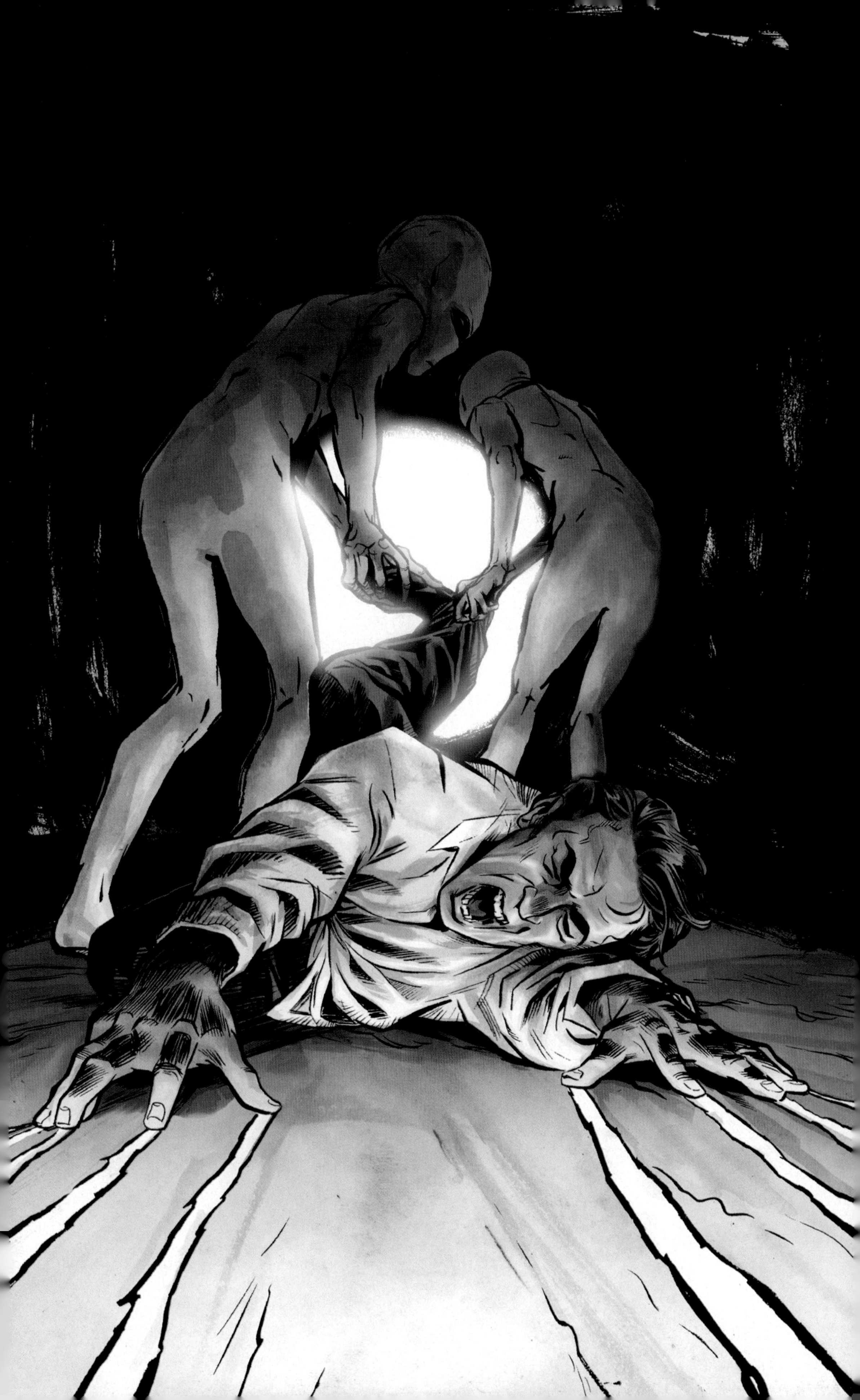

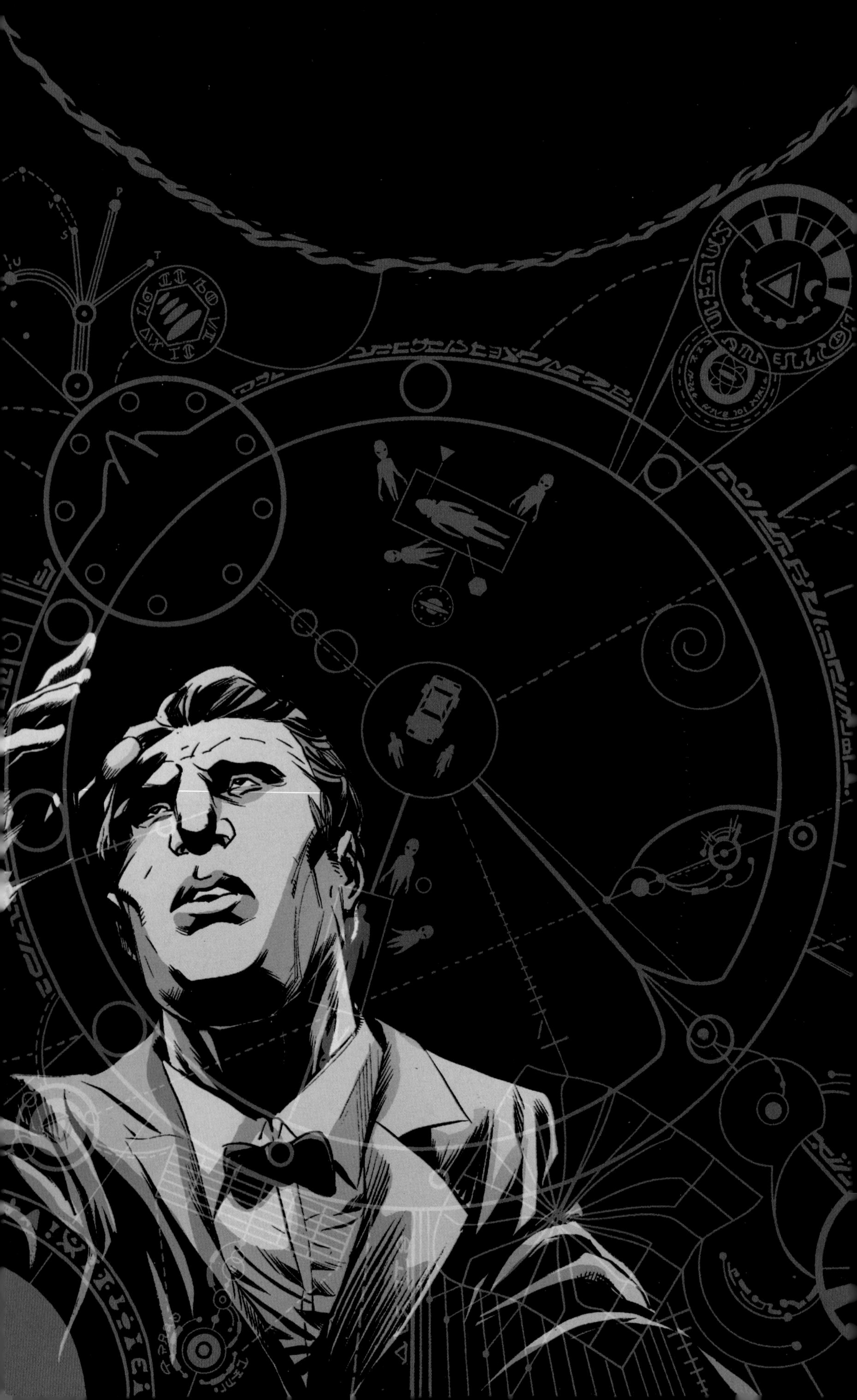

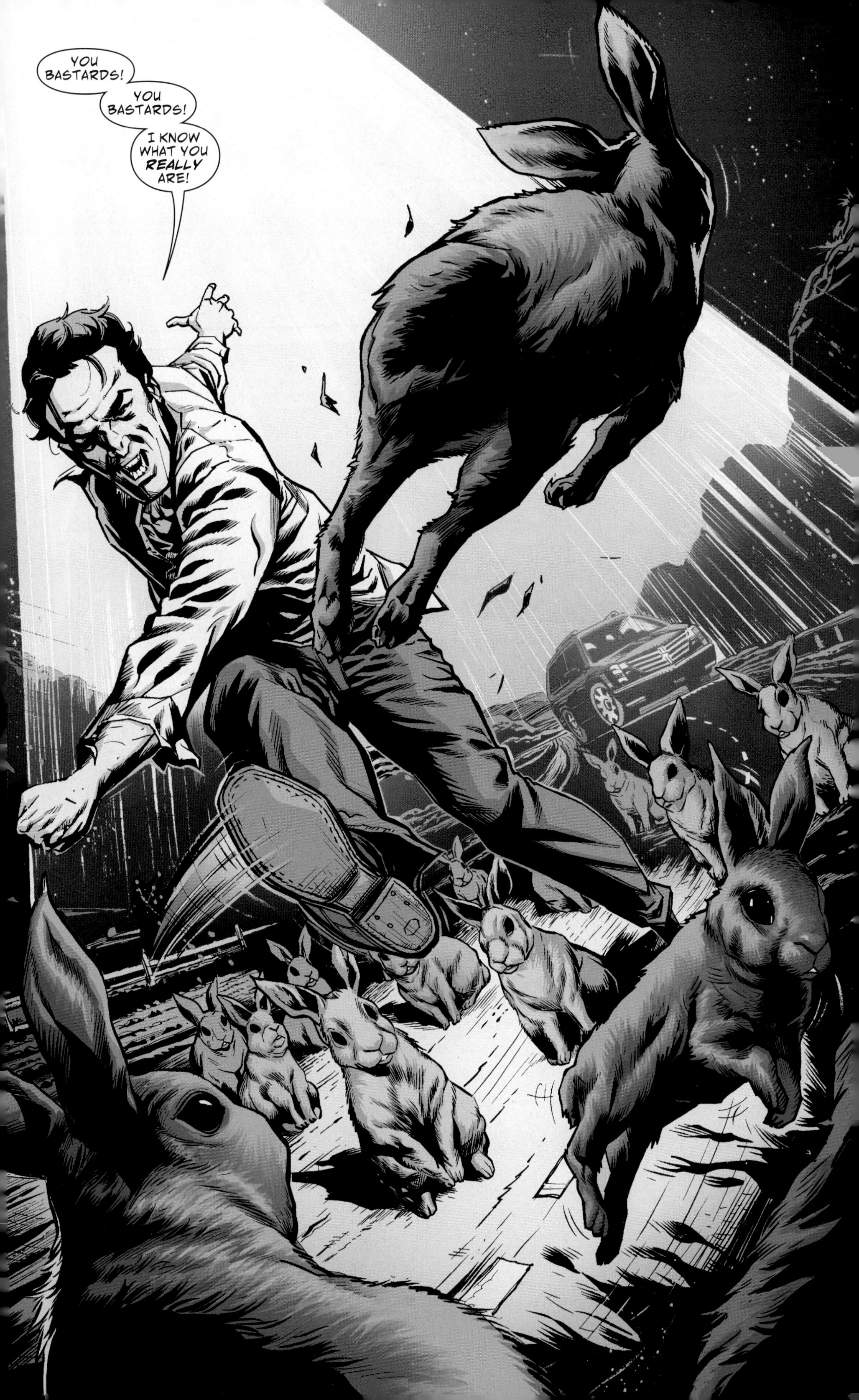
YOU BASTARDS!
YOU BASTARDS!
I KNOW WHAT YOU REALLY ARE!

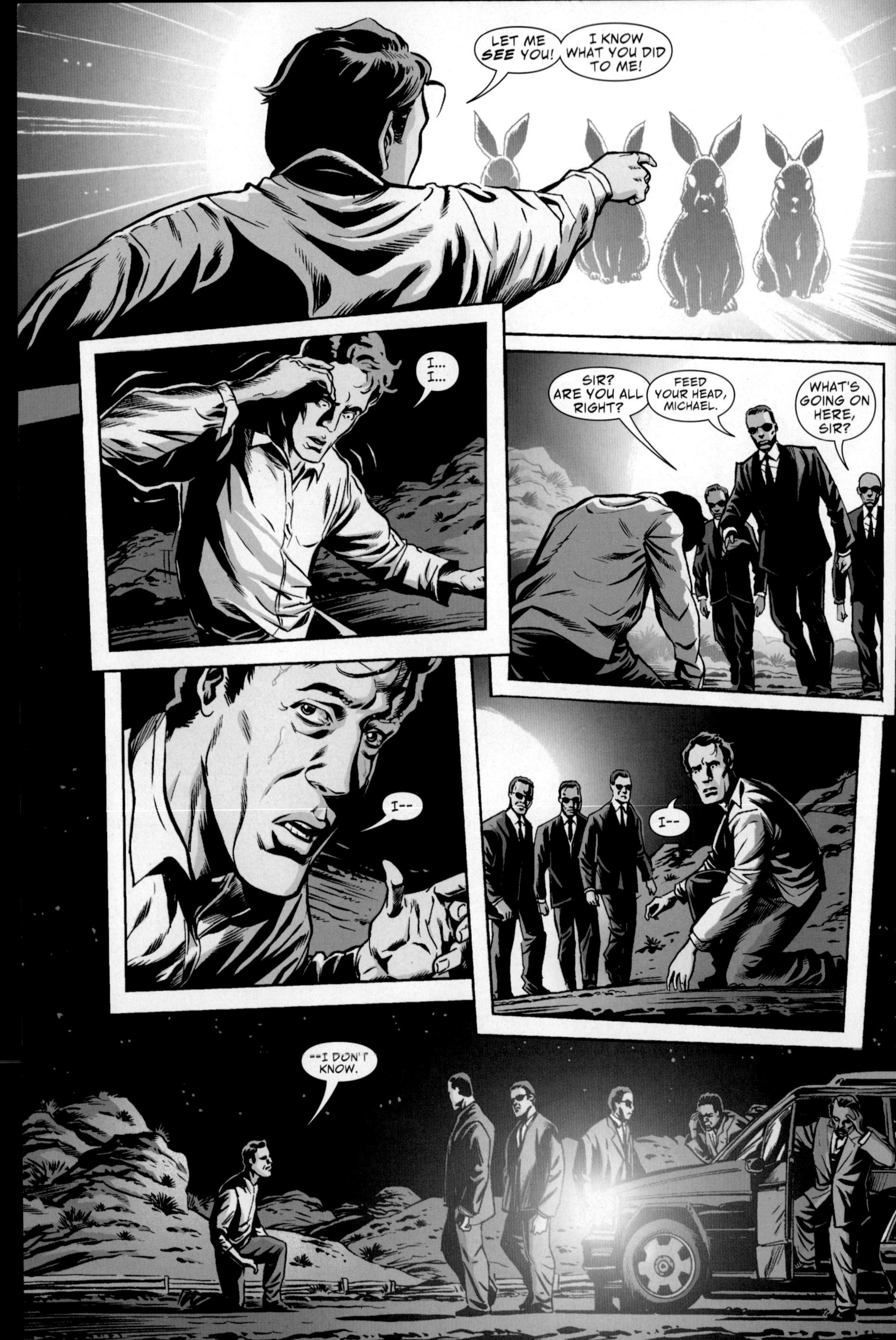
LET ME SEE YOU!
I KNOW WHAT YOU DID TO ME!
I... I...
SIR? ARE YOU ALL RIGHT?
FEED YOUR HEAD, MICHAEL.
WHAT'S GOING ON HERE, SIR?
I--
I--
--I DON'T KNOW.

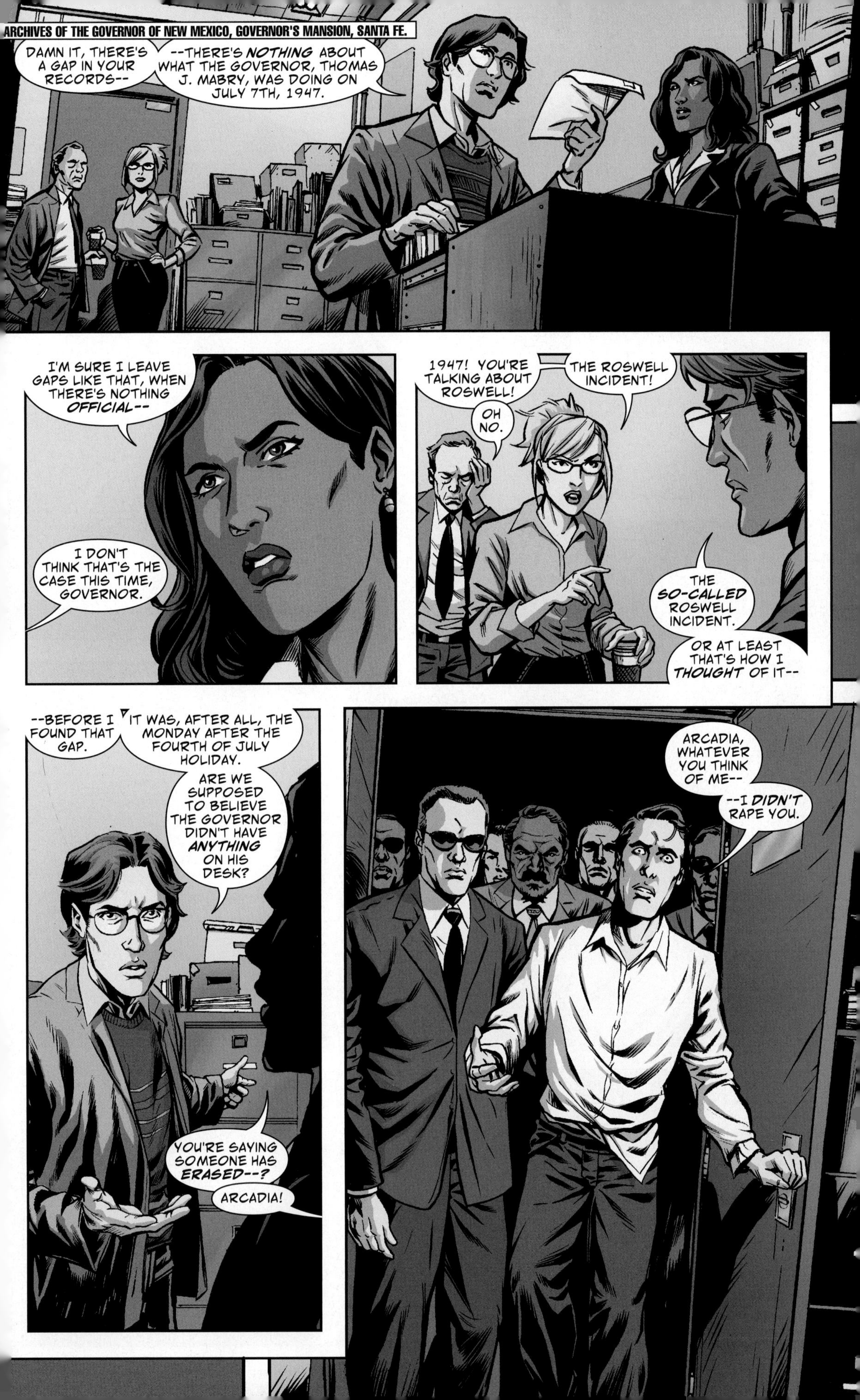
ARCHIVES OF THE GOVERNOR OF NEW MEXICO, GOVERNOR'S MANSION, SANTA FE.
DAMN IT, THERE'S A GAP IN YOUR RECORDS--
--THERE'S NOTHING ABOUT WHAT THE GOVERNOR, THOMAS J. MABRY, WAS DOING ON JULY 7TH, 1947.
I'M SURE I LEAVE GAPS LIKE THAT, WHEN THERE'S NOTHING OFFICIAL--
I DON'T THINK THAT'S THE CASE THIS TIME, GOVERNOR.
1947! YOU'RE TALKING ABOUT ROSWELL!
THE ROSWELL INCIDENT!
OH NO.
THE SO-CALLED ROSWELL INCIDENT.
OR AT LEAST THAT'S HOW I THOUGHT OF IT--
--BEFORE I FOUND THAT GAP.
IT WAS, AFTER ALL, THE MONDAY AFTER THE FOURTH OF JULY HOLIDAY.
ARE WE SUPPOSED TO BELIEVE THE GOVERNOR DIDN'T HAVE ANYTHING ON HIS DESK?
YOU'RE SAYING SOMEONE HAS ERASED--?
ARCADIA!
ARCADIA, WHATEVER YOU THINK OF ME--
--I DIDN'T RAPE YOU.

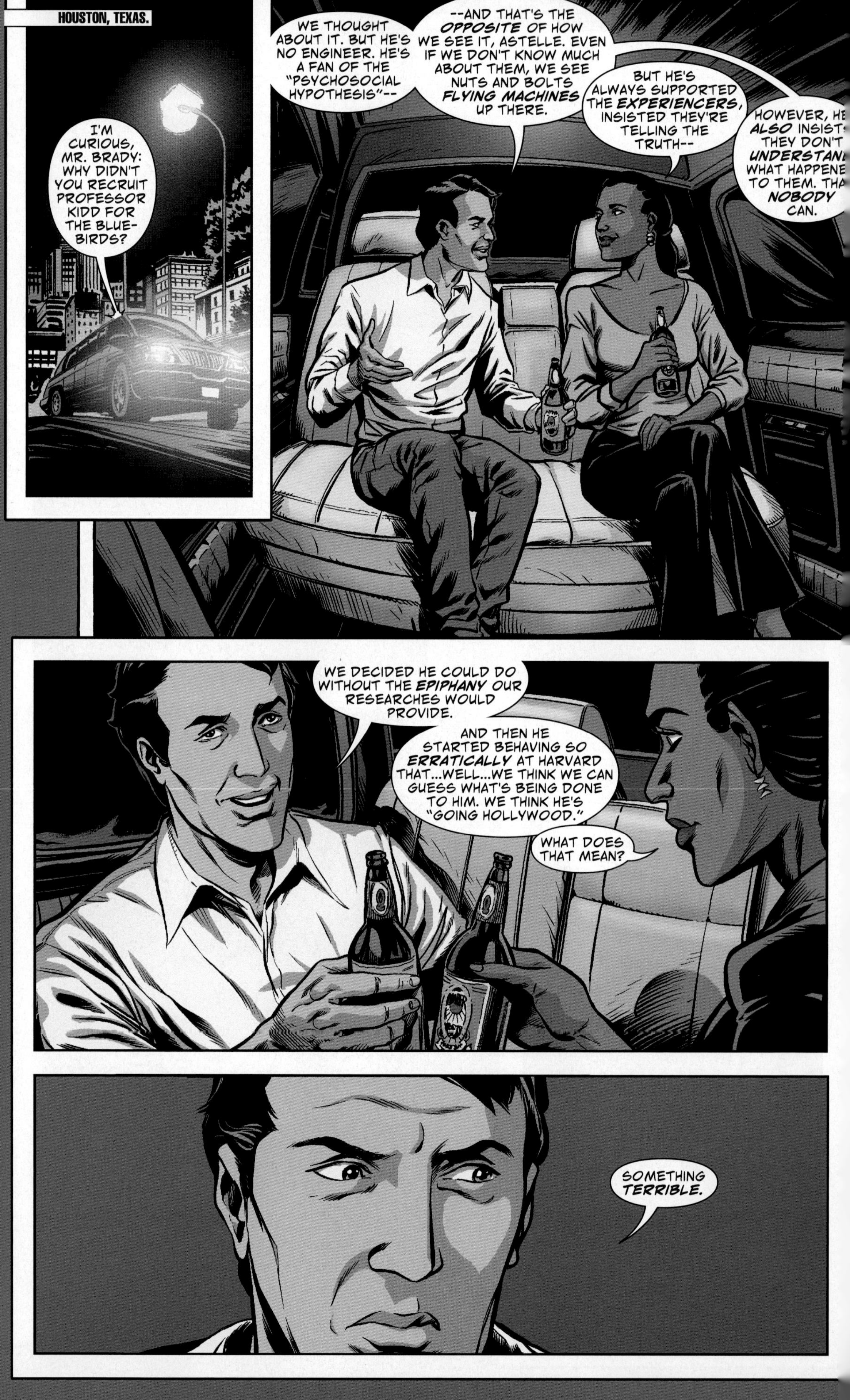
HOUSTON, TEXAS.
I'M CURIOUS, MR. BRADY: WHY DIDN'T YOU RECRUIT PROFESSOR KIDD FOR THE BLUE-BIRDS?
WE THOUGHT ABOUT IT. BUT HE'S NO ENGINEER. HE'S A FAN OF THE "PSYCHOSOCIAL HYPOTHESIS"--
--AND THAT'S THE OPPOSITE OF HOW WE SEE IT, ASTELLE. EVEN IF WE DON'T KNOW MUCH ABOUT THEM, WE SEE NUTS AND BOLTS FLYING MACHINES UP THERE.
BUT HE'S ALWAYS SUPPORTED THE EXPERIENCERS, INSISTED THEY'RE TELLING THE TRUTH--
HOWEVER, HE ALSO INSISTS THEY DON'T UNDERSTAN WHAT HAPPENE TO THEM. THA NOBODY CAN.
WE DECIDED HE COULD DO WITHOUT THE EPIPHANY OUR RESEARCHES WOULD PROVIDE.
AND THEN HE STARTED BEHAVING SO ERRATICALLY AT HARVARD THAT...WELL...WE THINK WE CAN GUESS WHAT'S BEING DONE TO HIM. WE THINK HE'S "GOING HOLLYWOOD."
WHAT DOES THAT MEAN?
SOMETHING TERRIBLE.

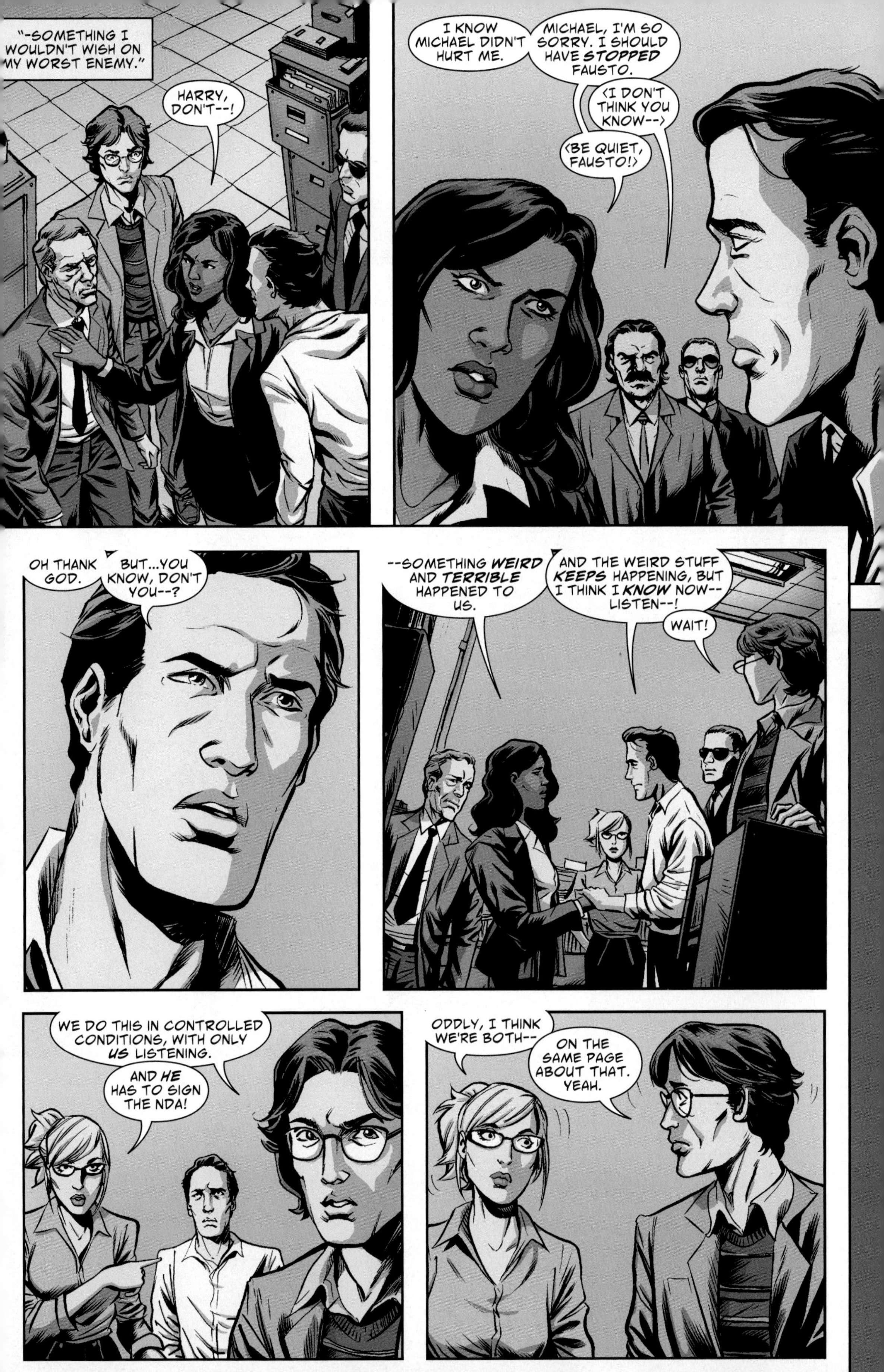
"-SOMETHING I WOULDN'T WISH ON MY WORST ENEMY."
HARRY, DON'T--!
I KNOW MICHAEL DIDN'T HURT ME.
MICHAEL, I'M SO SORRY. I SHOULD HAVE STOPPED FAUSTO.
‹I DON'T THINK YOU KNOW--›
‹BE QUIET, FAUSTO!›
OH THANK GOD.
BUT...YOU KNOW, DON'T YOU--?
--SOMETHING WEIRD AND TERRIBLE HAPPENED TO US.
AND THE WEIRD STUFF KEEPS HAPPENING, BUT I THINK I KNOW NOW-- LISTEN--!
WAIT!
WE DO THIS IN CONTROLLED CONDITIONS, WITH ONLY US LISTENING.
AND HE HAS TO SIGN THE NDA!
ODDLY, I THINK WE'RE BOTH--
ON THE SAME PAGE ABOUT THAT. YEAH.

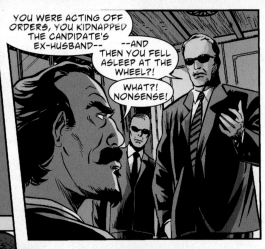

YOU WERE ACTING OFF ORDERS, YOU KIDNAPPED THE CANDIDATE'S EX-HUSBAND--

--AND THEN YOU FELL ASLEEP AT THE WHEEL?!

WHAT?! NONSENSE!

I REMEMBER NOTHING OF THE SORT.

I ASSUME YOU HAVE EVIDENCE OF THIS ALLEGED INCIDENT?

EVIDENCE--?

FAUSTO--IF I MAY CALL YOU FAUSTO--

--OR, IF I MAY NOT, BECAUSE HONESTLY? FUCK YOU--

--WE'RE THE OFFICIAL CANDIDATE SECURITY TEAM FOR A PRESIDENTIAL ELECTION.

YOU GO HOME NOW. THANK YOU FOR YOUR SERVICE. WE'LL TAKE IT FROM HERE.

SUCH UNPROFESSIONAL LANGUAGE. IT CHILLS ME, SIR. TO MY MUSCULAR, TATTOOED CORE.

WE WILL ONLY LEAVE THE GOVERNOR'S SIDE--

--ON THE GOVERNOR'S ORDERS.

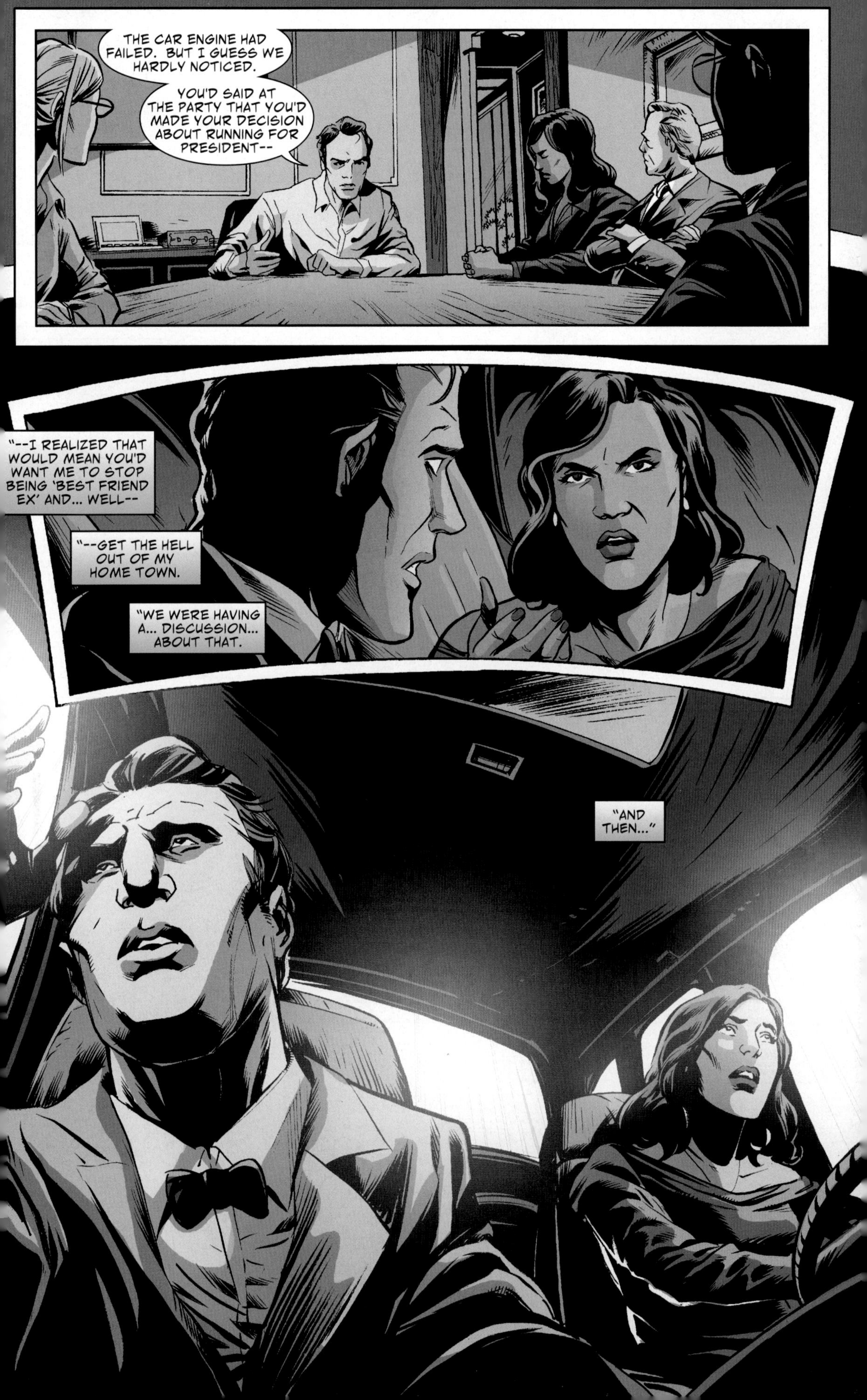
THE CAR ENGINE HAD FAILED. BUT I GUESS WE HARDLY NOTICED.
YOU'D SAID AT THE PARTY THAT YOU'D MADE YOUR DECISION ABOUT RUNNING FOR PRESIDENT--
"--I REALIZED THAT WOULD MEAN YOU'D WANT ME TO STOP BEING 'BEST FRIEND EX' AND... WELL--
"--GET THE HELL OUT OF MY HOME TOWN.
"WE WERE HAVING A... DISCUSSION... ABOUT THAT.
"AND THEN..."

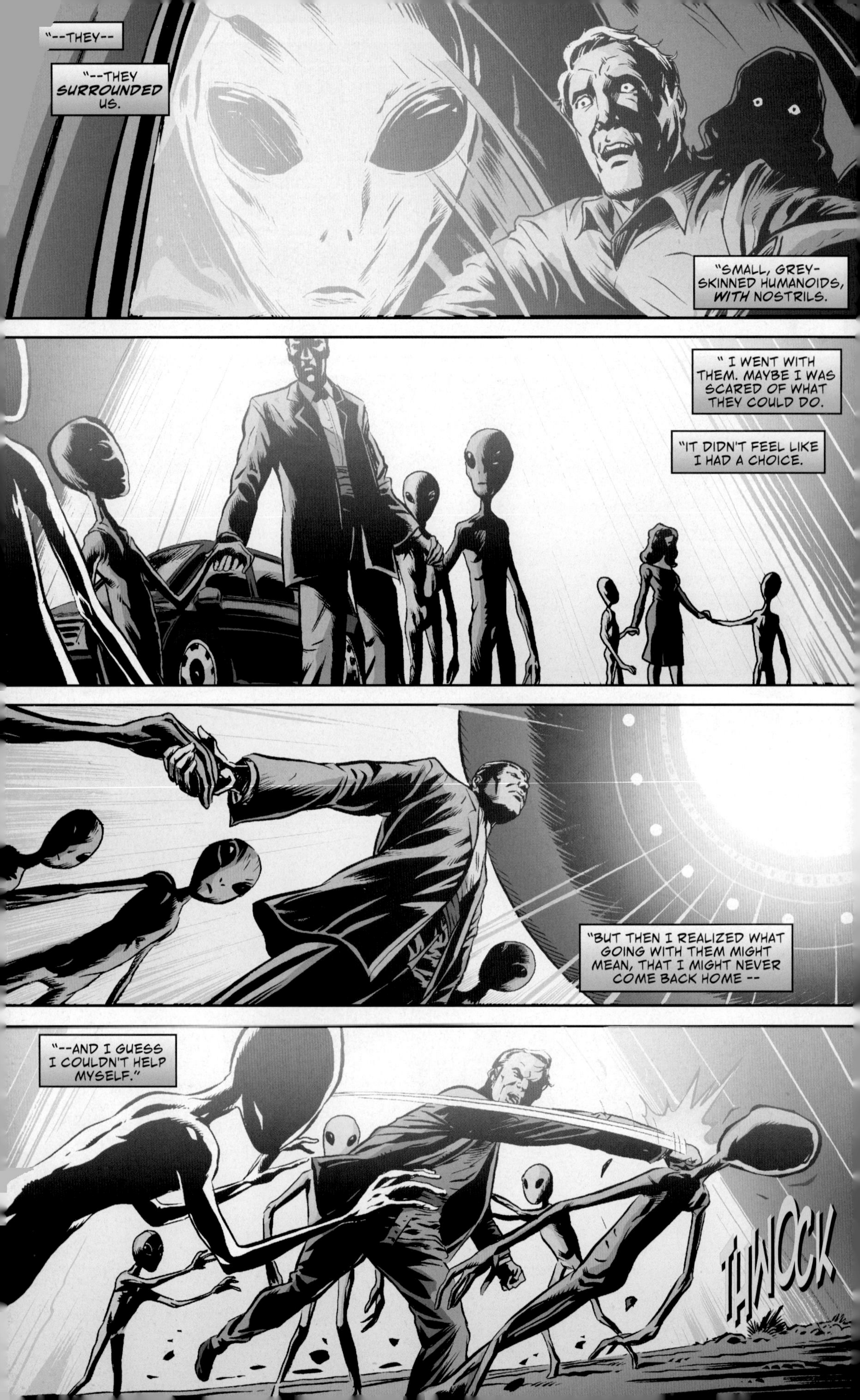
"--THEY--
"--THEY SURROUNDED US.
"SMALL, GREY-SKINNED HUMANOIDS, WITH NOSTRILS.
" I WENT WITH THEM. MAYBE I WAS SCARED OF WHAT THEY COULD DO.
"IT DIDN'T FEEL LIKE I HAD A CHOICE.
"BUT THEN I REALIZED WHAT GOING WITH THEM MIGHT MEAN, THAT I MIGHT NEVER COME BACK HOME --
"--AND I GUESS I COULDN'T HELP MYSELF."
THWOCK

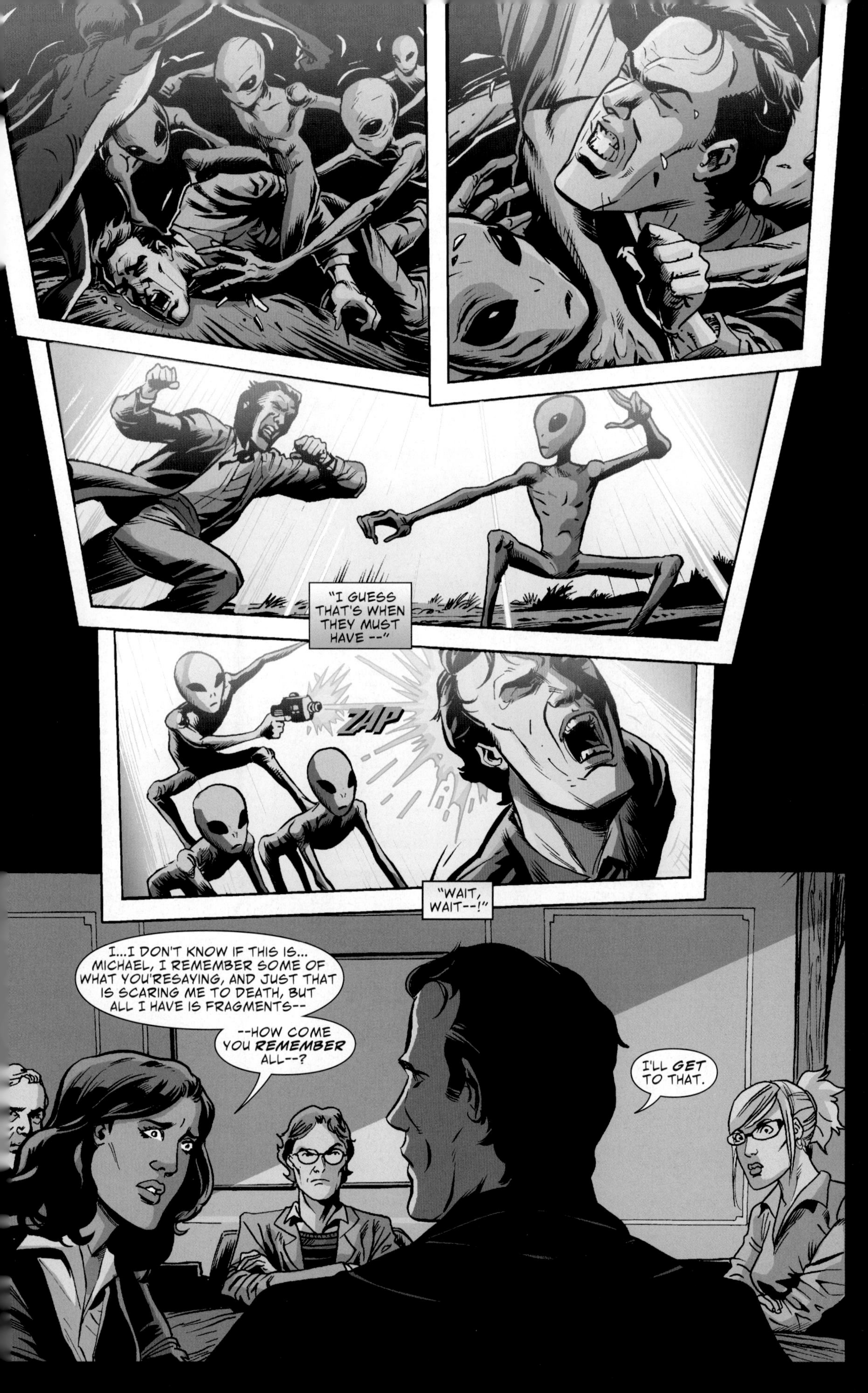
"I GUESS THAT'S WHEN THEY MUST HAVE --"
ZAP
"WAIT, WAIT--!"
I...I DON'T KNOW IF THIS IS... MICHAEL, I REMEMBER SOME OF WHAT YOU'RESAYING, AND JUST THAT IS SCARING ME TO DEATH, BUT ALL I HAVE IS FRAGMENTS--
--HOW COME YOU REMEMBER ALL--?
I'LL GET TO THAT.

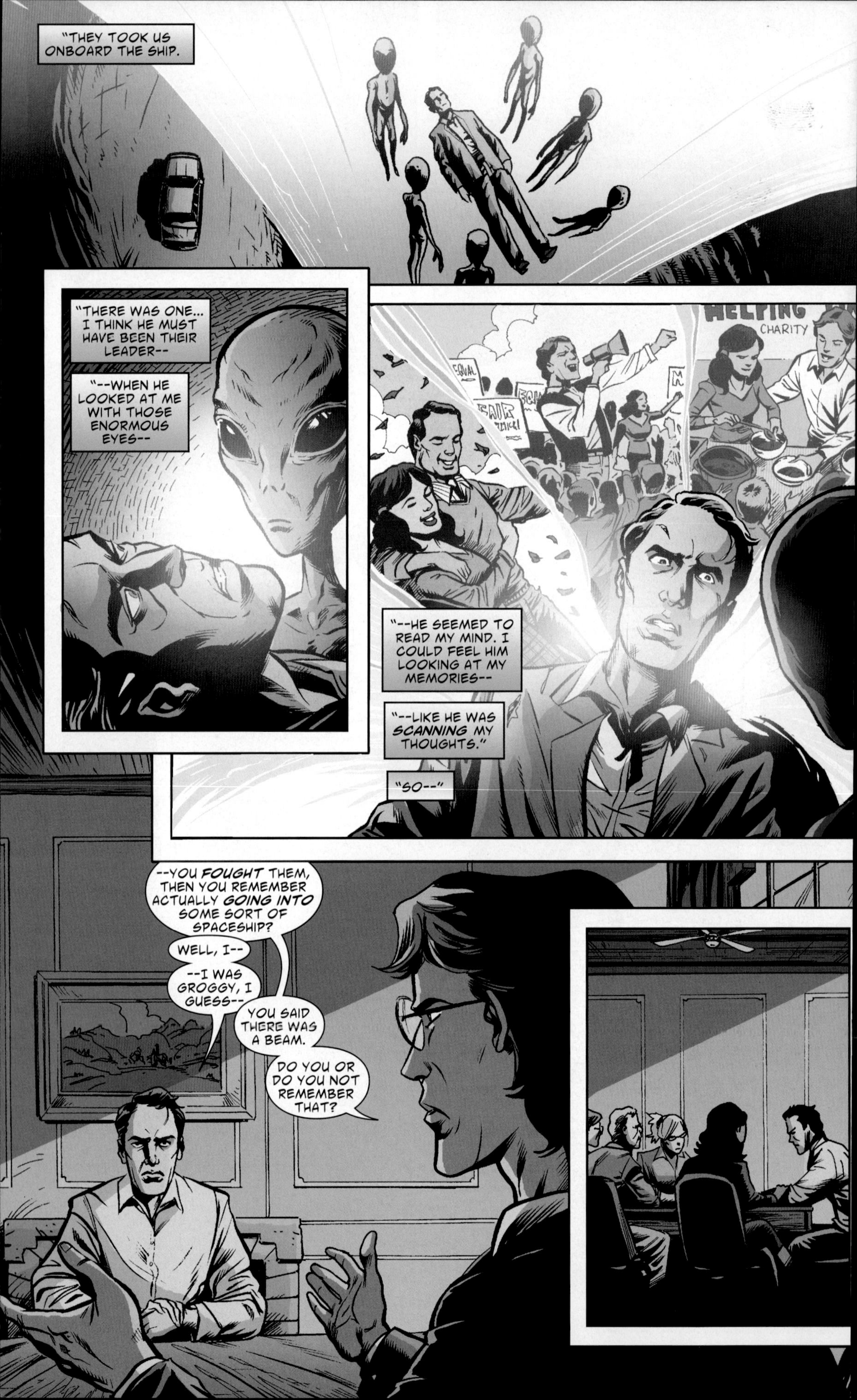
"THEY TOOK US ONBOARD THE SHIP.
"THERE WAS ONE... I THINK HE MUST HAVE BEEN THEIR LEADER--
"--WHEN HE LOOKED AT ME WITH THOSE ENORMOUS EYES--
HELPING
CHARITY
EQUAL
FAIR
"--HE SEEMED TO READ MY MIND. I COULD FEEL HIM LOOKING AT MY MEMORIES--
"--LIKE HE WAS *SCANNING* MY THOUGHTS."
"SO--"
--YOU *FOUGHT* THEM, THEN YOU REMEMBER ACTUALLY *GOING INTO* SOME SORT OF SPACESHIP?
WELL, I--
--I WAS GROGGY, I GUESS--
YOU SAID THERE WAS A BEAM.
DO YOU OR DO YOU NOT REMEMBER THAT?

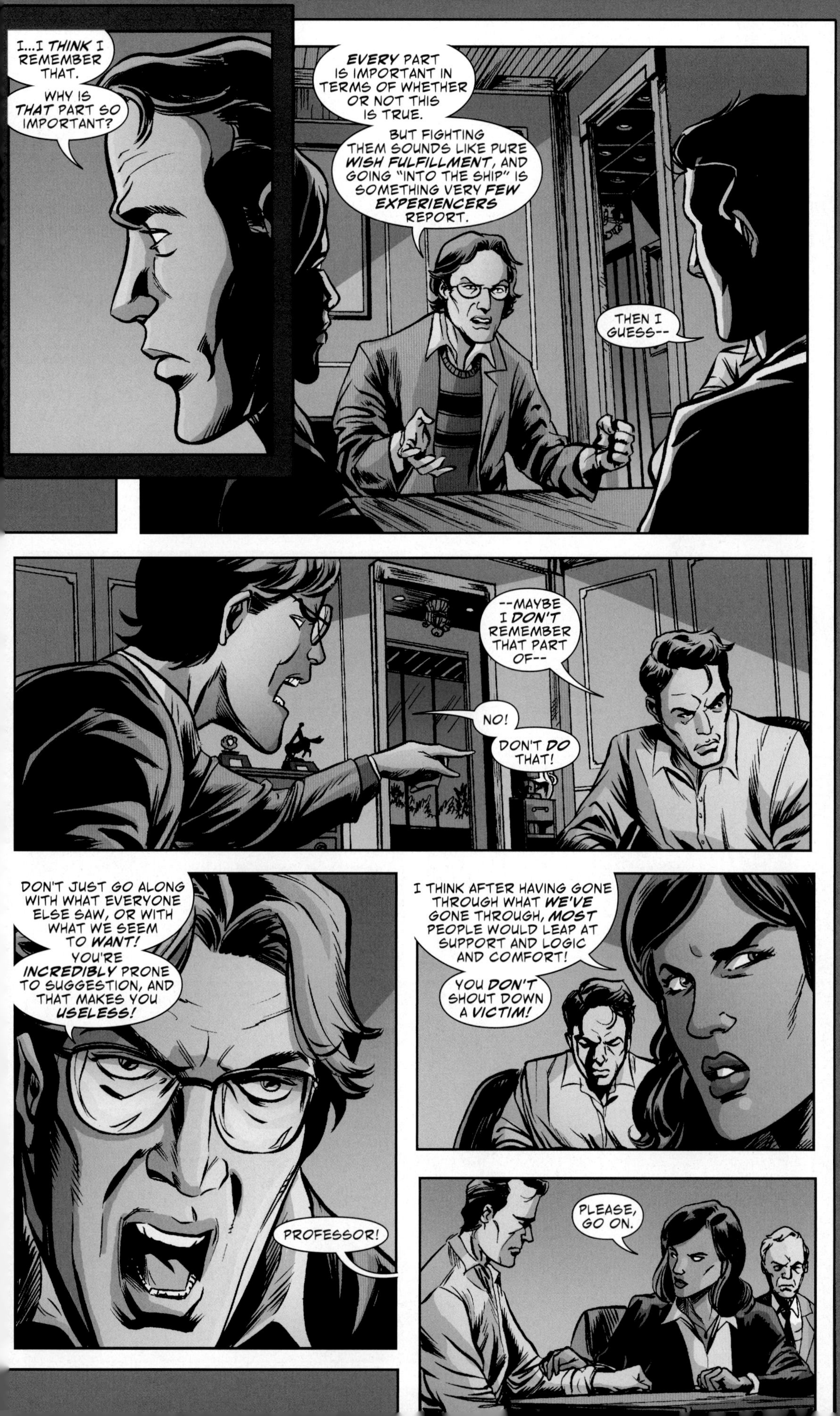
I...I THINK I REMEMBER THAT.
WHY IS THAT PART SO IMPORTANT?
EVERY PART IS IMPORTANT IN TERMS OF WHETHER OR NOT THIS IS TRUE.
BUT FIGHTING THEM SOUNDS LIKE PURE WISH FULFILLMENT, AND GOING "INTO THE SHIP" IS SOMETHING VERY FEW EXPERIENCERS REPORT.
THEN I GUESS--
--MAYBE I DON'T REMEMBER THAT PART OF--
NO!
DON'T DO THAT!
DON'T JUST GO ALONG WITH WHAT EVERYONE ELSE SAW, OR WITH WHAT WE SEEM TO WANT!
YOU'RE INCREDIBLY PRONE TO SUGGESTION, AND THAT MAKES YOU USELESS!
PROFESSOR!
I THINK AFTER HAVING GONE THROUGH WHAT WE'VE GONE THROUGH, MOST PEOPLE WOULD LEAP AT SUPPORT AND LOGIC AND COMFORT!
YOU DON'T SHOUT DOWN A VICTIM!
PLEASE, GO ON.

"THEY LED ME INTO SOME SORT OF MEDICAL AREA.

"I COULD HEAR YOU TALKING, NEARBY, YOU SOUNDED CALM, LIKE YOU WERE DREAMING.

"I NEVER HEARD *THEM* TALK, I JUST KNEW WHAT THEY WANTED ME TO DO.

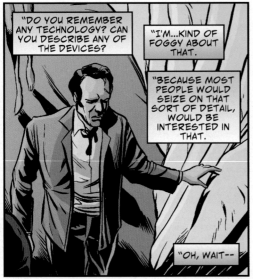

"DO YOU REMEMBER ANY TECHNOLOGY? CAN YOU DESCRIBE ANY OF THE DEVICES?

"I'M...KIND OF FOGGY ABOUT THAT.

"BECAUSE MOST PEOPLE WOULD SEIZE ON THAT SORT OF DETAIL, WOULD BE INTERESTED IN THAT.

"OH, WAIT--

"--THERE WAS A ROW OF...THEY LOOKED PART HUMAN, AND PART...ALIEN!"

OF COURSE THERE WAS.

NO, PLEASE, CONTINUE!

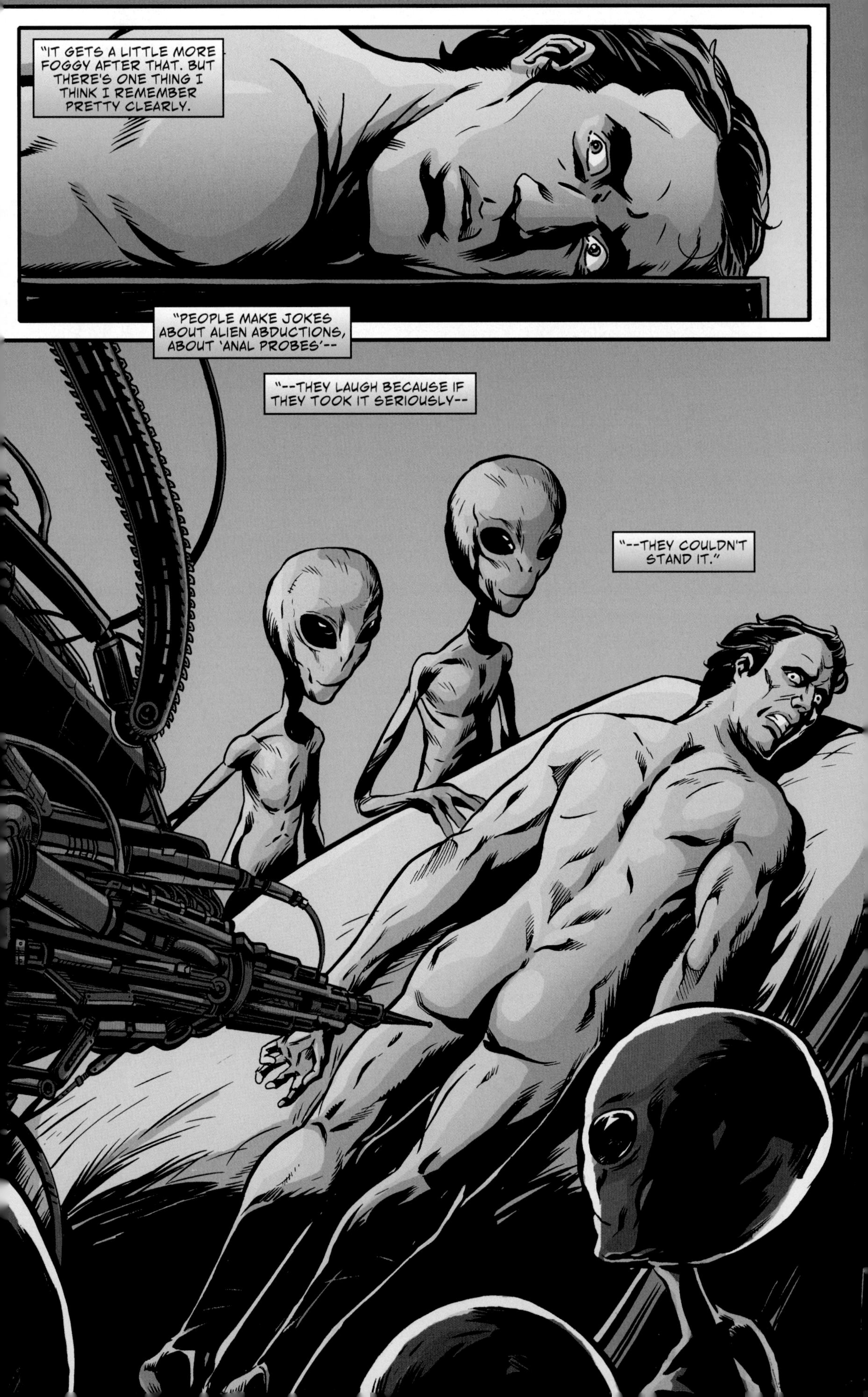
"IT GETS A LITTLE MORE FOGGY AFTER THAT. BUT THERE'S ONE THING I THINK I REMEMBER PRETTY CLEARLY.
"PEOPLE MAKE JOKES ABOUT ALIEN ABDUCTIONS, ABOUT 'ANAL PROBES'--
"--THEY LAUGH BECAUSE IF THEY TOOK IT SERIOUSLY--
"--THEY COULDN'T STAND IT."

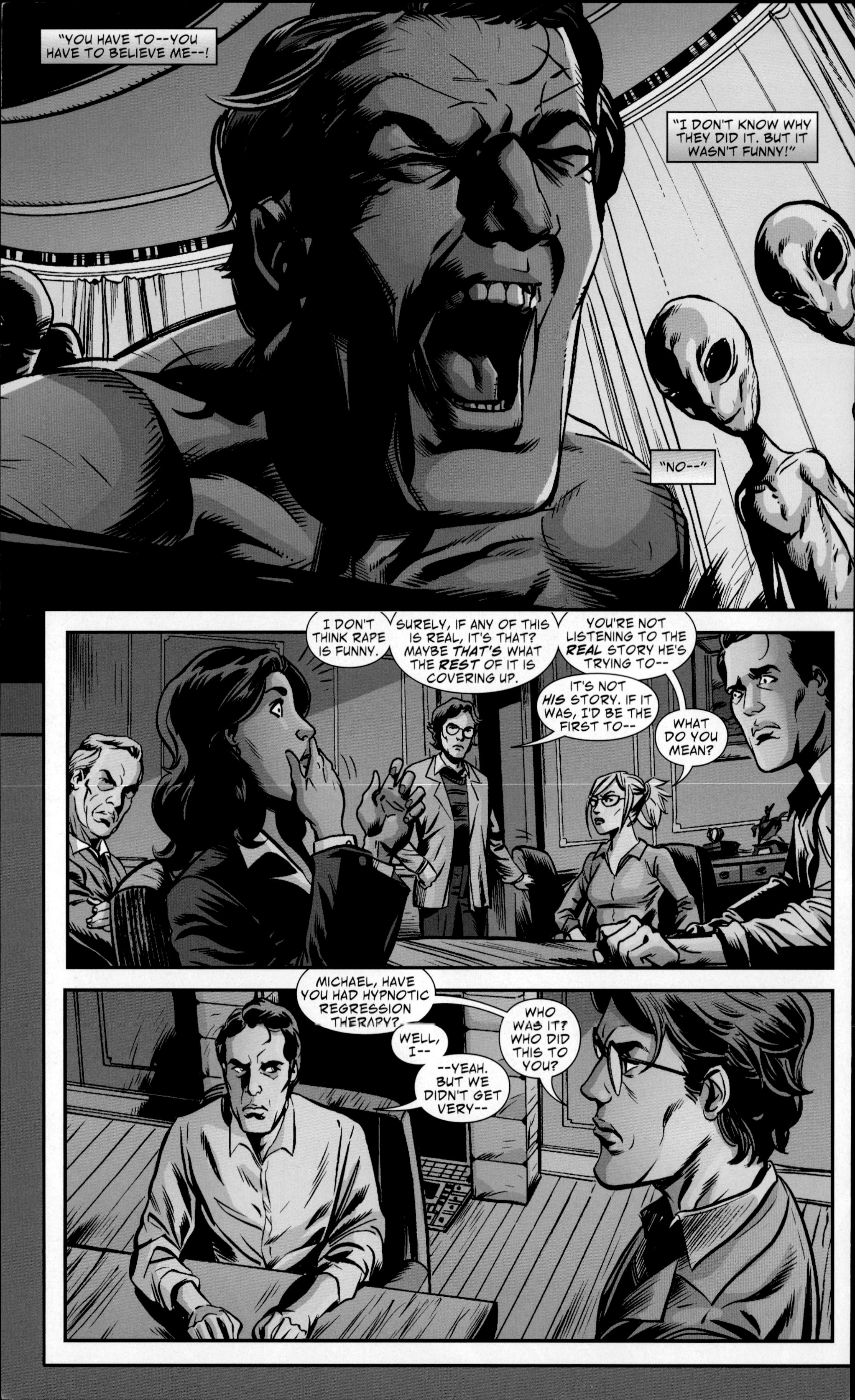
"YOU HAVE TO--YOU HAVE TO BELIEVE ME--!
"I DON'T KNOW WHY THEY DID IT. BUT IT WASN'T FUNNY!"
"NO--"
I DON'T THINK RAPE IS FUNNY.
SURELY, IF ANY OF THIS IS REAL, IT'S THAT? MAYBE *THAT'S* WHAT THE *REST* OF IT IS COVERING UP.
YOU'RE NOT LISTENING TO THE *REAL* STORY HE'S TRYING TO--
IT'S NOT *HIS* STORY. IF IT WAS, I'D BE THE FIRST TO--
WHAT DO YOU MEAN?
MICHAEL, HAVE YOU HAD HYPNOTIC REGRESSION THERAPY?
WELL, I--
--YEAH. BUT WE DIDN'T GET VERY--
WHO WAS IT? WHO DID THIS TO YOU?

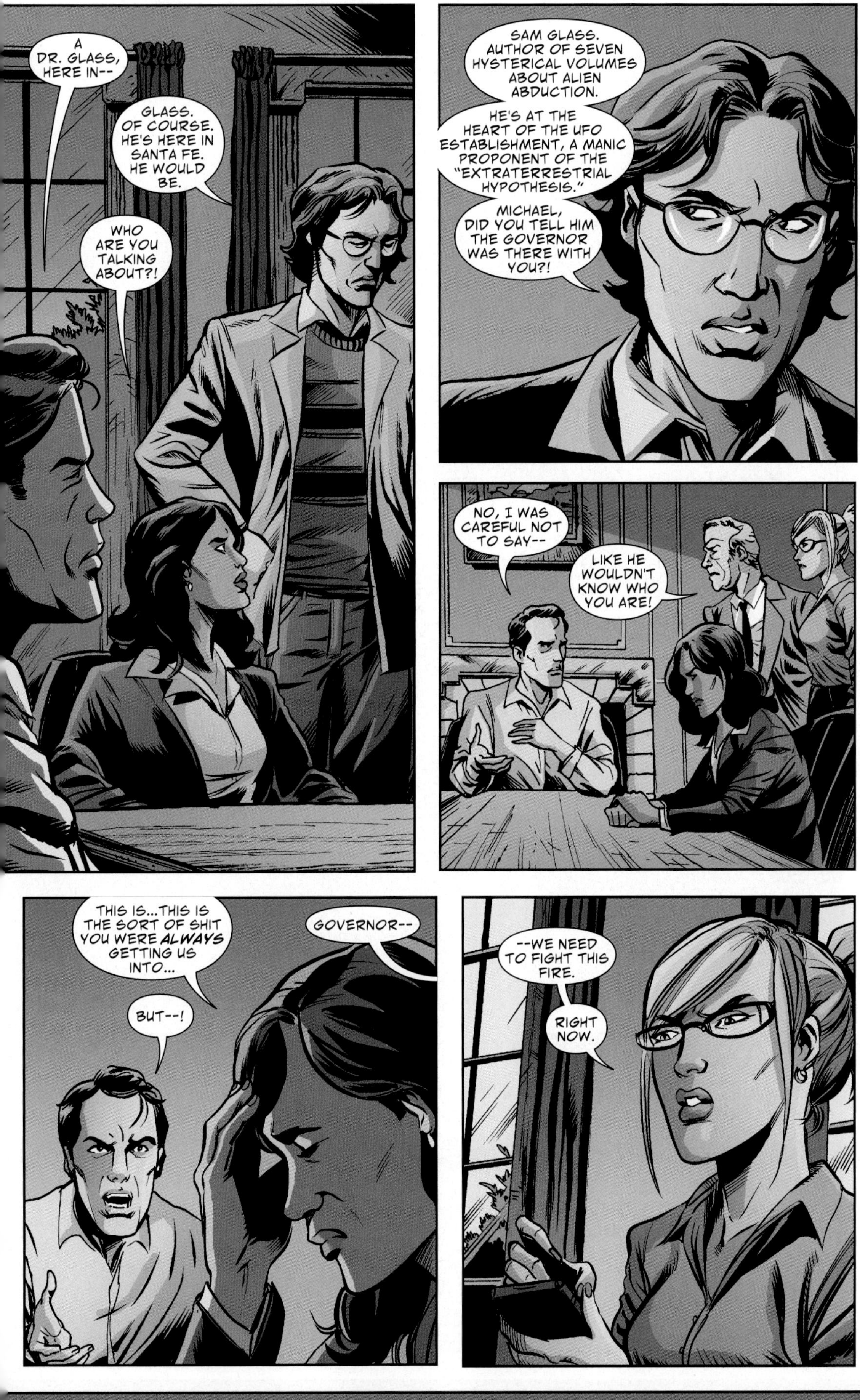
A DR. GLASS, HERE IN--
GLASS. OF COURSE. HE'S HERE IN SANTA FE. HE WOULD BE.
WHO ARE YOU TALKING ABOUT?!
SAM GLASS. AUTHOR OF SEVEN HYSTERICAL VOLUMES ABOUT ALIEN ABDUCTION.
HE'S AT THE HEART OF THE UFO ESTABLISHMENT, A MANIC PROPONENT OF THE "EXTRATERRESTRIAL HYPOTHESIS."
MICHAEL, DID YOU TELL HIM THE GOVERNOR WAS THERE WITH YOU?!
NO, I WAS CAREFUL NOT TO SAY--
LIKE HE WOULDN'T KNOW WHO YOU ARE!
THIS IS...THIS IS THE SORT OF SHIT YOU WERE ALWAYS GETTING US INTO...
GOVERNOR--
BUT--!
--WE NEED TO FIGHT THIS FIRE.
RIGHT NOW.

AND I KEPT THE TAPE, BUT HE DOESN'T NAME HIS FELLOW ABDUCTEE! THE IDENTITIES OF THE ONES WHO TOOK HIM FROM ME CHECK OUT, AND THEY WERE KIND OF, YOU KNOW--

--TOO BROWN TO BE MEN IN BLACK.

ONE OF THE GOVERNOR'S HIT SQUADS, THEN.

THAT BITCH HAS US UNDER HER THUMB.

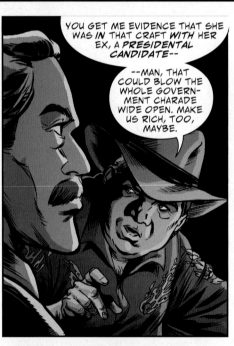

YOU GET ME EVIDENCE THAT SHE WAS IN THAT CRAFT WITH HER EX, A PRESIDENTIAL CANDIDATE--

--MAN, THAT COULD BLOW THE WHOLE GOVERN-MENT CHARADE WIDE OPEN. MAKE US RICH, TOO, MAYBE.

THEY STEAL OUR FARMERS' LAND FOR THE MILITARY, THEY LET THEIR GREY ALIEN FRIENDS STEAL OUR BODIES--

--OH, HEY, THERE'S THAT GUY I WANTED YOU TO MEET.

YOU, ME AND HIM, WE COULD BE THE ONES WHO CUT THROUGH THE DISINFORMATION AND THE CONSPIRACY THEORY BULLSHIT AND DRAG US ALL OUT OF THE DARK SIDE--

MAJOR STAN ABRAMOWITZ. HE'S OFTEN IN HERE.

REMEMBER, HE DOESN'T LIKE PEOPLE KNOWING HE WAS IN THE MILITARY.

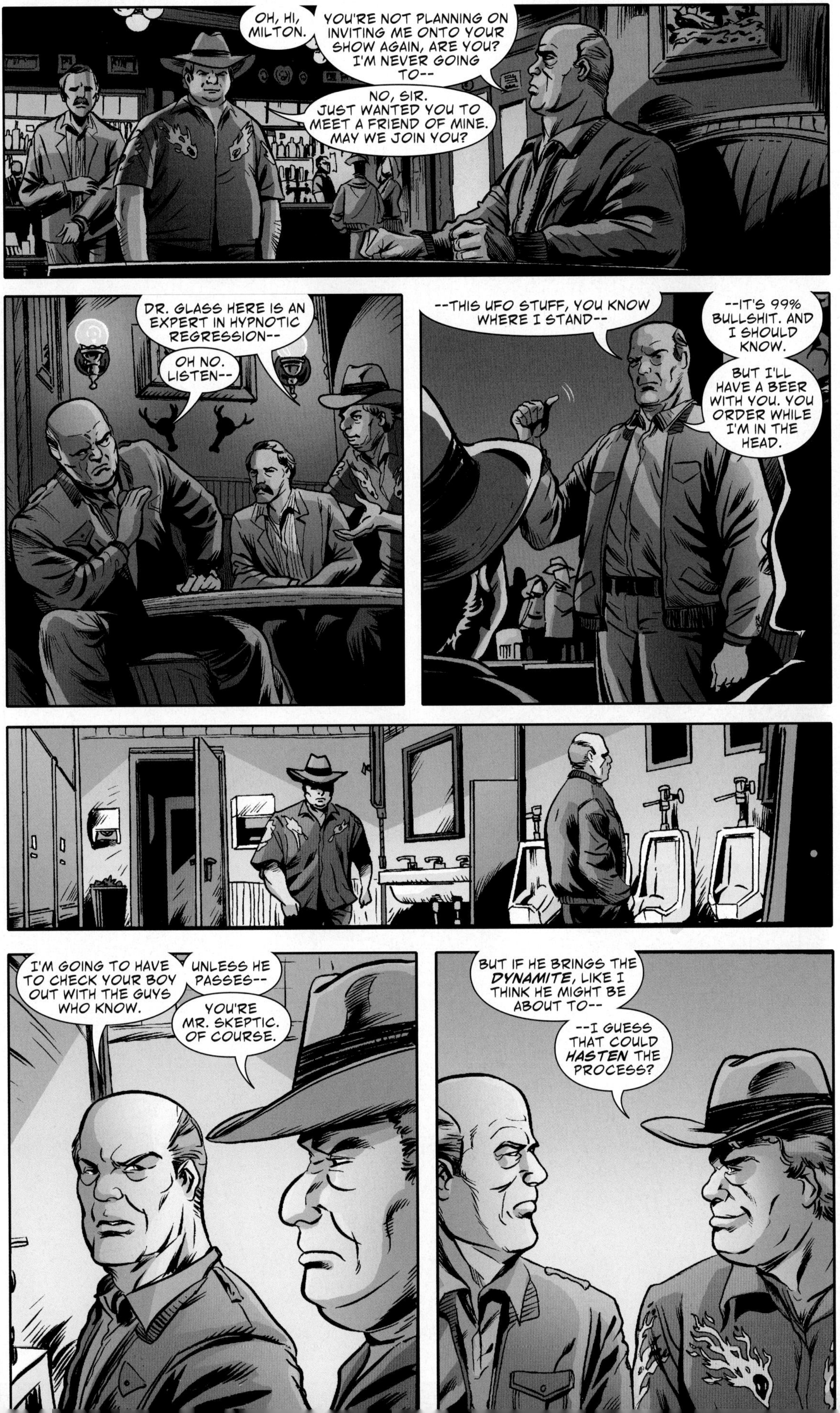
OH, HI, MILTON.
YOU'RE NOT PLANNING ON INVITING ME ONTO YOUR SHOW AGAIN, ARE YOU? I'M NEVER GOING TO--
NO, SIR. JUST WANTED YOU TO MEET A FRIEND OF MINE. MAY WE JOIN YOU?
DR. GLASS HERE IS AN EXPERT IN HYPNOTIC REGRESSION--
OH NO. LISTEN--
--THIS UFO STUFF, YOU KNOW WHERE I STAND--
--IT'S 99% BULLSHIT. AND I SHOULD KNOW.
BUT I'LL HAVE A BEER WITH YOU. YOU ORDER WHILE I'M IN THE HEAD.
I'M GOING TO HAVE TO CHECK YOUR BOY OUT WITH THE GUYS WHO KNOW.
UNLESS HE PASSES--
YOU'RE MR. SKEPTIC. OF COURSE.
BUT IF HE BRINGS THE DYNAMITE, LIKE I THINK HE MIGHT BE ABOUT TO--
--I GUESS THAT COULD HASTEN THE PROCESS?

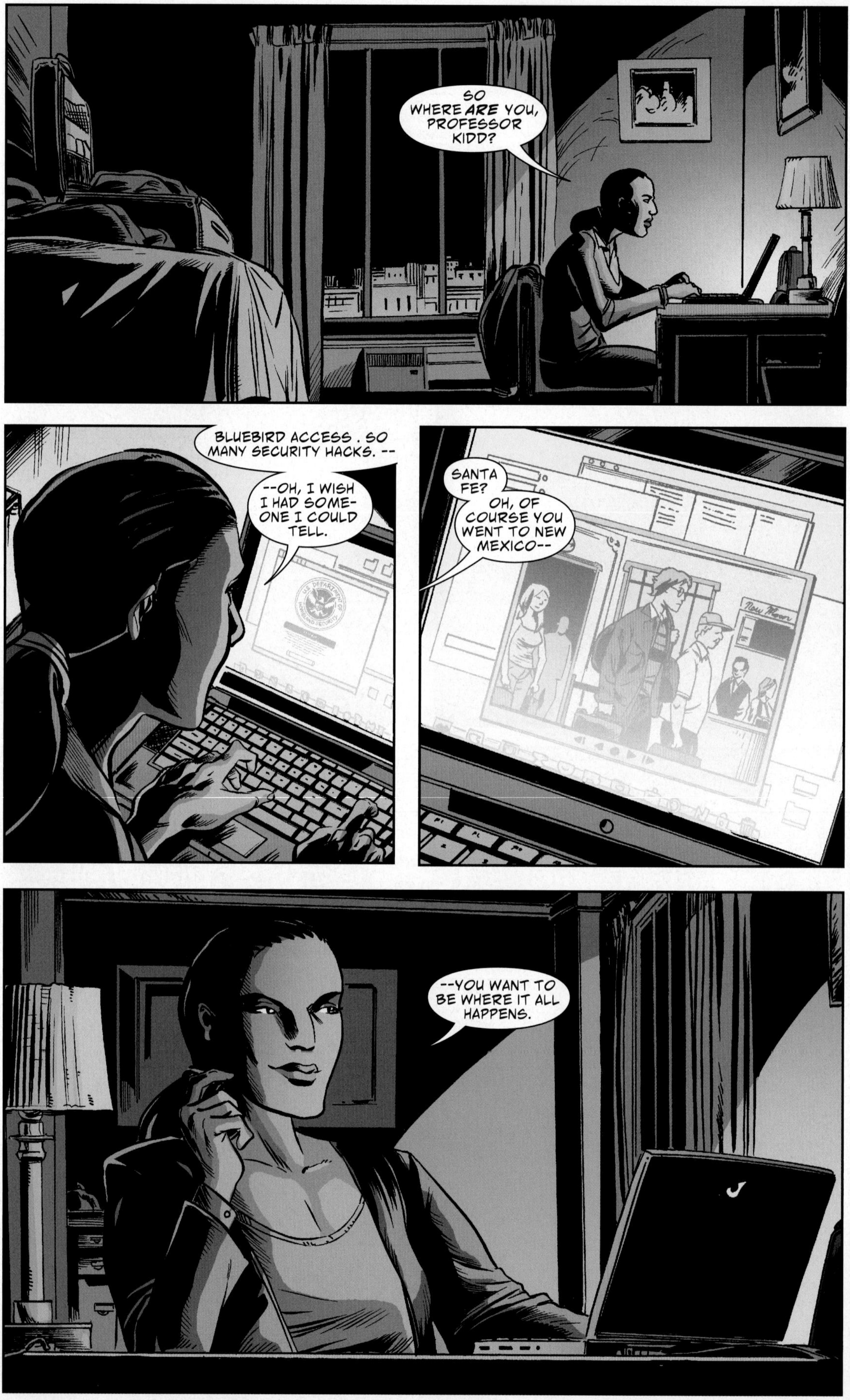
SO WHERE ARE YOU, PROFESSOR KIDD?
BLUEBIRD ACCESS . SO MANY SECURITY HACKS. --
--OH, I WISH I HAD SOME-ONE I COULD TELL.
SANTA FE?
OH, OF COURSE YOU WENT TO NEW MEXICO--
--YOU WANT TO BE WHERE IT ALL HAPPENS.

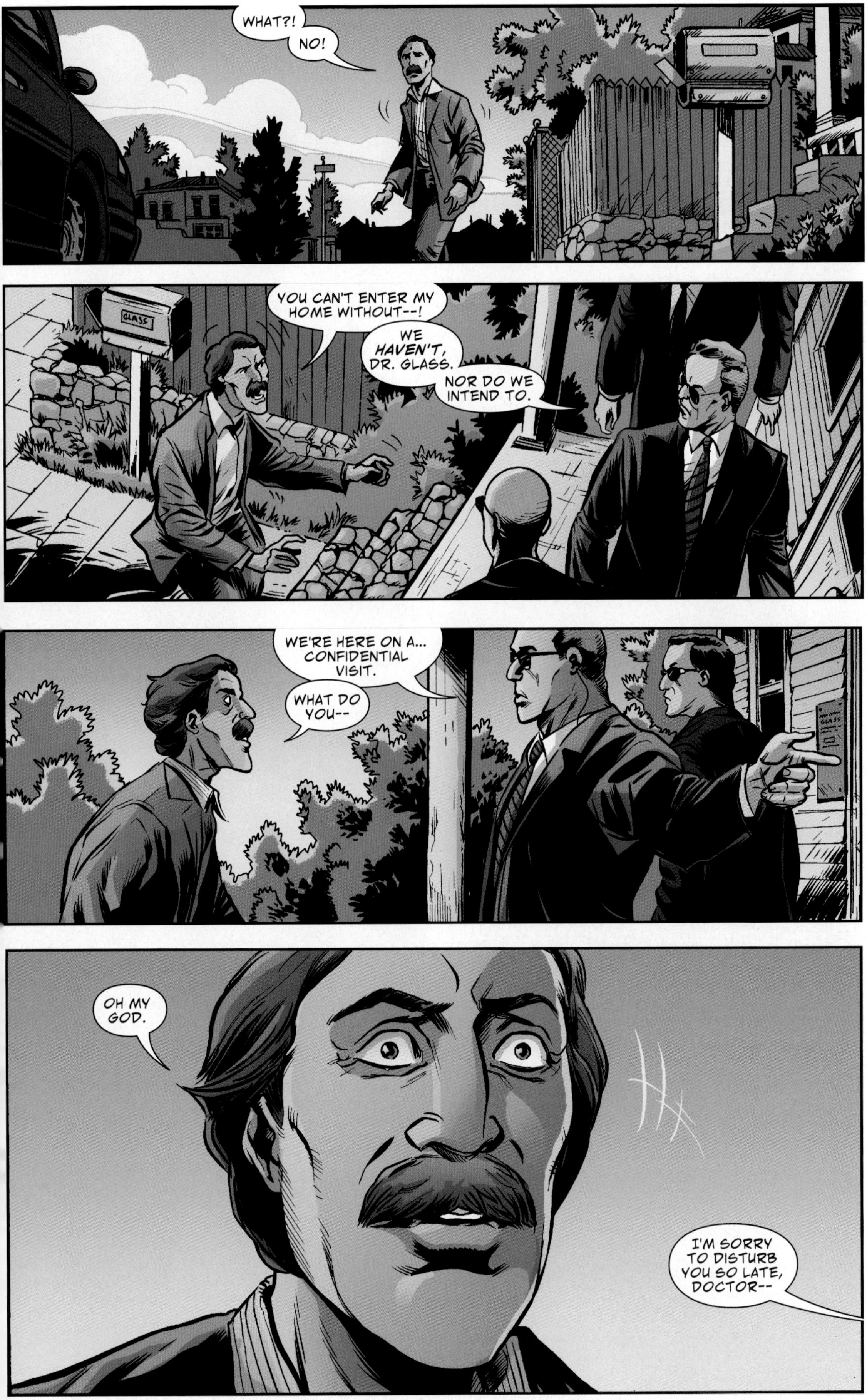
WHAT?!
NO!
GLASS
YOU CAN'T ENTER MY HOME WITHOUT--!
WE HAVEN'T, DR. GLASS.
NOR DO WE INTEND TO.
WE'RE HERE ON A... CONFIDENTIAL VISIT.
WHAT DO YOU--
OH MY GOD.
I'M SORRY TO DISTURB YOU SO LATE, DOCTOR--

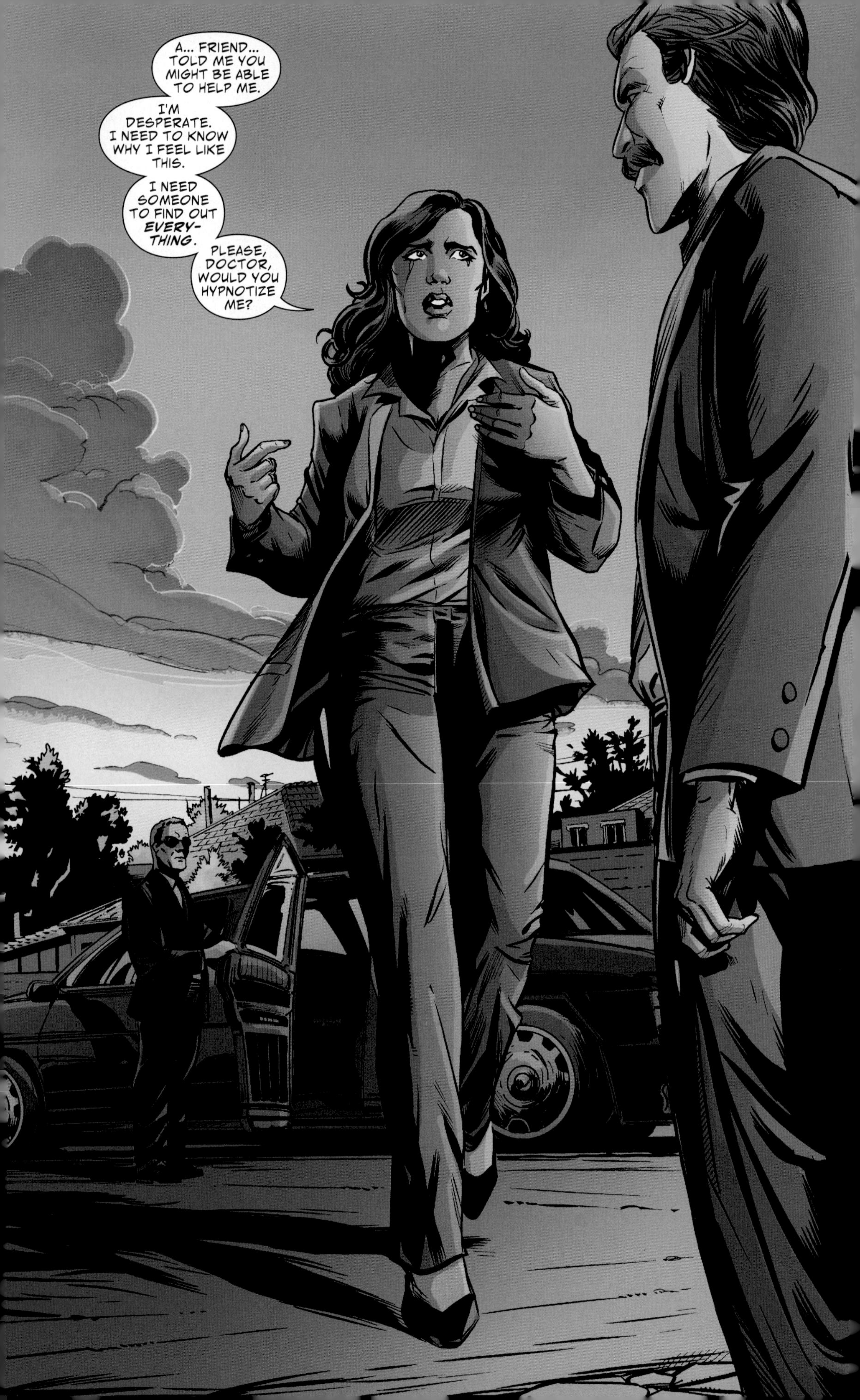
A... FRIEND... TOLD ME YOU MIGHT BE ABLE TO HELP ME.
I'M DESPERATE. I NEED TO KNOW WHY I FEEL LIKE THIS.
I NEED SOMEONE TO FIND OUT *EVERY-THING*.
PLEASE, DOCTOR, WOULD YOU HYPNOTIZE ME?

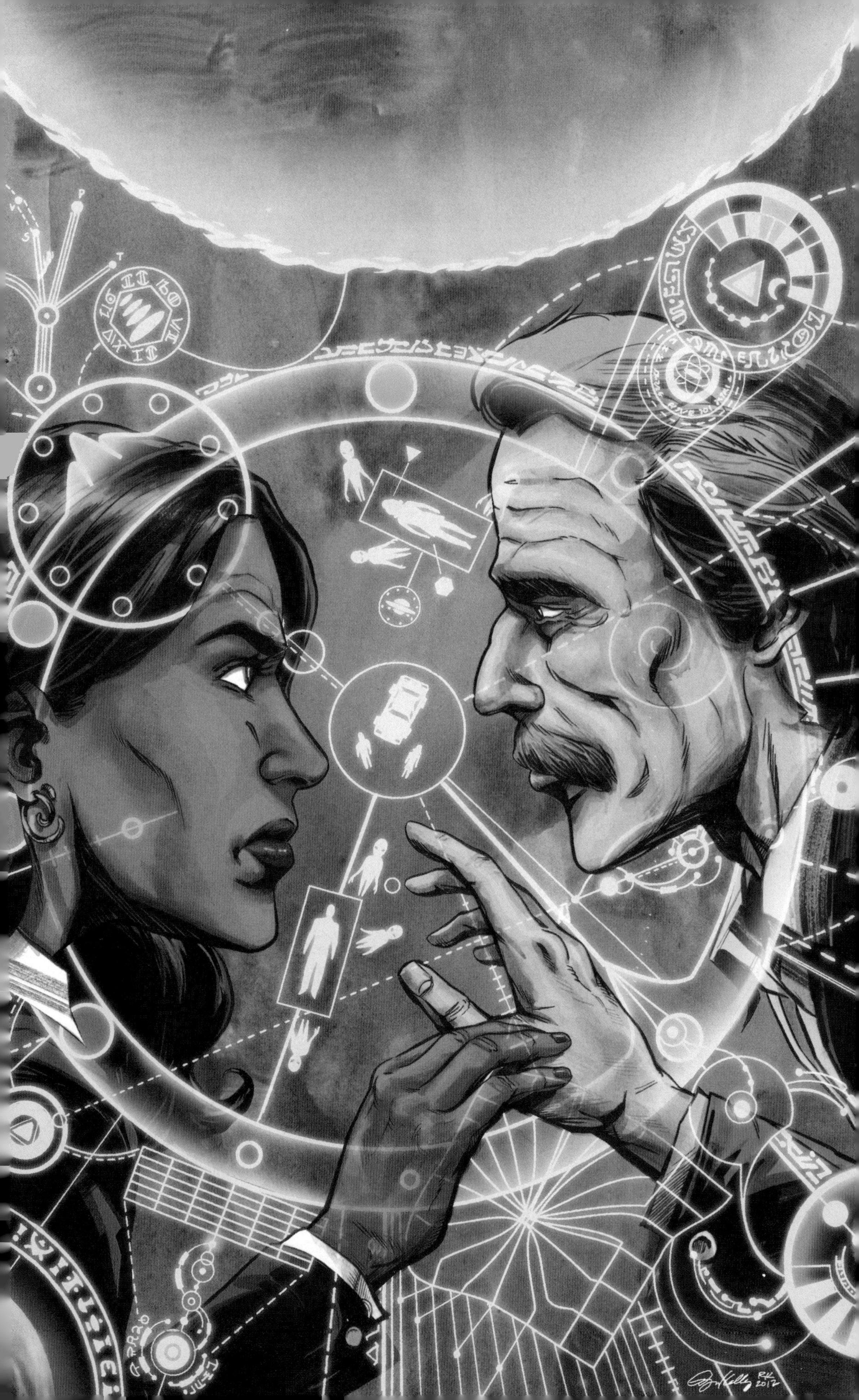

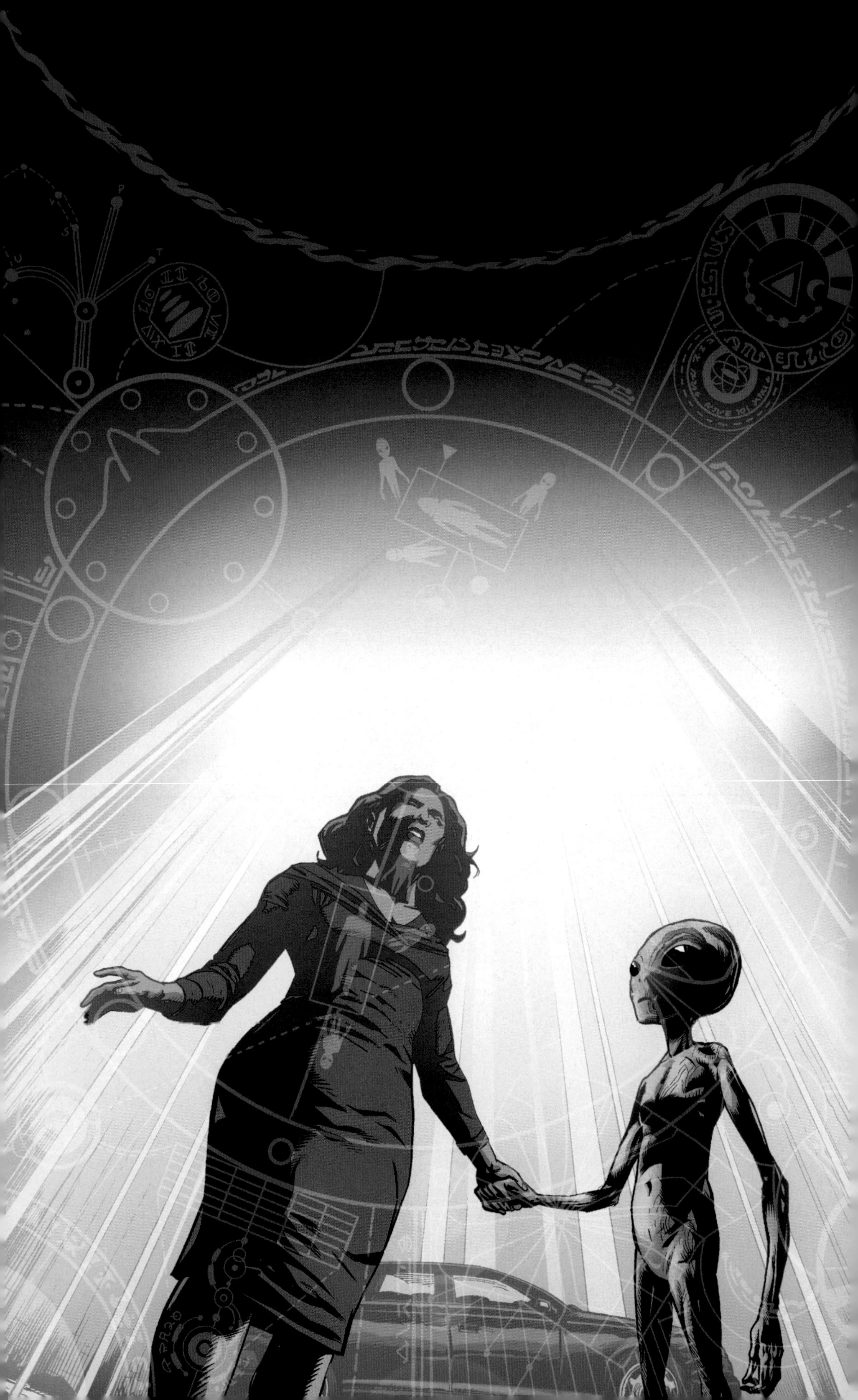

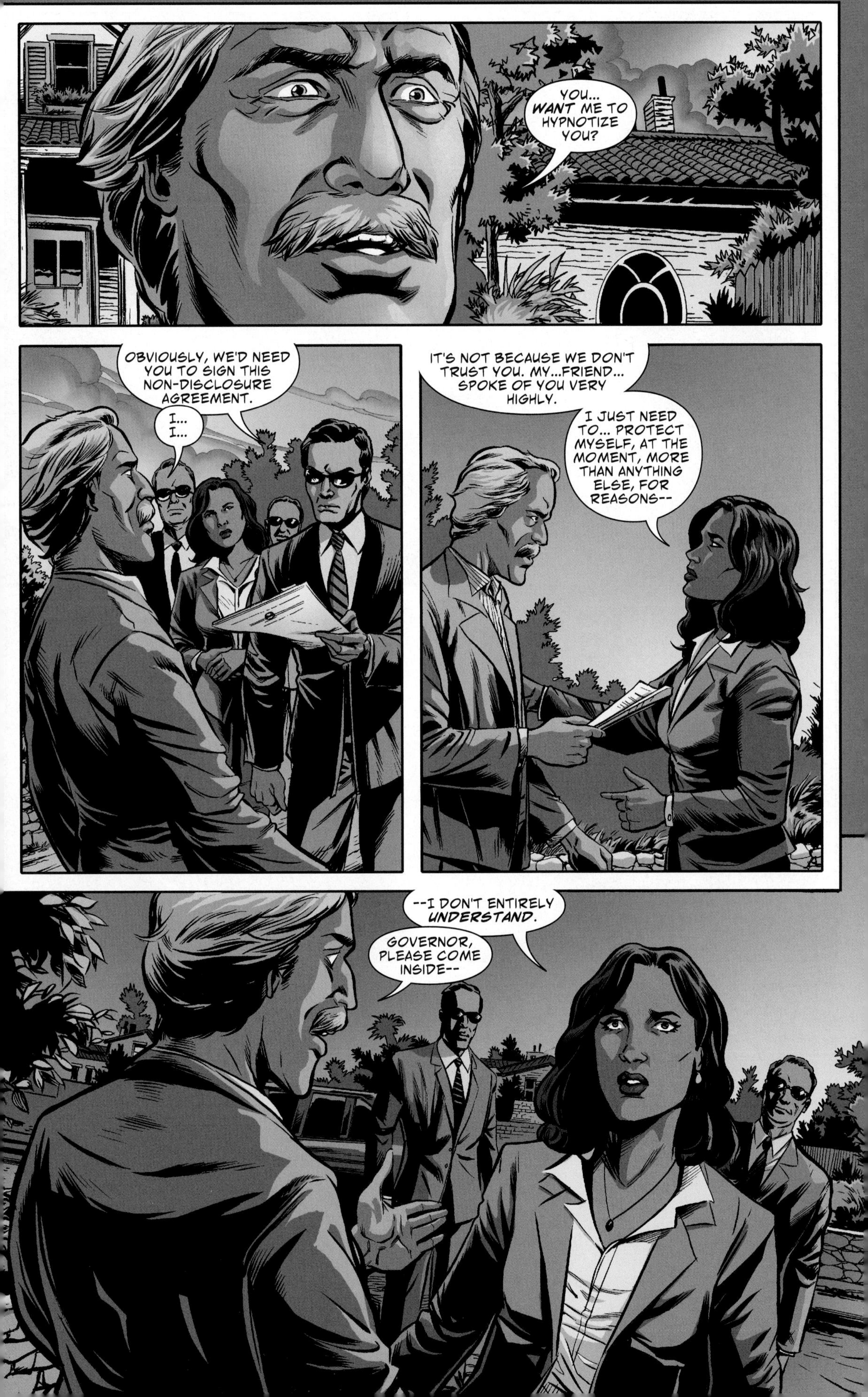
YOU... WANT ME TO HYPNOTIZE YOU?
OBVIOUSLY, WE'D NEED YOU TO SIGN THIS NON-DISCLOSURE AGREEMENT.
I... I...
IT'S NOT BECAUSE WE DON'T TRUST YOU. MY...FRIEND... SPOKE OF YOU VERY HIGHLY.
I JUST NEED TO... PROTECT MYSELF, AT THE MOMENT, MORE THAN ANYTHING ELSE, FOR REASONS--
--I DON'T ENTIRELY UNDERSTAND.
GOVERNOR, PLEASE COME INSIDE--

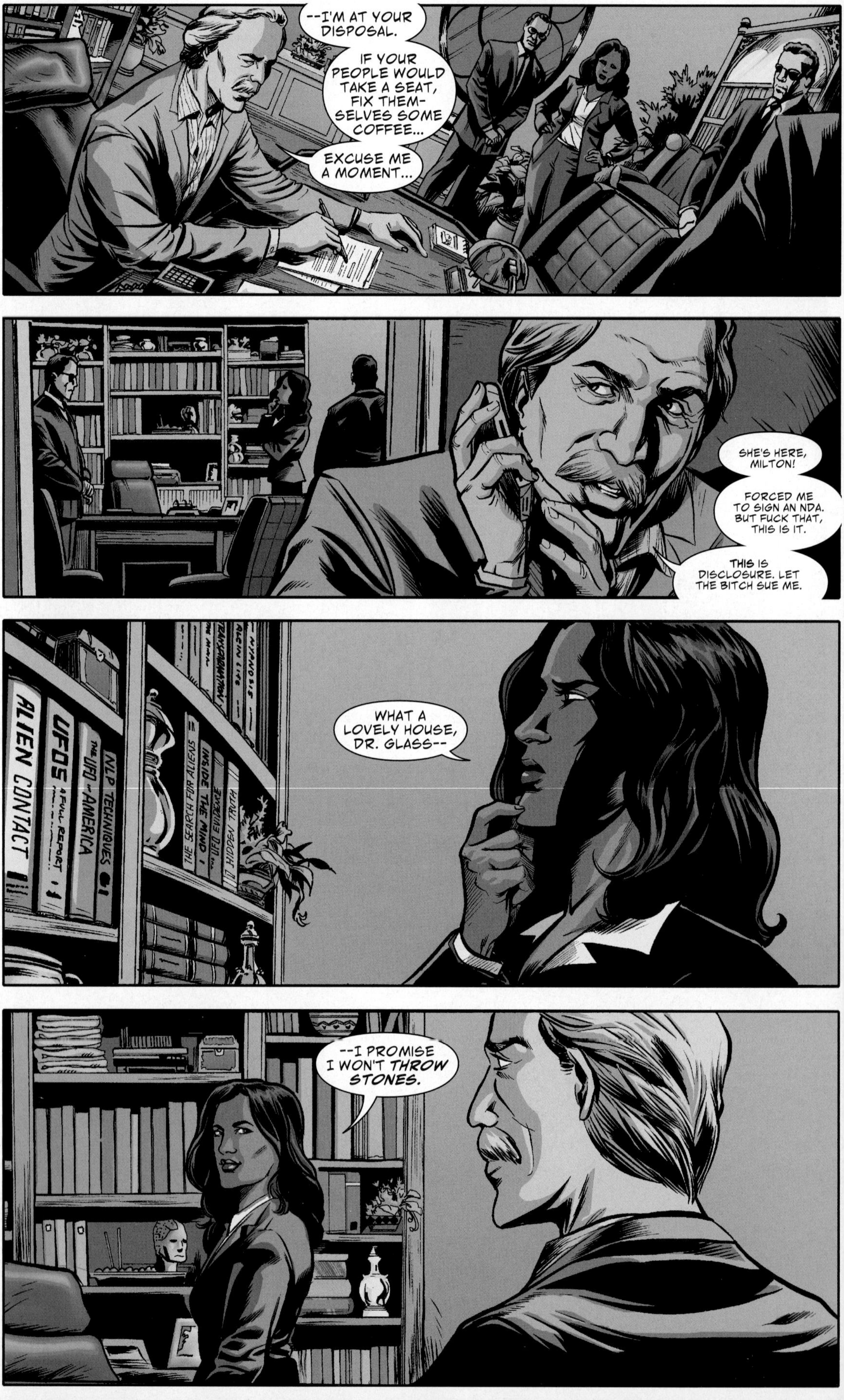
--I'M AT YOUR DISPOSAL.
IF YOUR PEOPLE WOULD TAKE A SEAT, FIX THEM-SELVES SOME COFFEE...
EXCUSE ME A MOMENT...
SHE'S HERE, MILTON!
FORCED ME TO SIGN AN NDA. BUT FUCK THAT, THIS IS IT.
THIS IS DISCLOSURE. LET THE BITCH SUE ME.
ALIEN CONTACT
UFOS
NLP TECHNIQUES
THE SEARCH FOR ALIENS
INSIDE THE MIND
HIDDEN TRUTH
WHAT A LOVELY HOUSE, DR. GLASS--
--I PROMISE I WON'T THROW STONES.

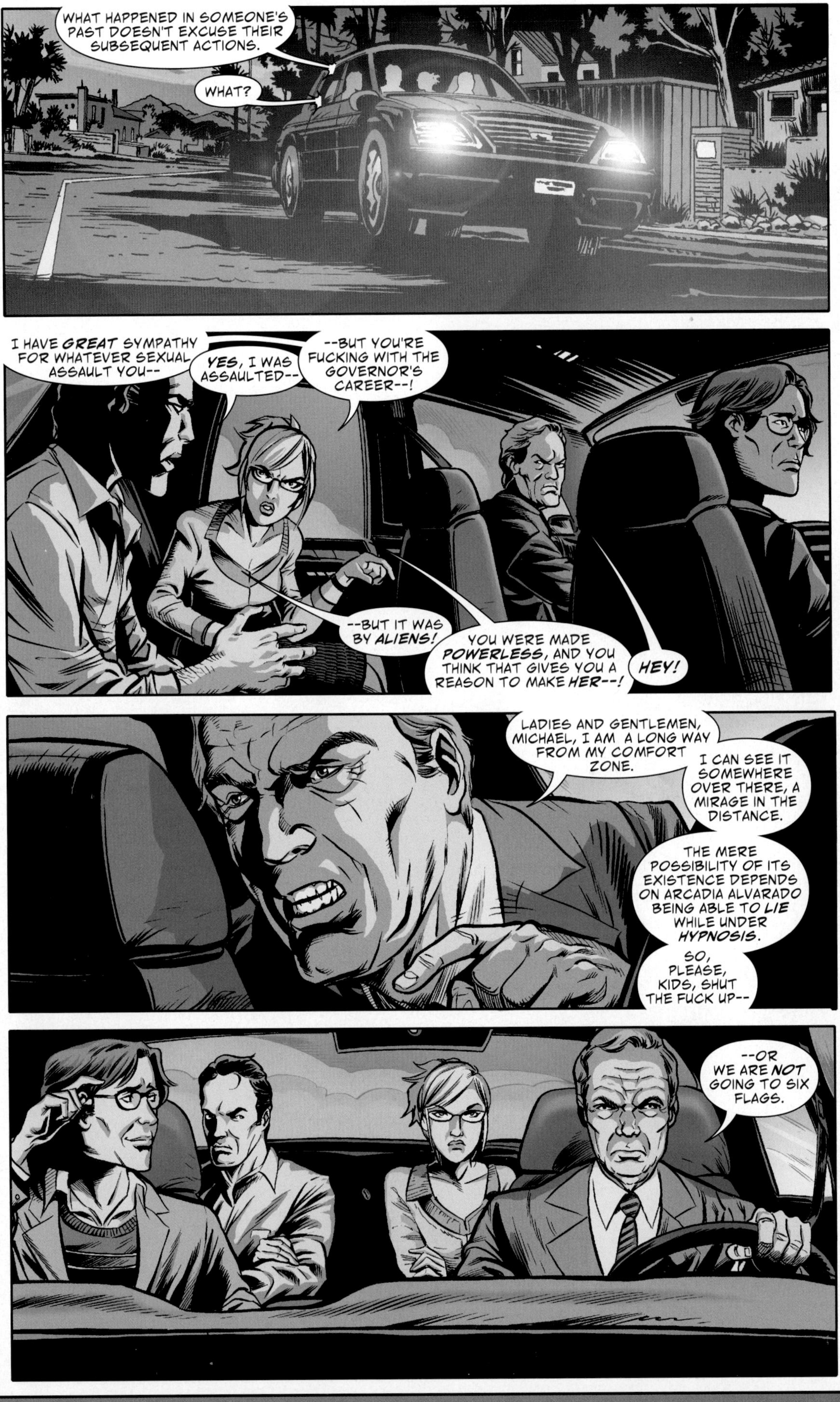
WHAT HAPPENED IN SOMEONE'S PAST DOESN'T EXCUSE THEIR SUBSEQUENT ACTIONS.
WHAT?
I HAVE GREAT SYMPATHY FOR WHATEVER SEXUAL ASSAULT YOU--
YES, I WAS ASSAULTED--
--BUT YOU'RE FUCKING WITH THE GOVERNOR'S CAREER--!
--BUT IT WAS BY ALIENS!
YOU WERE MADE POWERLESS, AND YOU THINK THAT GIVES YOU A REASON TO MAKE HER--!
HEY!
LADIES AND GENTLEMEN, MICHAEL, I AM A LONG WAY FROM MY COMFORT ZONE.
I CAN SEE IT SOMEWHERE OVER THERE, A MIRAGE IN THE DISTANCE.
THE MERE POSSIBILITY OF ITS EXISTENCE DEPENDS ON ARCADIA ALVARADO BEING ABLE TO LIE WHILE UNDER HYPNOSIS.
SO, PLEASE, KIDS, SHUT THE FUCK UP--
--OR WE ARE NOT GOING TO SIX FLAGS.

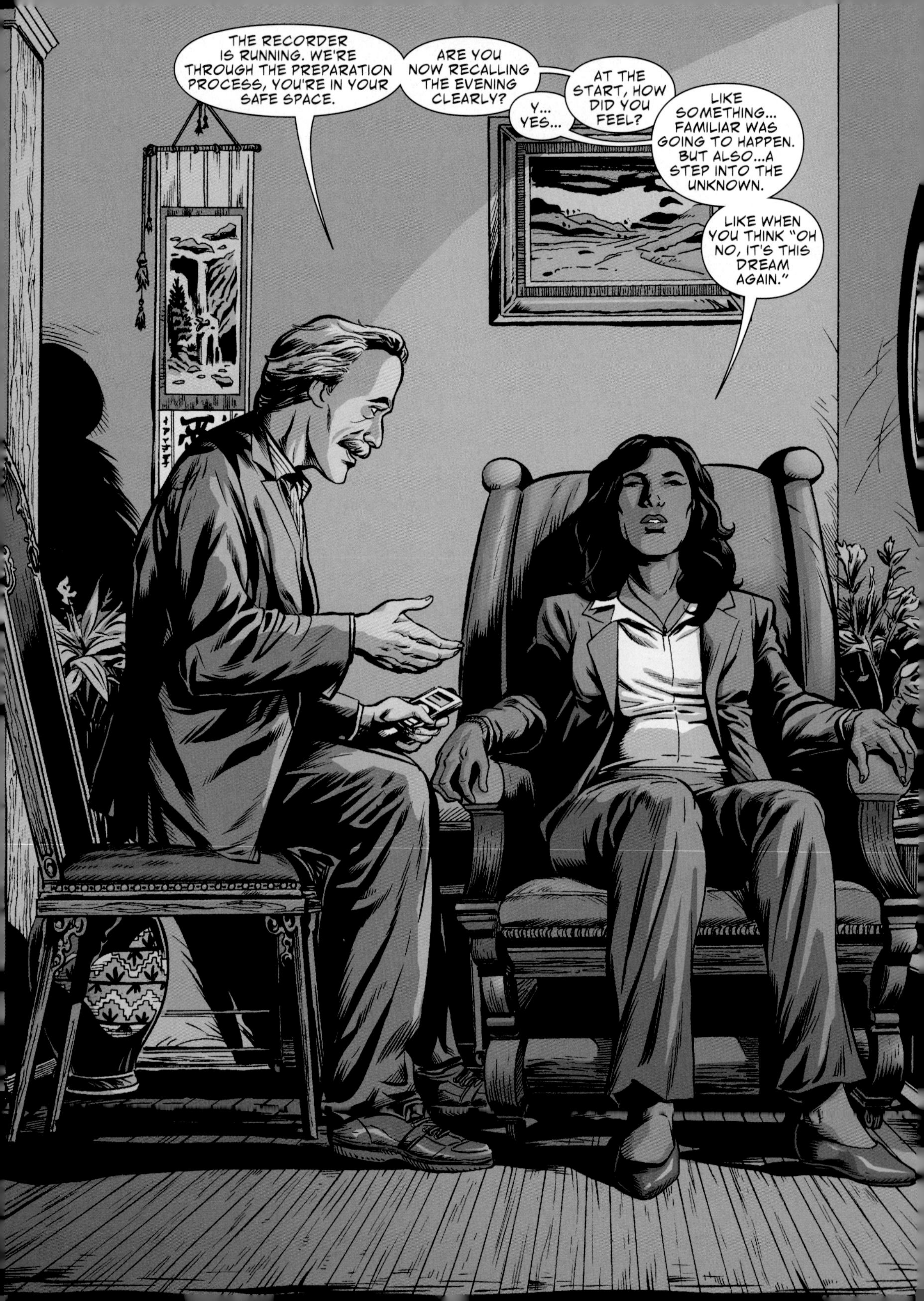
THE RECORDER IS RUNNING. WE'RE THROUGH THE PREPARATION PROCESS, YOU'RE IN YOUR SAFE SPACE.
ARE YOU NOW RECALLING THE EVENING CLEARLY?
Y... YES...
AT THE START, HOW DID YOU FEEL?
LIKE SOMETHING... FAMILIAR WAS GOING TO HAPPEN. BUT ALSO...A STEP INTO THE UNKNOWN.
LIKE WHEN YOU THINK "OH NO, IT'S THIS DREAM AGAIN."

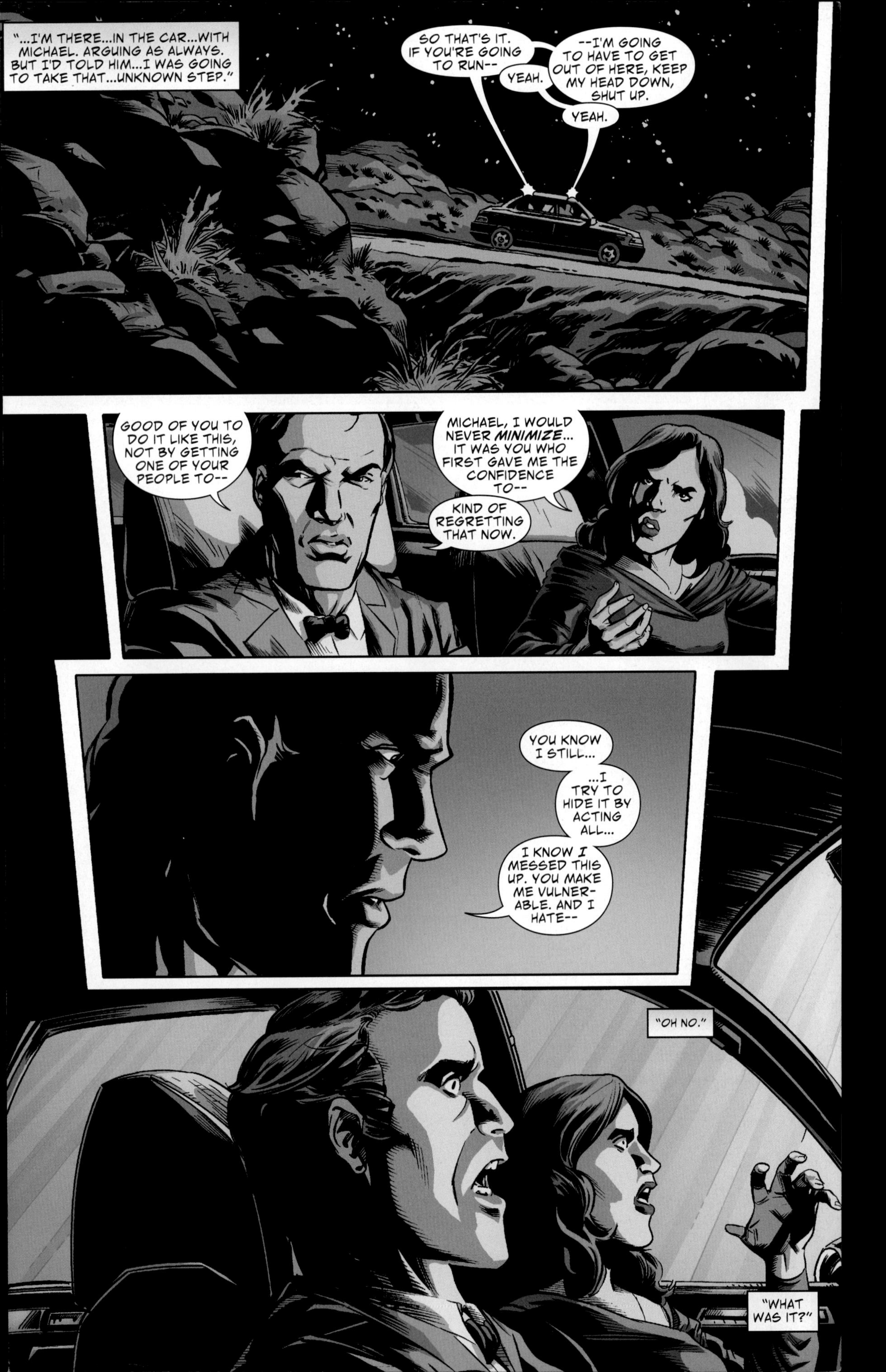
"...I'M THERE...IN THE CAR...WITH MICHAEL. ARGUING AS ALWAYS. BUT I'D TOLD HIM...I WAS GOING TO TAKE THAT...UNKNOWN STEP."
SO THAT'S IT. IF YOU'RE GOING TO RUN--
YEAH.
--I'M GOING TO HAVE TO GET OUT OF HERE, KEEP MY HEAD DOWN, SHUT UP.
YEAH.
GOOD OF YOU TO DO IT LIKE THIS, NOT BY GETTING ONE OF YOUR PEOPLE TO--
MICHAEL, I WOULD NEVER *MINIMIZE*... IT WAS YOU WHO FIRST GAVE ME THE CONFIDENCE TO--
KIND OF REGRETTING THAT NOW.
YOU KNOW I STILL...
...I TRY TO HIDE IT BY ACTING ALL...
I KNOW *I* MESSED THIS UP. YOU MAKE ME VULNER-ABLE. AND I HATE--
"OH NO."
"WHAT WAS IT?"

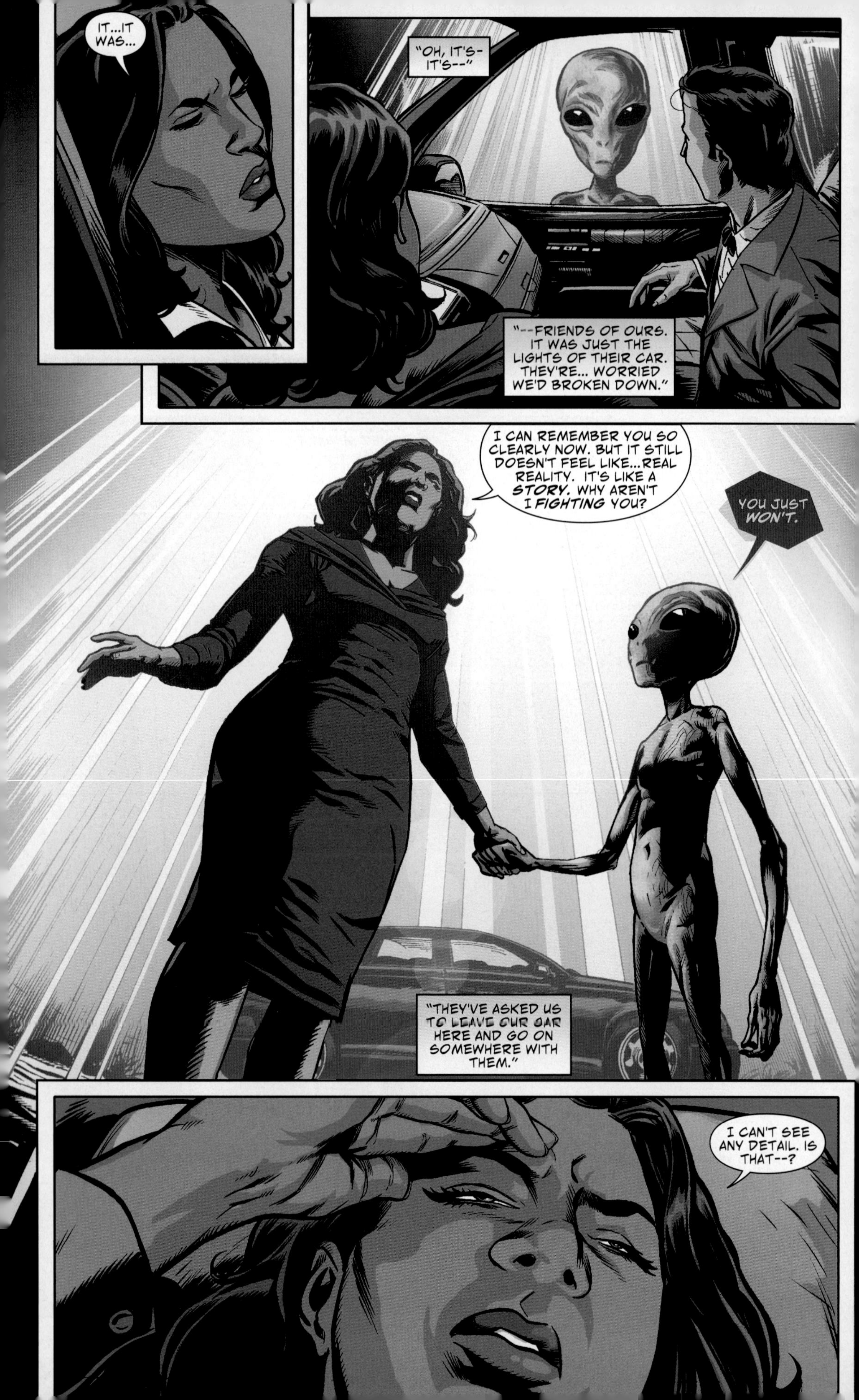
IT...IT WAS...
"OH, IT'S-IT'S--"
"--FRIENDS OF OURS. IT WAS JUST THE LIGHTS OF THEIR CAR. THEY'RE... WORRIED WE'D BROKEN DOWN."
I CAN REMEMBER YOU SO CLEARLY NOW. BUT IT STILL DOESN'T FEEL LIKE...REAL REALITY. IT'S LIKE A *STORY*. WHY AREN'T I *FIGHTING* YOU?
YOU JUST *WON'T*.
"THEY'VE ASKED US TO LEAVE OUR CAR HERE AND GO ON SOMEWHERE WITH THEM."
I CAN'T SEE ANY DETAIL. IS THAT--?

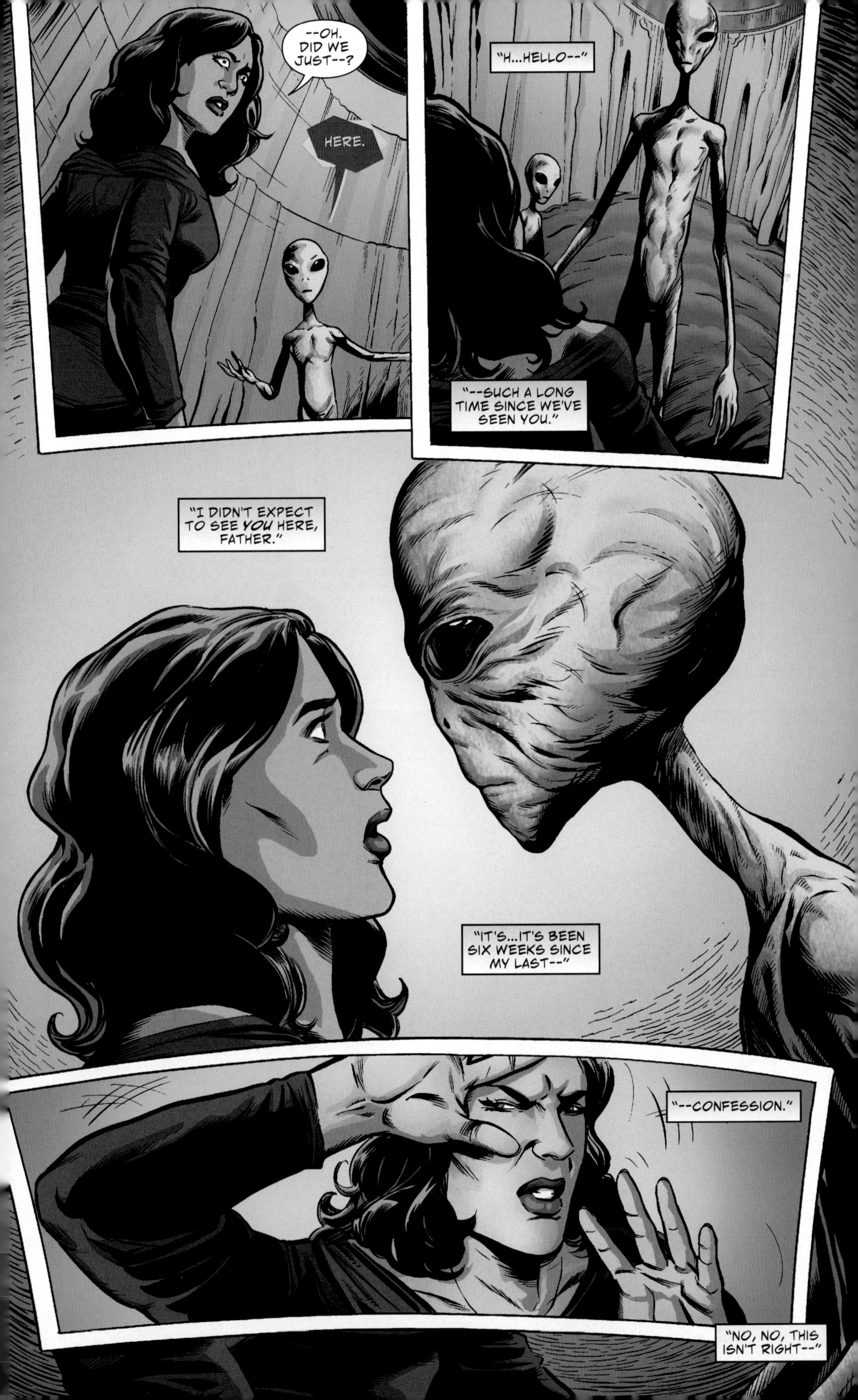
--OH. DID WE JUST--?
HERE.
"H...HELLO--"
"--SUCH A LONG TIME SINCE WE'VE SEEN YOU."
"I DIDN'T EXPECT TO SEE *YOU* HERE, FATHER."
"IT'S...IT'S BEEN SIX WEEKS SINCE MY LAST--"
"--CONFESSION."
"NO, NO, THIS ISN'T RIGHT--"

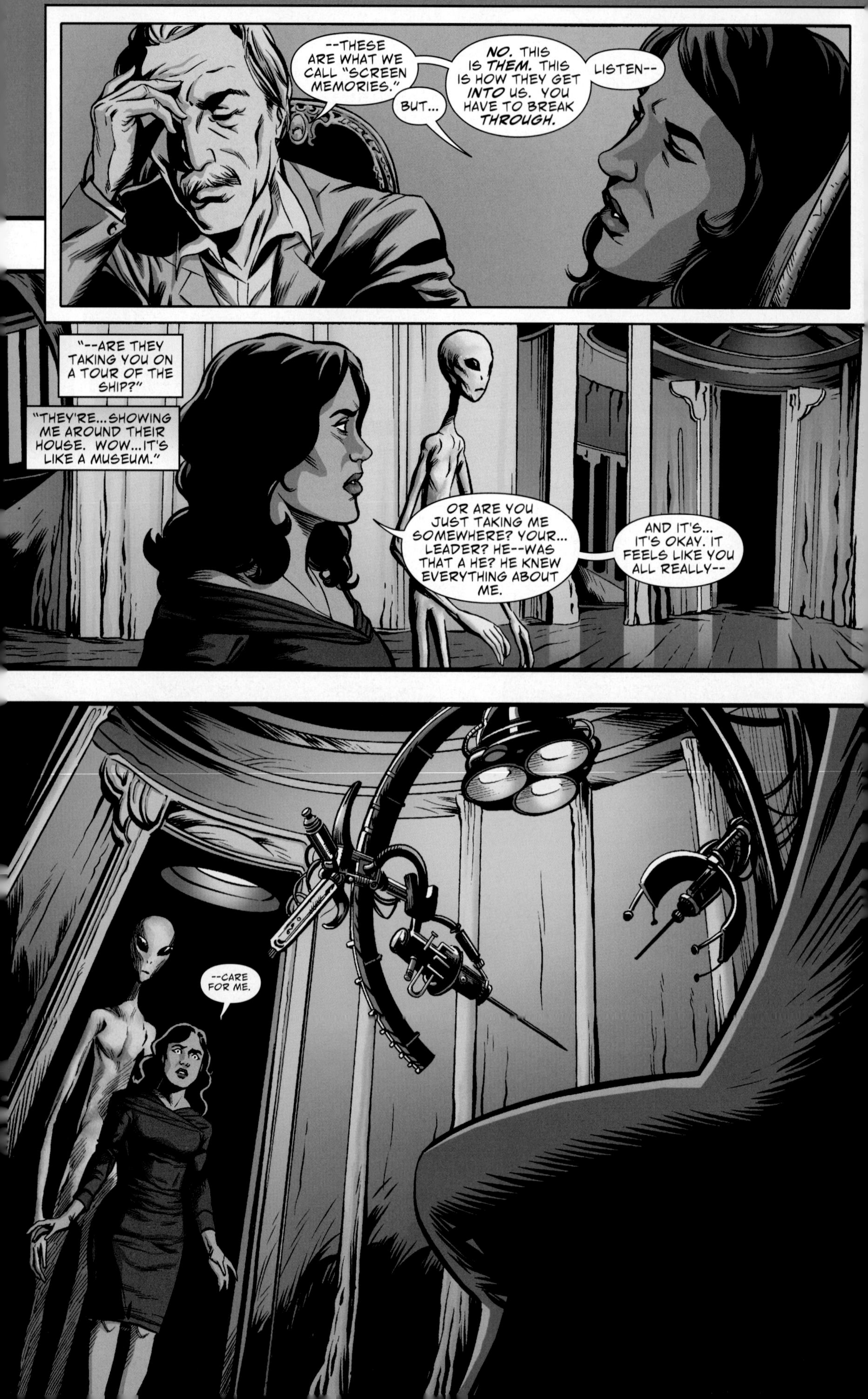
--THESE ARE WHAT WE CALL "SCREEN MEMORIES."
BUT...
NO. THIS IS THEM. THIS IS HOW THEY GET INTO US. YOU HAVE TO BREAK THROUGH.
LISTEN--
"--ARE THEY TAKING YOU ON A TOUR OF THE SHIP?"
"THEY'RE...SHOWING ME AROUND THEIR HOUSE. WOW...IT'S LIKE A MUSEUM."
OR ARE YOU JUST TAKING ME SOMEWHERE? YOUR... LEADER? HE--WAS THAT A HE? HE KNEW EVERYTHING ABOUT ME.
AND IT'S... IT'S OKAY. IT FEELS LIKE YOU ALL REALLY--
--CARE FOR ME.

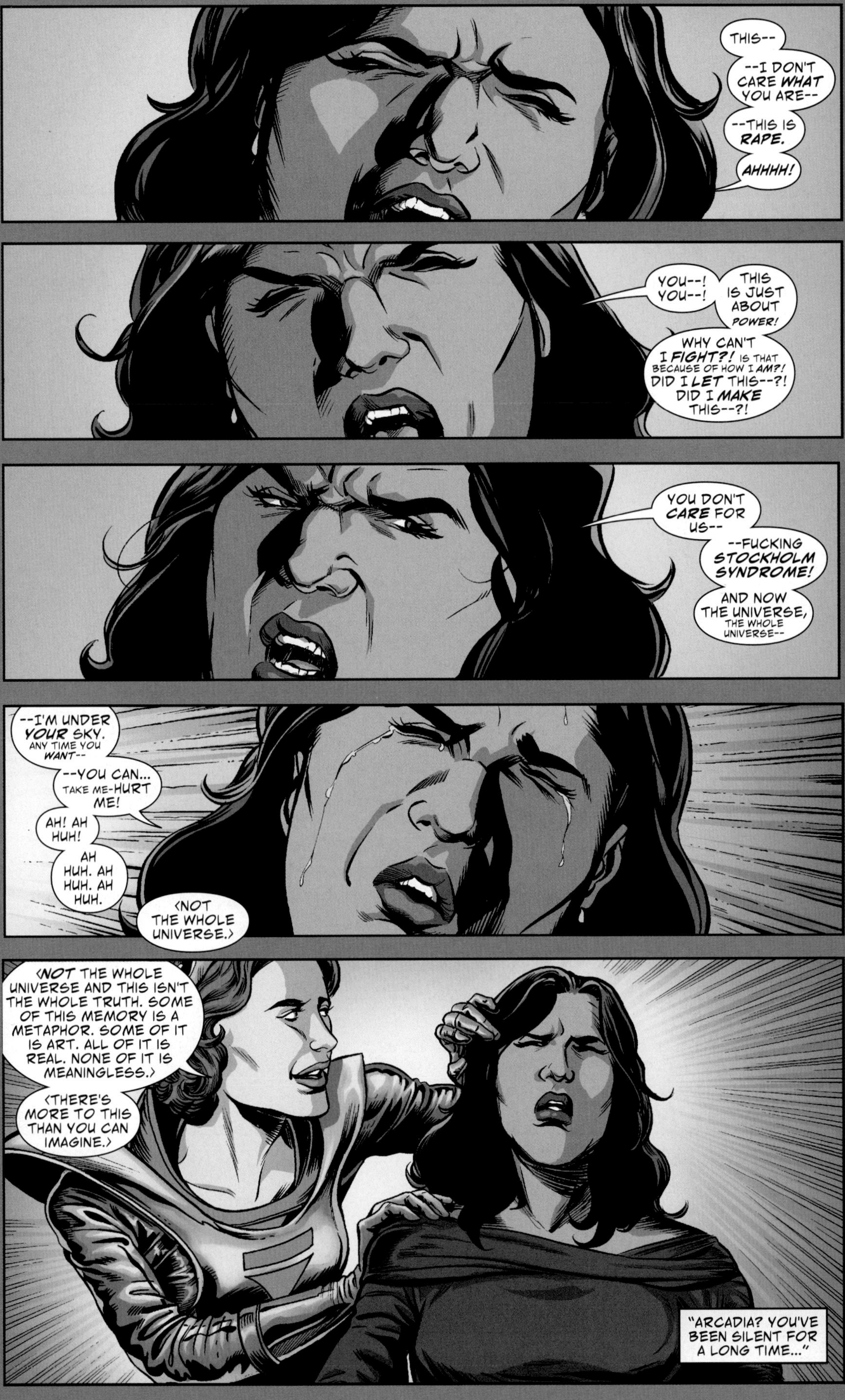
THIS--
--I DON'T CARE WHAT YOU ARE--
--THIS IS RAPE.
AHHHH!
YOU--! YOU--!
THIS IS JUST ABOUT POWER!
WHY CAN'T I FIGHT?! IS THAT BECAUSE OF HOW I AM?! DID I LET THIS--?! DID I MAKE THIS--?!
YOU DON'T CARE FOR US--
--FUCKING STOCKHOLM SYNDROME!
AND NOW THE UNIVERSE, THE WHOLE UNIVERSE--
--I'M UNDER YOUR SKY. ANY TIME YOU WANT--
--YOU CAN... TAKE ME-HURT ME!
AH! AH HUH!
AH HUH. AH HUH. AH HUH.
<NOT THE WHOLE UNIVERSE.>
<NOT THE WHOLE UNIVERSE AND THIS ISN'T THE WHOLE TRUTH. SOME OF THIS MEMORY IS A METAPHOR. SOME OF IT IS ART. ALL OF IT IS REAL. NONE OF IT IS MEANINGLESS.>
<THERE'S MORE TO THIS THAN YOU CAN IMAGINE.>
"ARCADIA? YOU'VE BEEN SILENT FOR A LONG TIME..."

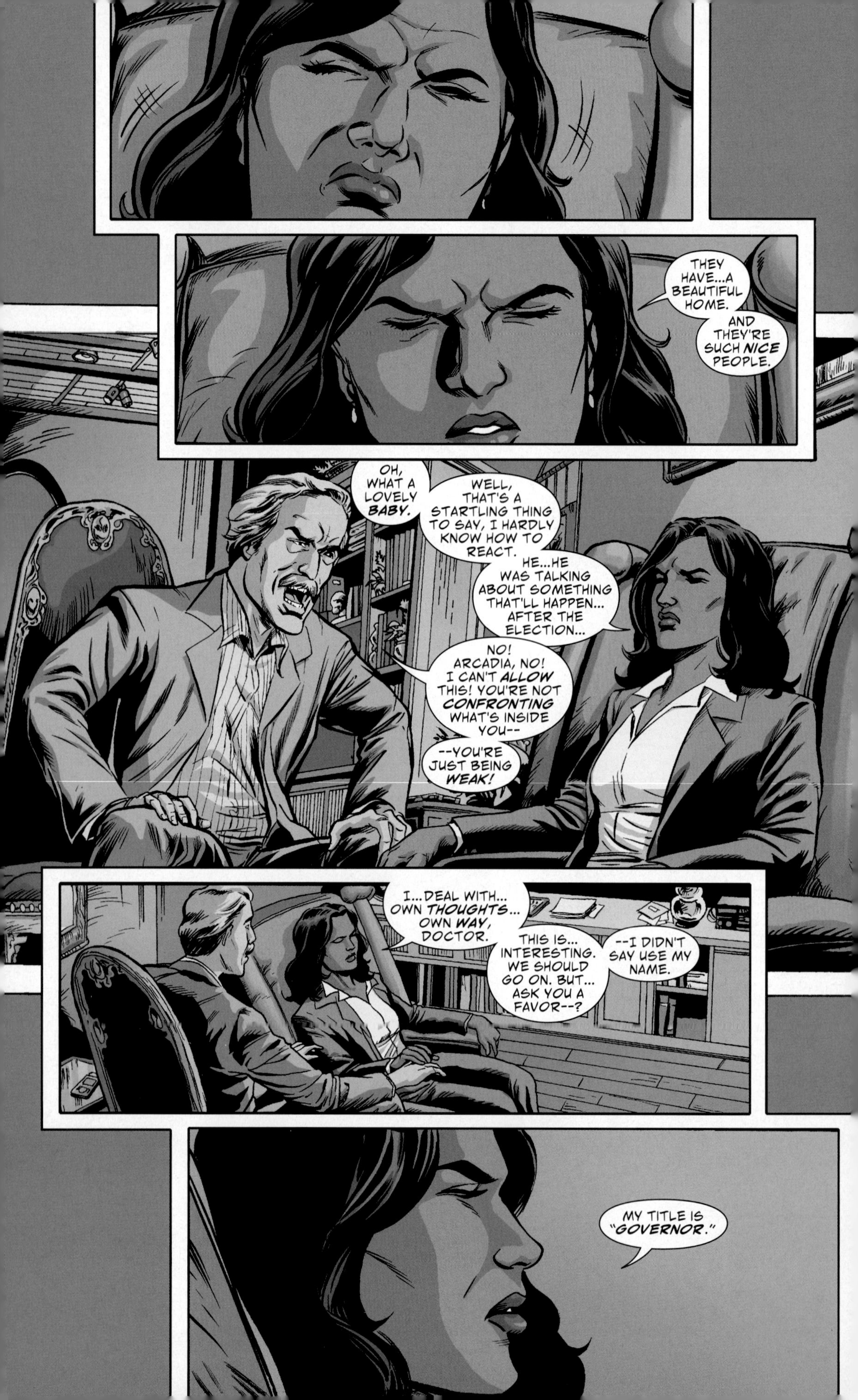
THEY HAVE...A BEAUTIFUL HOME.
AND THEY'RE SUCH NICE PEOPLE.
OH, WHAT A LOVELY BABY.
WELL, THAT'S A STARTLING THING TO SAY, I HARDLY KNOW HOW TO REACT.
HE...HE WAS TALKING ABOUT SOMETHING THAT'LL HAPPEN... AFTER THE ELECTION...
NO! ARCADIA, NO! I CAN'T ALLOW THIS! YOU'RE NOT CONFRONTING WHAT'S INSIDE YOU--
--YOU'RE JUST BEING WEAK!
I...DEAL WITH... OWN THOUGHTS... OWN WAY, DOCTOR.
THIS IS... INTERESTING. WE SHOULD GO ON. BUT... ASK YOU A FAVOR--?
--I DIDN'T SAY USE MY NAME.
MY TITLE IS "GOVERNOR."

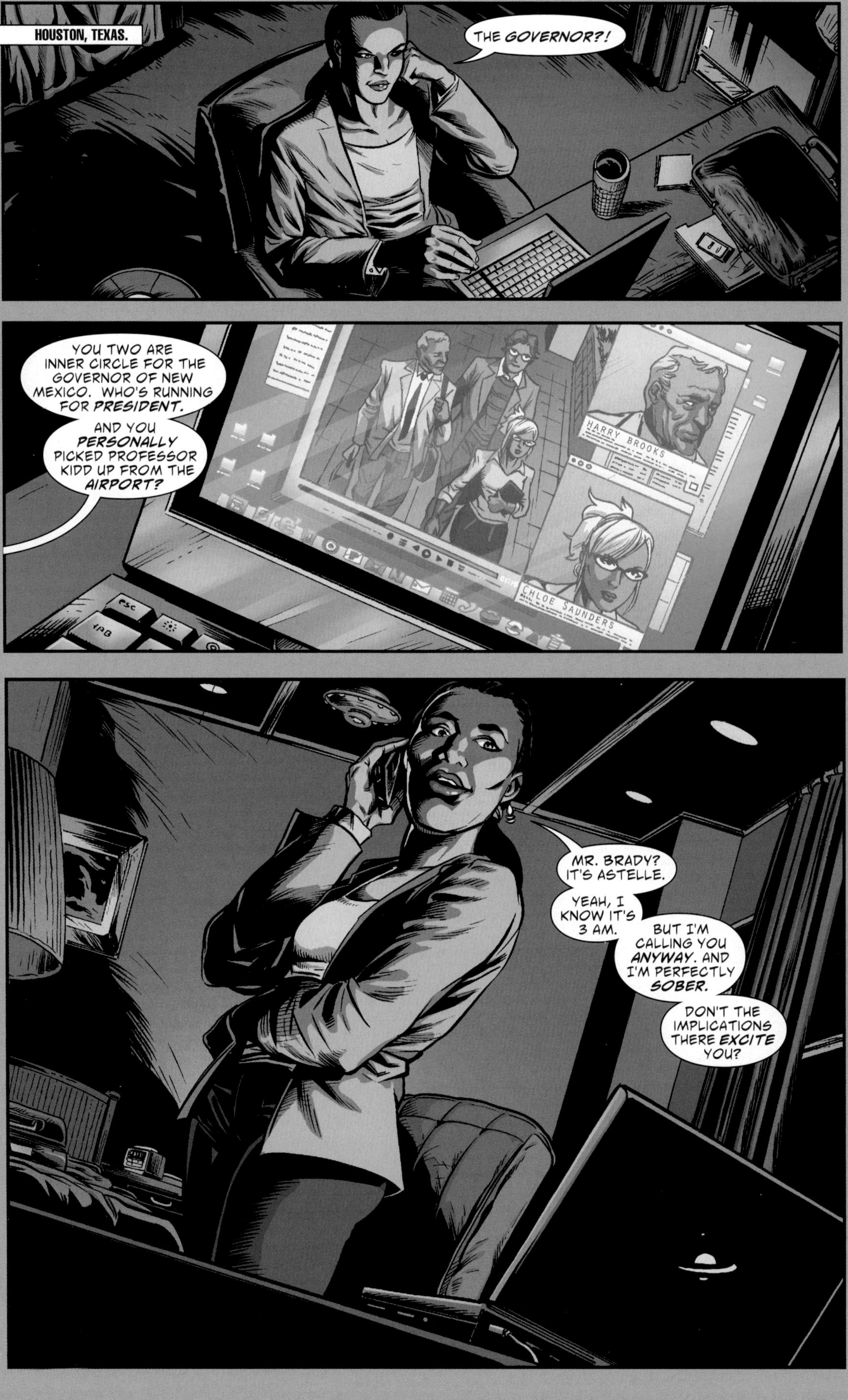
HOUSTON, TEXAS.
THE GOVERNOR?!
YOU TWO ARE INNER CIRCLE FOR THE GOVERNOR OF NEW MEXICO. WHO'S RUNNING FOR PRESIDENT.
AND YOU PERSONALLY PICKED PROFESSOR KIDD UP FROM THE AIRPORT?
HARRY BROOKS
CHLOE SAUNDERS
MR. BRADY? IT'S ASTELLE.
YEAH, I KNOW IT'S 3 AM.
BUT I'M CALLING YOU ANYWAY. AND I'M PERFECTLY SOBER.
DON'T THE IMPLICATIONS THERE EXCITE YOU?

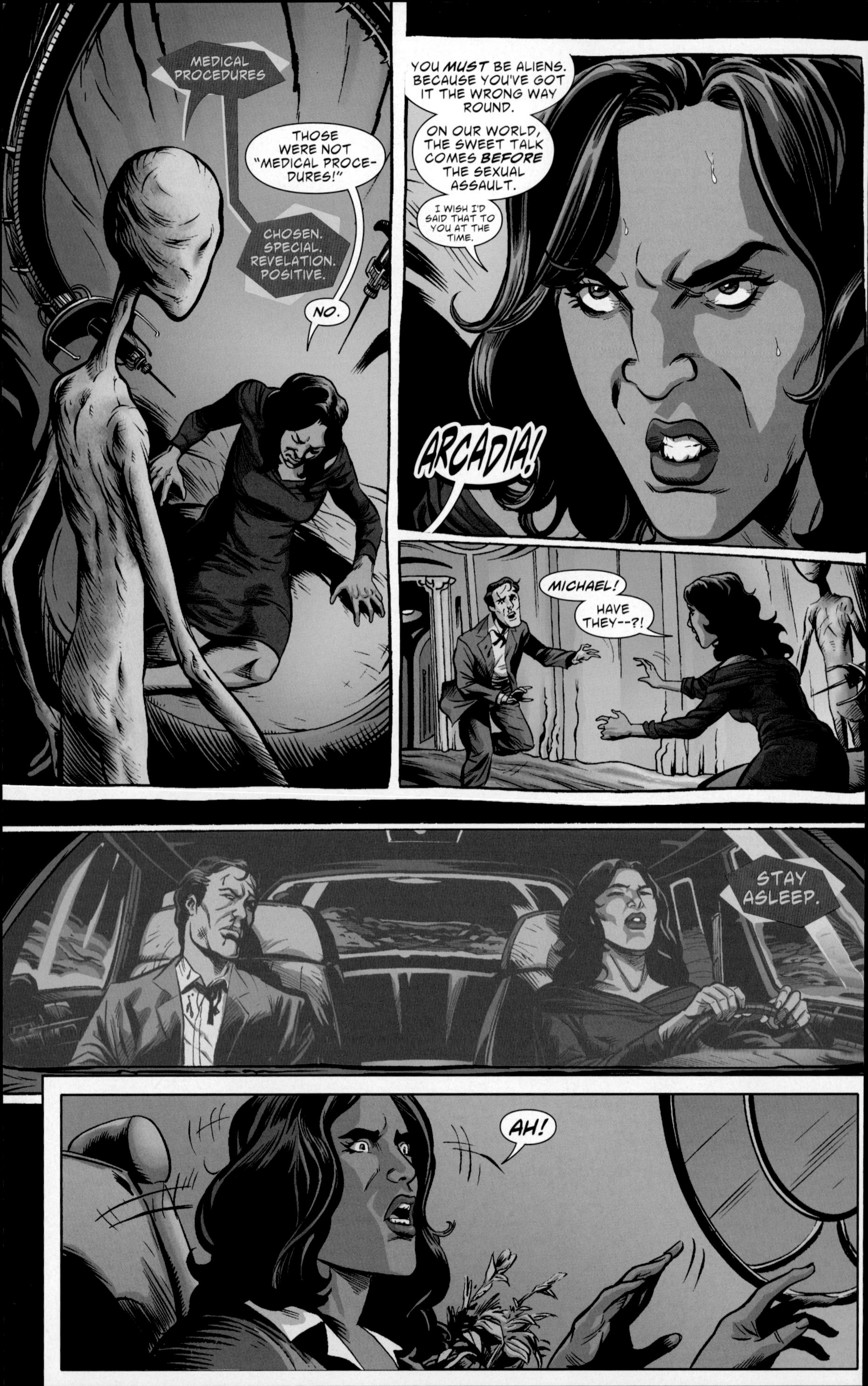
MEDICAL PROCEDURES
THOSE WERE NOT "MEDICAL PROCE-DURES!"
CHOSEN. SPECIAL. REVELATION. POSITIVE.
NO.
YOU MUST BE ALIENS. BECAUSE YOU'VE GOT IT THE WRONG WAY ROUND.
ON OUR WORLD, THE SWEET TALK COMES BEFORE THE SEXUAL ASSAULT.
I WISH I'D SAID THAT TO YOU AT THE TIME.
ARCADIA!
MICHAEL!
HAVE THEY--?!
STAY ASLEEP.
AH!

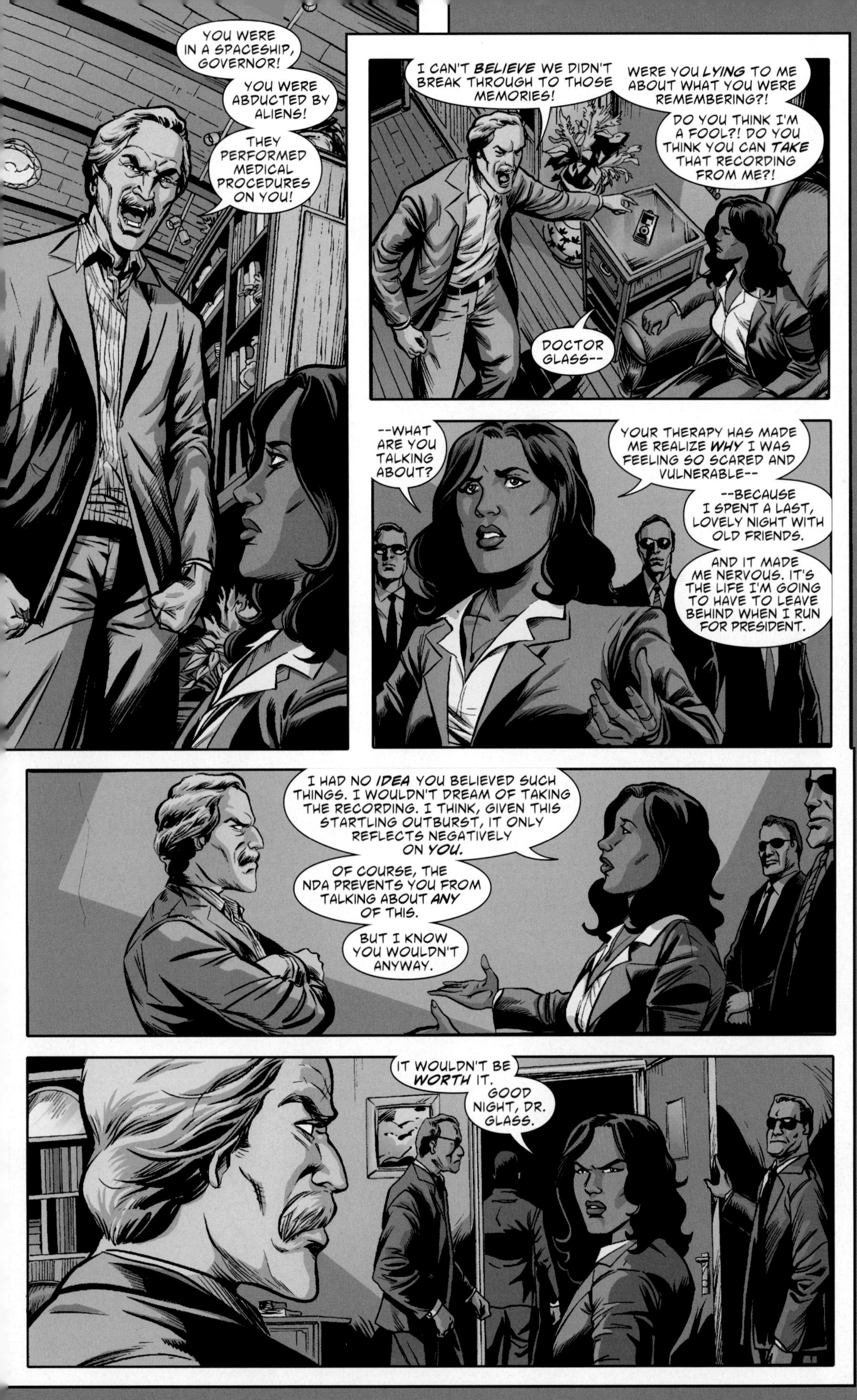
YOU WERE IN A SPACESHIP, GOVERNOR!
YOU WERE ABDUCTED BY ALIENS!
THEY PERFORMED MEDICAL PROCEDURES ON YOU!
I CAN'T BELIEVE WE DIDN'T BREAK THROUGH TO THOSE MEMORIES!
WERE YOU LYING TO ME ABOUT WHAT YOU WERE REMEMBERING?!
DO YOU THINK I'M A FOOL?! DO YOU THINK YOU CAN TAKE THAT RECORDING FROM ME?!
DOCTOR GLASS--
--WHAT ARE YOU TALKING ABOUT?
YOUR THERAPY HAS MADE ME REALIZE WHY I WAS FEELING SO SCARED AND VULNERABLE--
--BECAUSE I SPENT A LAST, LOVELY NIGHT WITH OLD FRIENDS.
AND IT MADE ME NERVOUS. IT'S THE LIFE I'M GOING TO HAVE TO LEAVE BEHIND WHEN I RUN FOR PRESIDENT.
I HAD NO IDEA YOU BELIEVED SUCH THINGS. I WOULDN'T DREAM OF TAKING THE RECORDING. I THINK, GIVEN THIS STARTLING OUTBURST, IT ONLY REFLECTS NEGATIVELY ON YOU.
OF COURSE, THE NDA PREVENTS YOU FROM TALKING ABOUT ANY OF THIS.
BUT I KNOW YOU WOULDN'T ANYWAY.
IT WOULDN'T BE WORTH IT.
GOOD NIGHT, DR. GLASS.

SHE THINKS SHE *PLAYED* ME! BUT I *STILL* WANT TO GO ON YOUR SHOW. THE RECORDING'S NO USE, BUT THOSE GUYS SMASHED MY DOOR, AND I CAN SAY WHAT I *THINK* WAS--!

NO.

WHAT?!

I'D FACE DOWN A LAWSUIT FUNDED BY CAMPAIGN DONATIONS IF IT GOT US *FULL DISCLOSURE.*

BUT NOT FOR A BUNCH OF NOTHING LIKE *THAT.* YOU LET ME DOWN, GLASS!

BUT--!

LISTEN TO HIM, DOCTOR--

--YOU'RE BEING SET UP TO FAIL. THEY WANT TO *DISCREDIT* YOU.

CLASSIC PSY OPS. I RECOGNIZE THE WAY THESE GUYS WORK.

DON'T FALL FOR IT.

BUT--

BUT I'VE GOT SOME GOOD NEWS FOR YOU--

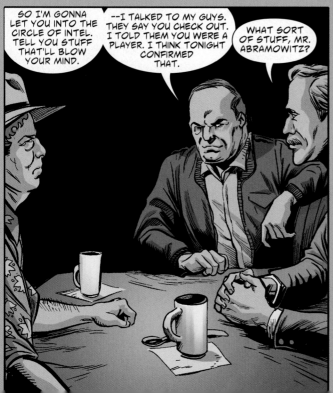

SO I'M GONNA LET YOU INTO THE CIRCLE OF INTEL. TELL YOU STUFF THAT'LL BLOW YOUR MIND.

--I TALKED TO MY GUYS. THEY SAY YOU CHECK OUT. I TOLD THEM YOU WERE A PLAYER. I THINK TONIGHT CONFIRMED THAT.

WHAT SORT OF STUFF, MR. ABRAMOWITZ?

FROM NOW ON, DOCTOR, PLEASE--

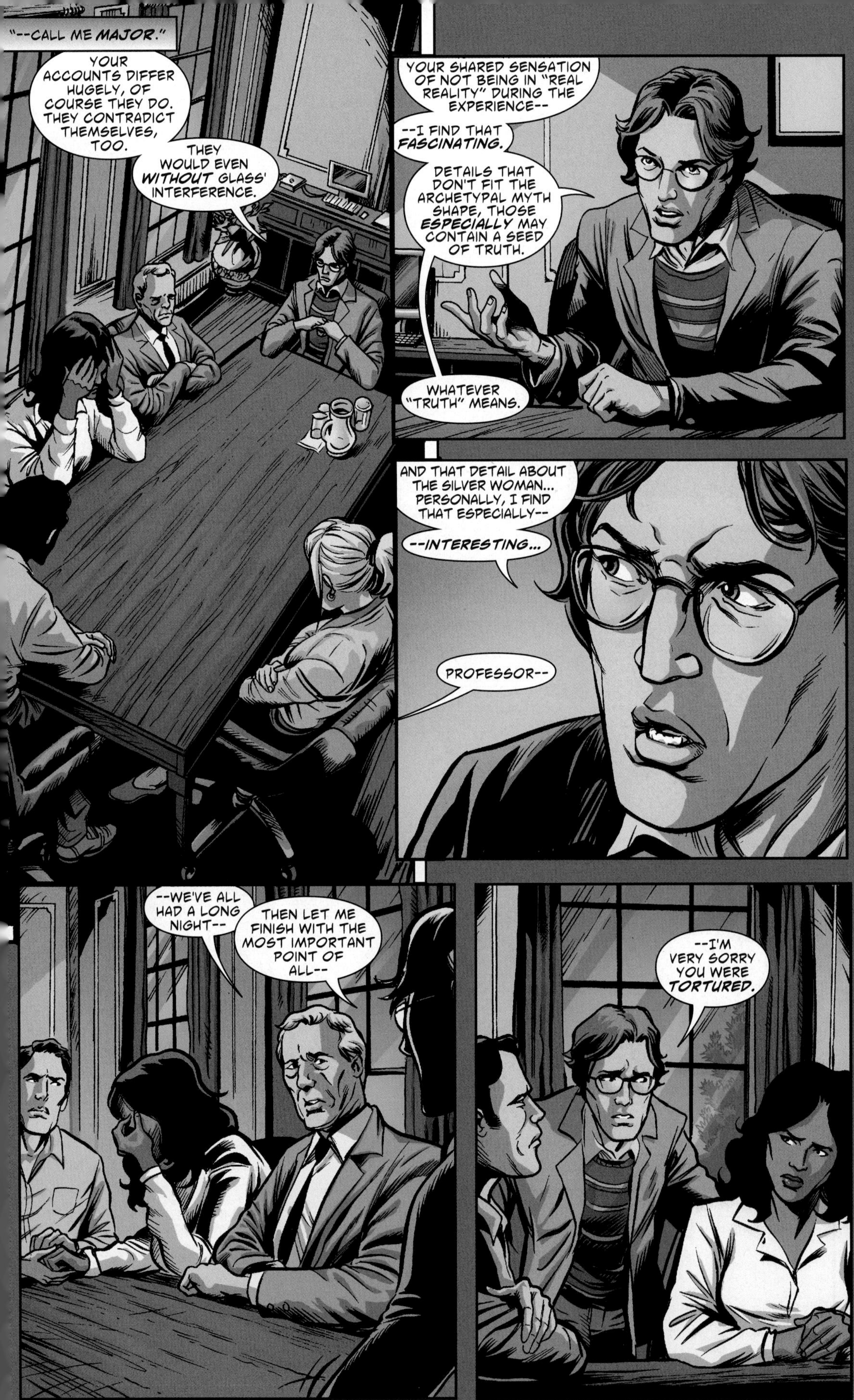
"--CALL ME MAJOR."
YOUR ACCOUNTS DIFFER HUGELY, OF COURSE THEY DO. THEY CONTRADICT THEMSELVES, TOO.
THEY WOULD EVEN WITHOUT GLASS' INTERFERENCE.
YOUR SHARED SENSATION OF NOT BEING IN "REAL REALITY" DURING THE EXPERIENCE--
--I FIND THAT FASCINATING.
DETAILS THAT DON'T FIT THE ARCHETYPAL MYTH SHAPE, THOSE ESPECIALLY MAY CONTAIN A SEED OF TRUTH.
WHATEVER "TRUTH" MEANS.
AND THAT DETAIL ABOUT THE SILVER WOMAN... PERSONALLY, I FIND THAT ESPECIALLY--
--INTERESTING...
PROFESSOR--
--WE'VE ALL HAD A LONG NIGHT--
THEN LET ME FINISH WITH THE MOST IMPORTANT POINT OF ALL--
--I'M VERY SORRY YOU WERE TORTURED.

I CAN'T CLAIM TO HAVE UNCOVERED ANY TRUTHS WHILE HYPNOTIZED--

--I THINK ALL IT GAVE US WAS SOME...CLUES. SOME *POINTERS.*

YOU HAVE THE CLEAREST VERSION OF IT NOW. MY HEAD FEELS...SCREWED AROUND WITH.

I'M SORRY I WAS ANGRY. WE'VE BOTH BEEN THROUGH--

NO, CHLOE WAS RIGHT, I DIDN'T THINK, I JUST GRABBED FOR THE FIRST HELP I COULD FIND.

YOU WERE ALWAYS THE STRONG ONE, KIDDER.

THAT'S SO NOT TRUE.

IF YOU STILL WANT ME TO GET LOST--

NO. YOU'RE PART OF THIS NOW. LISTEN, EARLIER YOU SAID THE WEIRD STUFF WAS STILL HAPPENING--?

YEAH--

--I THINK WHAT GLASS DID... STAYED WITH ME FOR A WHILE.

I DON'T THINK THEY...CAME BACK.

NOT *YET*--

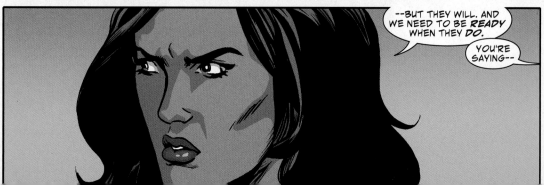

--BUT THEY WILL. AND WE NEED TO BE *READY* WHEN THEY *DO.*

YOU'RE SAYING--

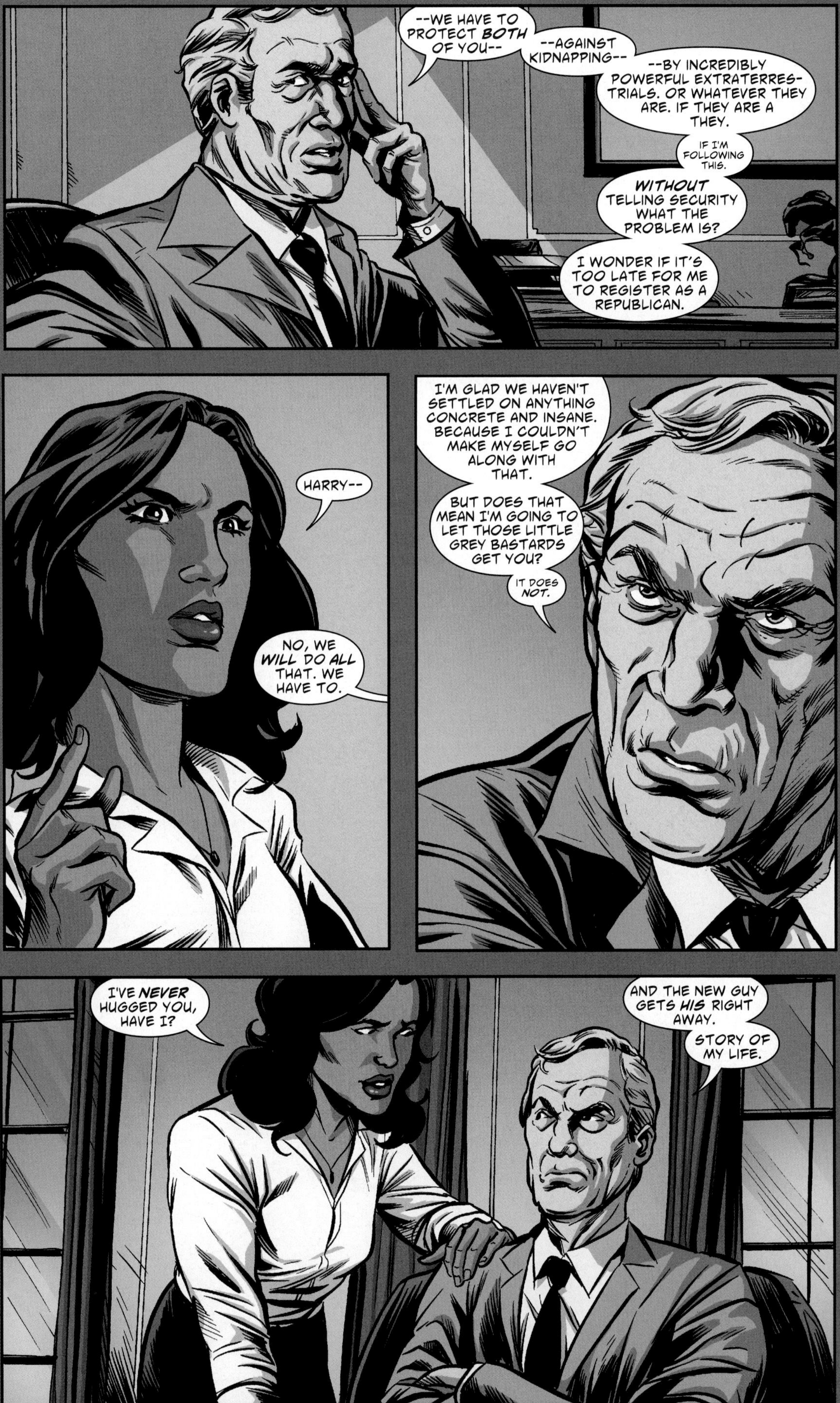
--WE HAVE TO PROTECT BOTH OF YOU--
--AGAINST KIDNAPPING--
--BY INCREDIBLY POWERFUL EXTRATERRES-TRIALS. OR WHATEVER THEY ARE. IF THEY ARE A THEY.
IF I'M FOLLOWING THIS.
WITHOUT TELLING SECURITY WHAT THE PROBLEM IS?
I WONDER IF IT'S TOO LATE FOR ME TO REGISTER AS A REPUBLICAN.
HARRY--
NO, WE WILL DO ALL THAT. WE HAVE TO.
I'M GLAD WE HAVEN'T SETTLED ON ANYTHING CONCRETE AND INSANE. BECAUSE I COULDN'T MAKE MYSELF GO ALONG WITH THAT.
BUT DOES THAT MEAN I'M GOING TO LET THOSE LITTLE GREY BASTARDS GET YOU?
IT DOES NOT.
I'VE NEVER HUGGED YOU, HAVE I?
AND THE NEW GUY GETS HIS RIGHT AWAY.
STORY OF MY LIFE.

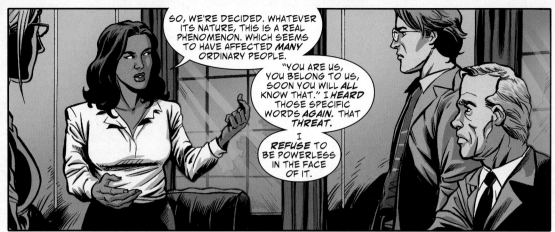

SO, WE'RE DECIDED. WHATEVER ITS NATURE, THIS IS A REAL PHENOMENON. WHICH SEEMS TO HAVE AFFECTED *MANY* ORDINARY PEOPLE.

"YOU ARE US, YOU BELONG TO US, SOON YOU WILL *ALL* KNOW THAT." I *HEARD* THOSE SPECIFIC WORDS *AGAIN*. THAT *THREAT*.

I *REFUSE* TO BE POWERLESS IN THE FACE OF IT.

I INTEND TO USE THE POWERS OF THE GOVERNOR'S OFFICE, AND THE ADDITIONAL OPPORTUNITIES GIVEN TO A CANDIDATE--

--TO INVESTIGATE AND UNCOVER THE *NATURE* OF THAT THREAT.

PROFESSOR, I WANT YOU TO FIND US SOME *THREADS* TO PULL AT.

I ALREADY HAVE SOME IN MIND. ANOMALIES IN THE MYTHOLOGY, PLACES TO VISIT, PEOPLE TO TALK TO.

EXCELLENT. CHLOE--

YEAH--

--I *STILL* THINK THIS IS *BULLSHIT*.

AND BEING THE NEXT PRESIDENT OF THE UNITED STATES, AND THUS A VERY CLEVER PERSON, YOU UNDERSTAND THAT THIS IS A *POSITIVE* REASON TO KEEP ME AROUND.

PERSUADING *YOU*, "SCULLY," IS THE WHOLE GAME. WE NEED *EVIDENCE*.

THE CAMPAIGN TRAIL WILL GIVE US ACCESS TO ANYWHERE WE MIGHT FIND IT.

IN THE SECRECY WE'LL NEED TO MAINTAIN, ESPECIALLY IF THAT GAP IN THE RECORDS INDICATES *OPPOSITION*.

SO--

--WHERE DO WE BEGIN?

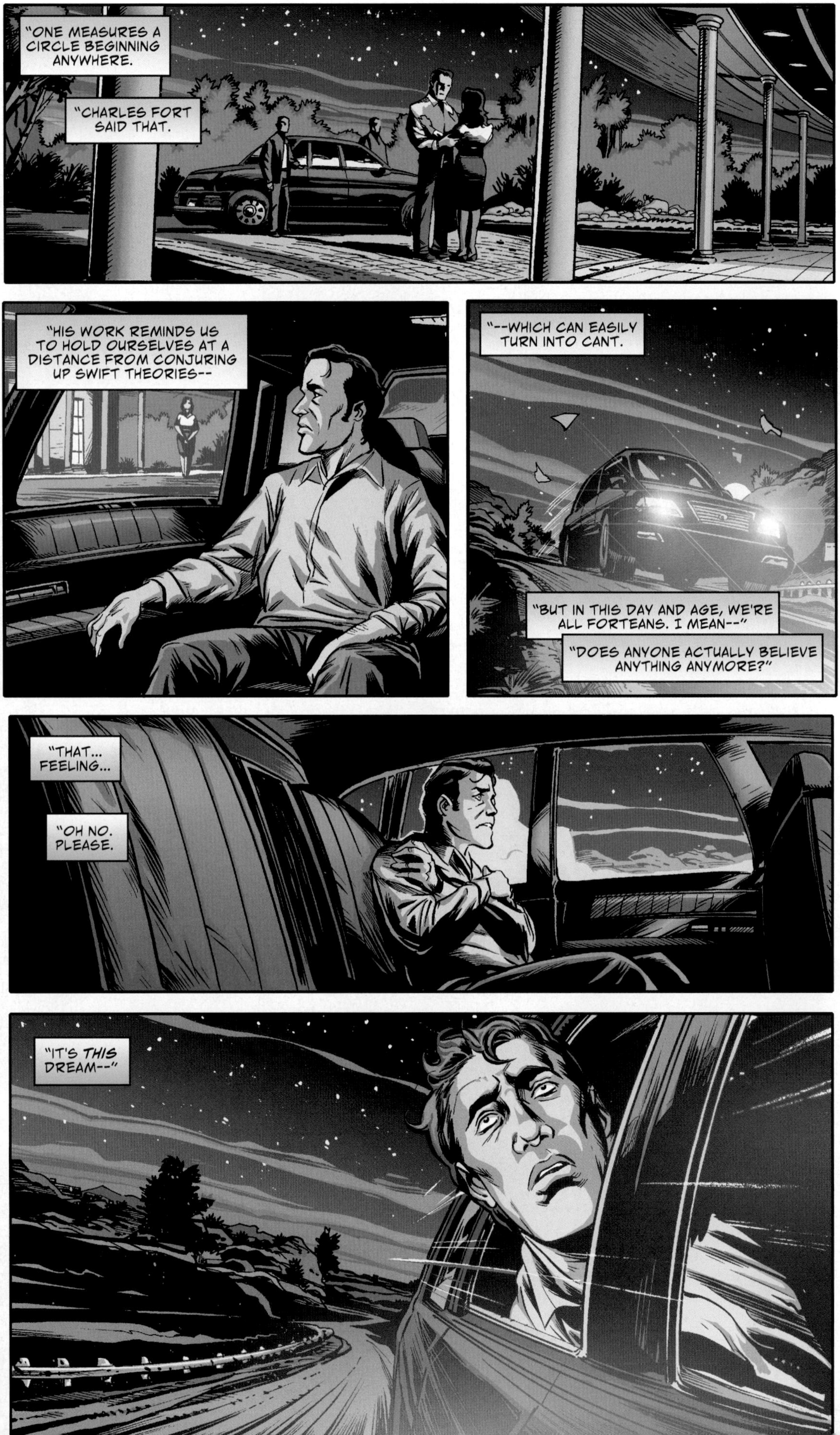
"ONE MEASURES A CIRCLE BEGINNING ANYWHERE.
"CHARLES FORT SAID THAT.
"HIS WORK REMINDS US TO HOLD OURSELVES AT A DISTANCE FROM CONJURING UP SWIFT THEORIES--
"--WHICH CAN EASILY TURN INTO CANT.
"BUT IN THIS DAY AND AGE, WE'RE ALL FORTEANS. I MEAN--"
"DOES ANYONE ACTUALLY BELIEVE ANYTHING ANYMORE?"
"THAT... FEELING...
"OH NO. PLEASE.
"IT'S *THIS* DREAM--"

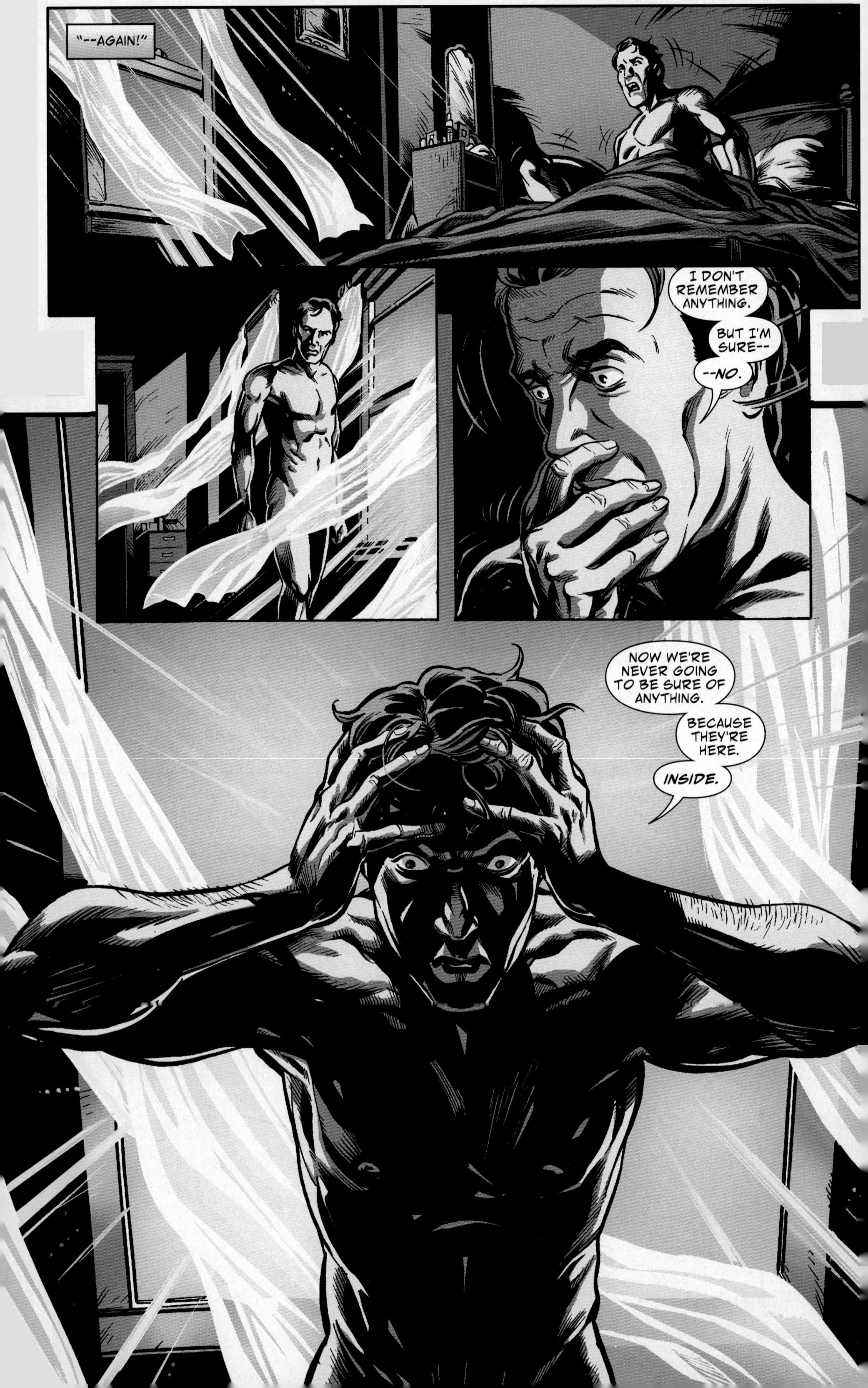
"--AGAIN!"
I DON'T REMEMBER ANYTHING.
BUT I'M SURE--
--NO.
NOW WE'RE NEVER GOING TO BE SURE OF ANYTHING.
BECAUSE THEY'RE HERE.
INSIDE.

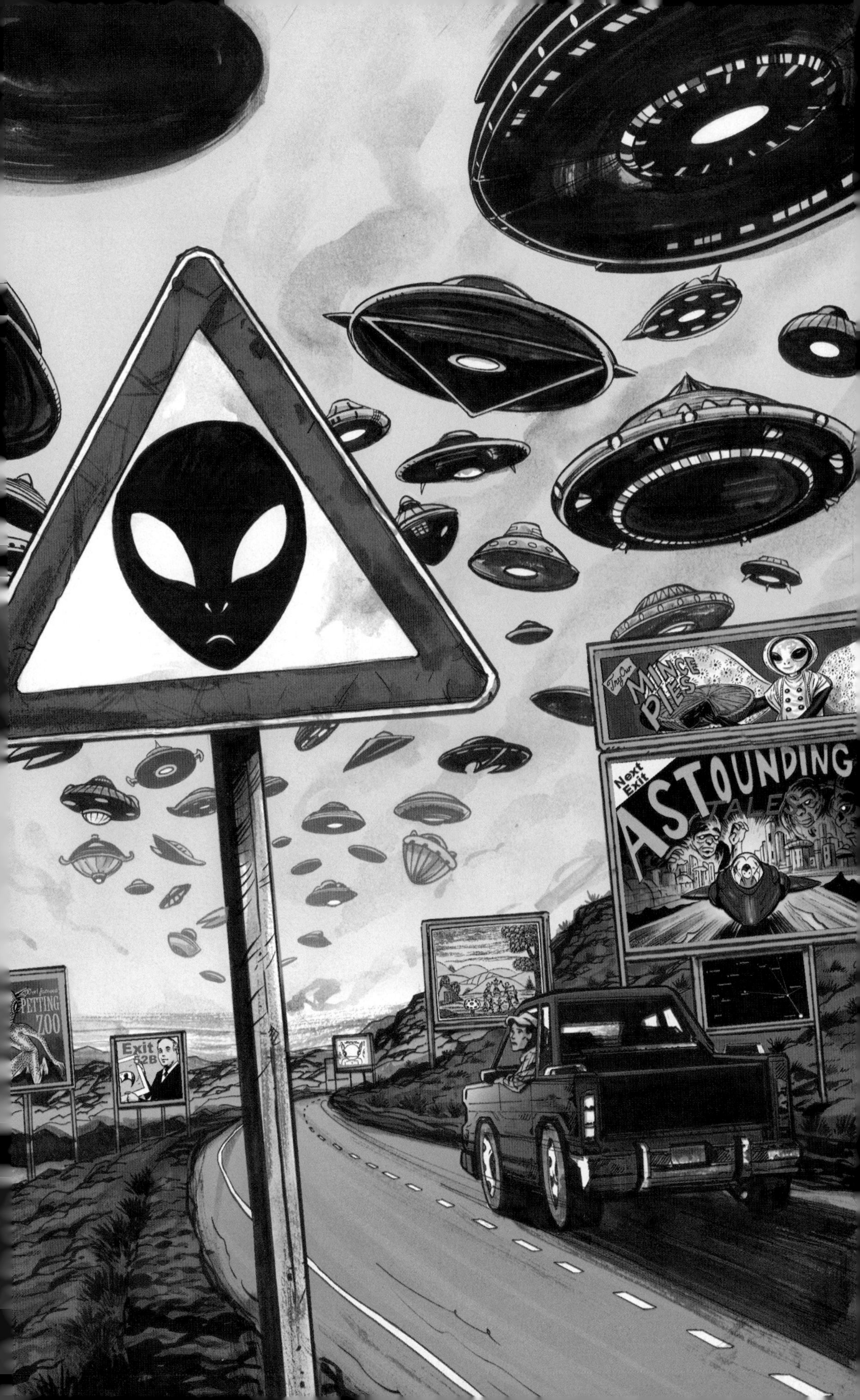
Try Our
MINCE PIES
Next Exit
ASTOUNDING
TALE
PETTING ZOO
Exit
52B

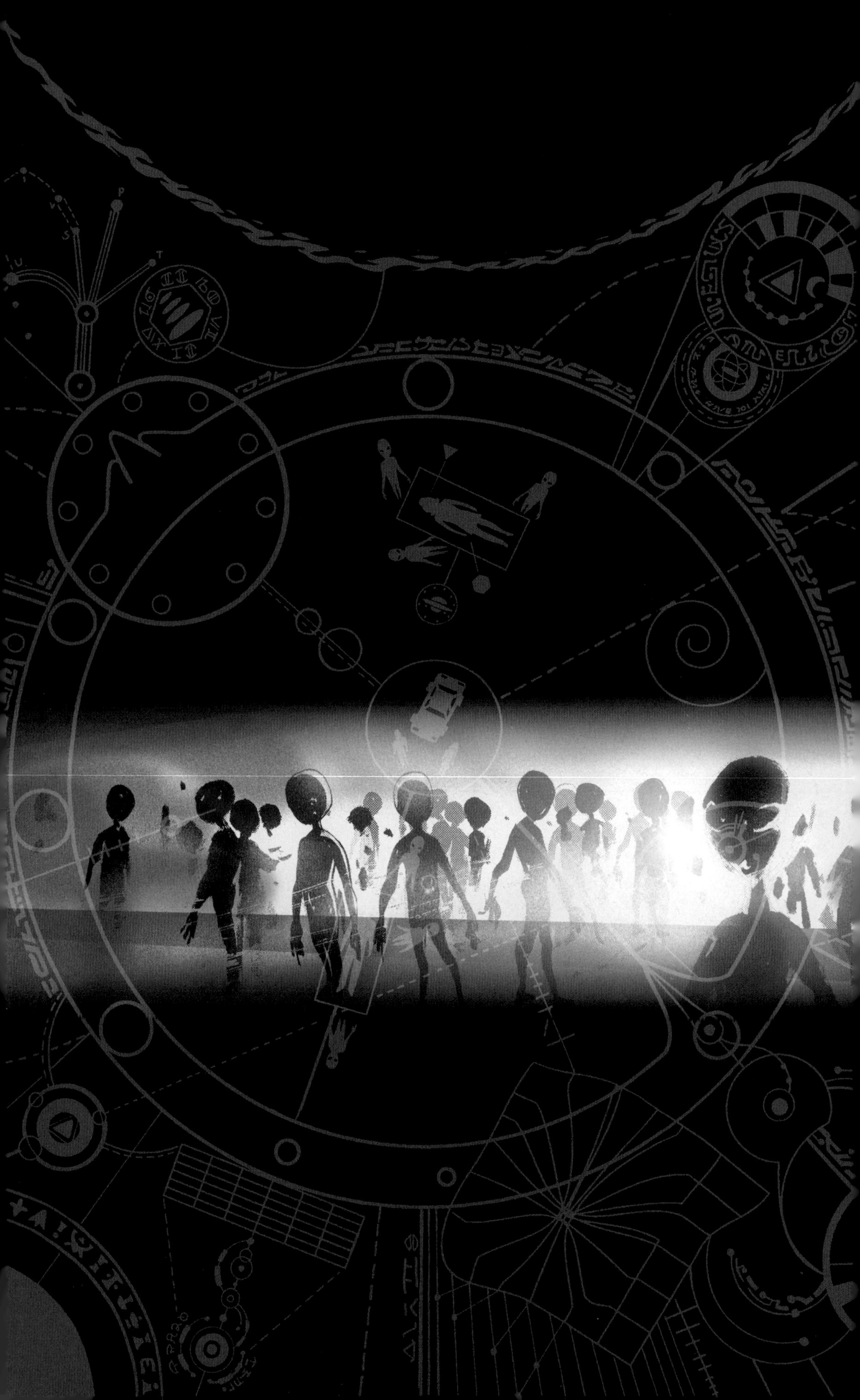

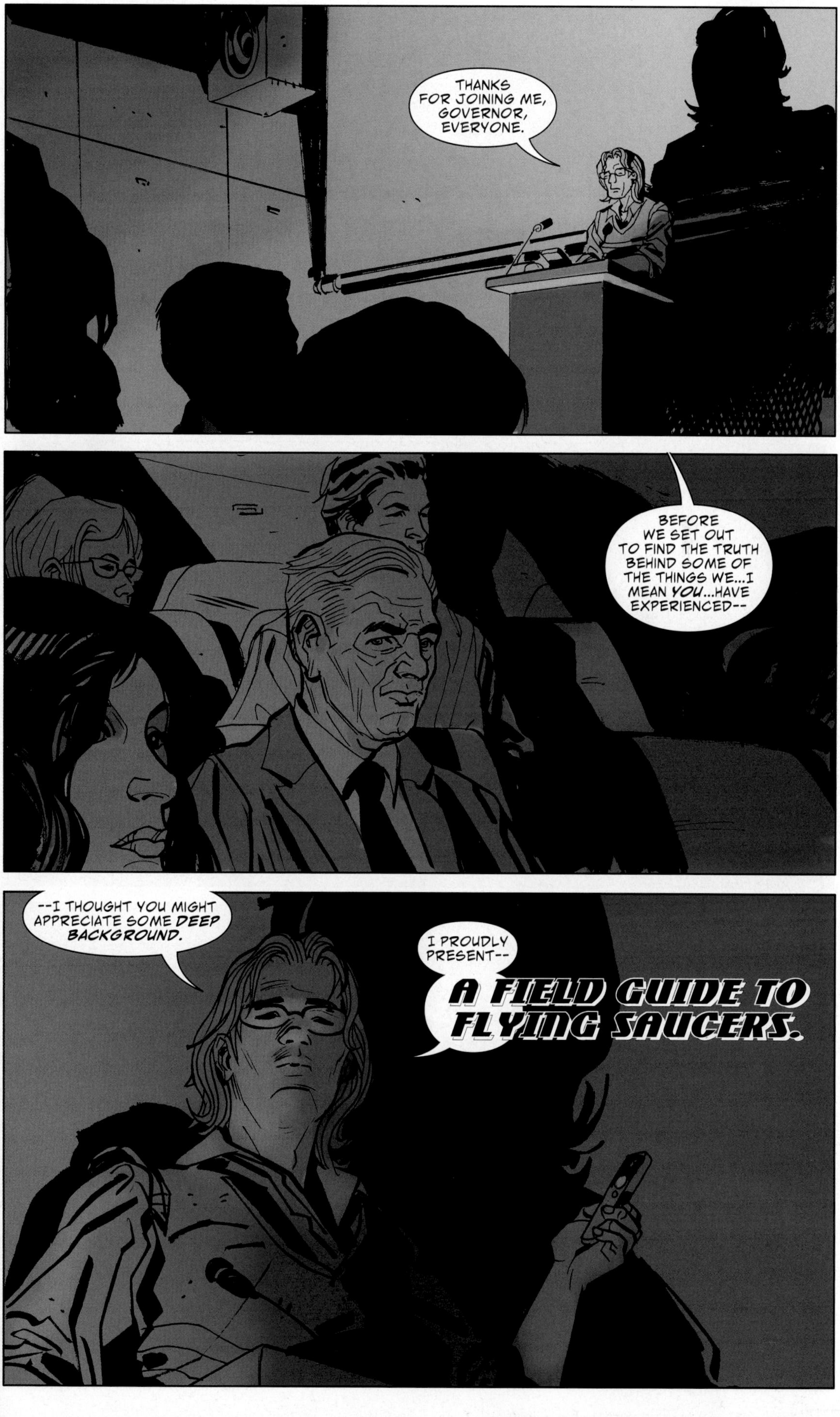
THANKS FOR JOINING ME, GOVERNOR, EVERYONE.
BEFORE WE SET OUT TO FIND THE TRUTH BEHIND SOME OF THE THINGS WE...I MEAN YOU...HAVE EXPERIENCED--
--I THOUGHT YOU MIGHT APPRECIATE SOME DEEP BACKGROUND.
I PROUDLY PRESENT--
A FIELD GUIDE TO FLYING SAUCERS.

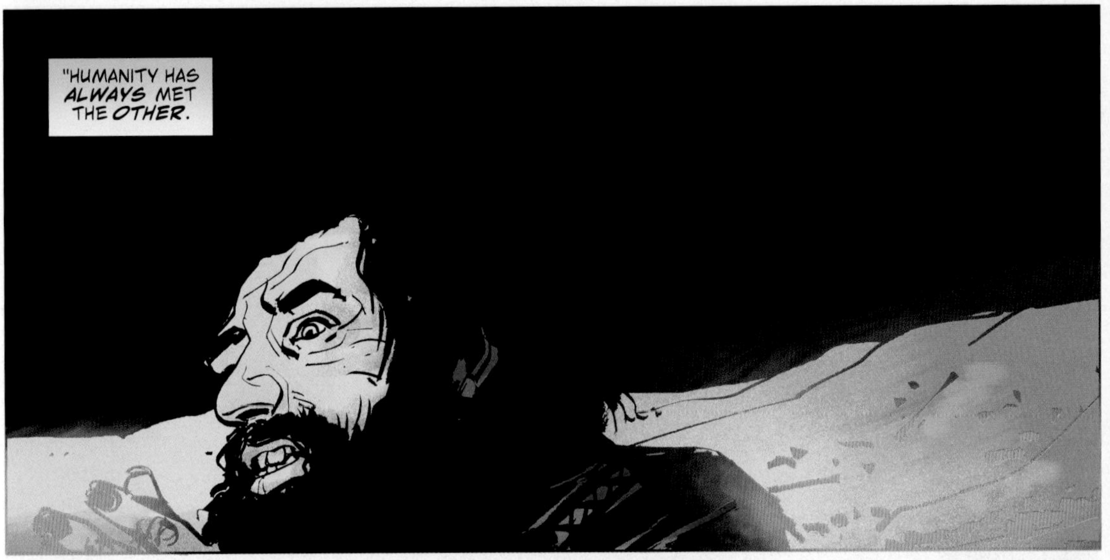
"HUMANITY HAS *ALWAYS* MET THE *OTHER*.

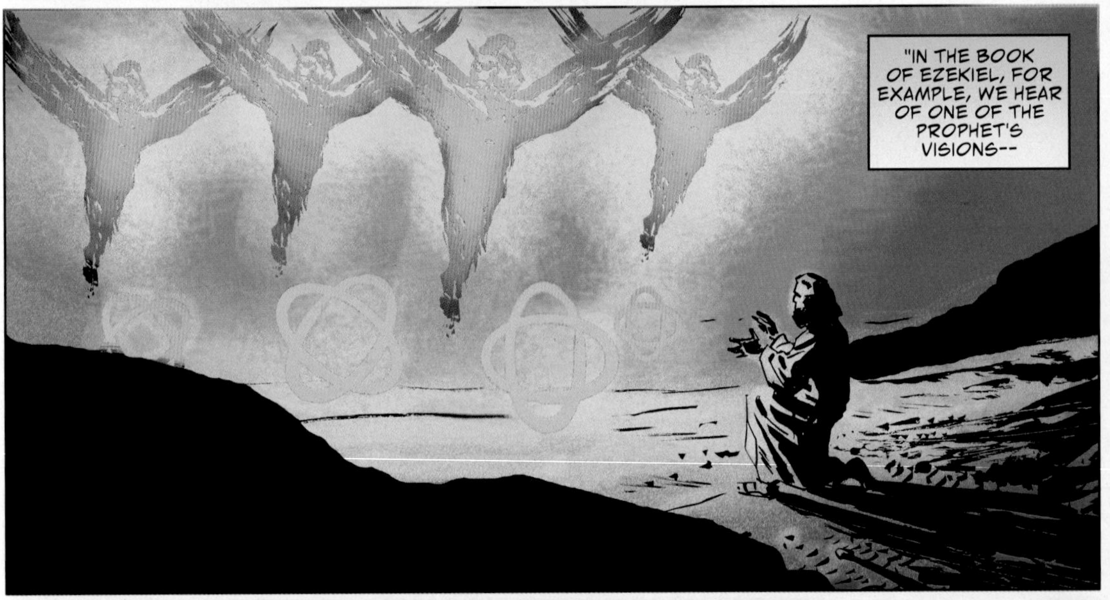
"IN THE BOOK OF EZEKIEL, FOR EXAMPLE, WE HEAR OF ONE OF THE PROPHET'S VISIONS--

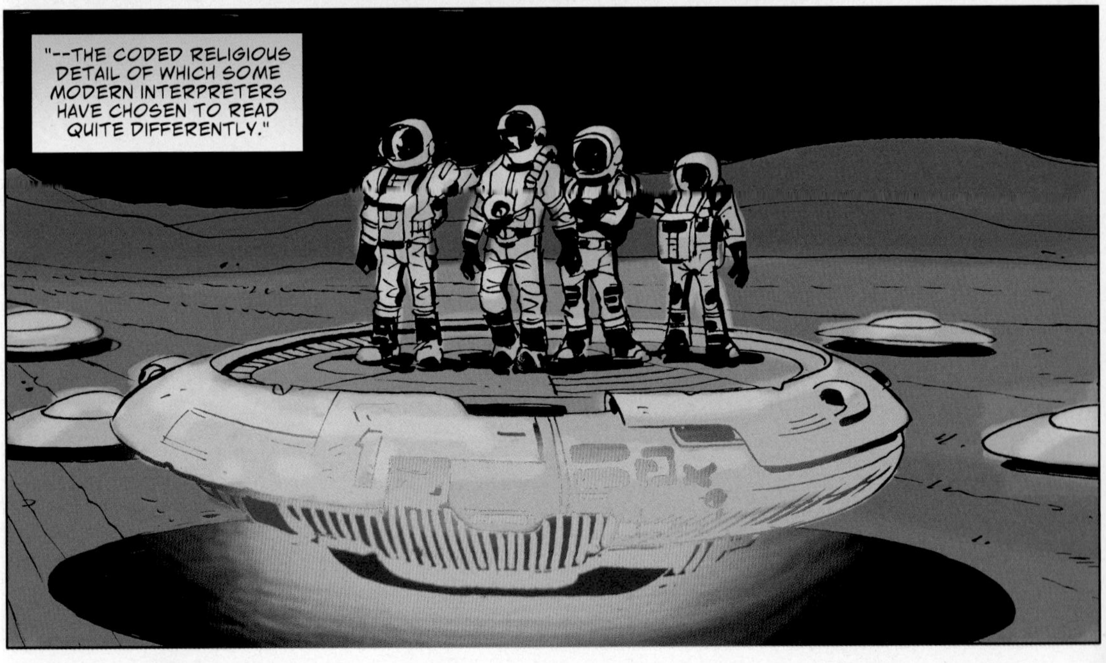
"--THE CODED RELIGIOUS DETAIL OF WHICH SOME MODERN INTERPRETERS HAVE CHOSEN TO READ QUITE DIFFERENTLY."

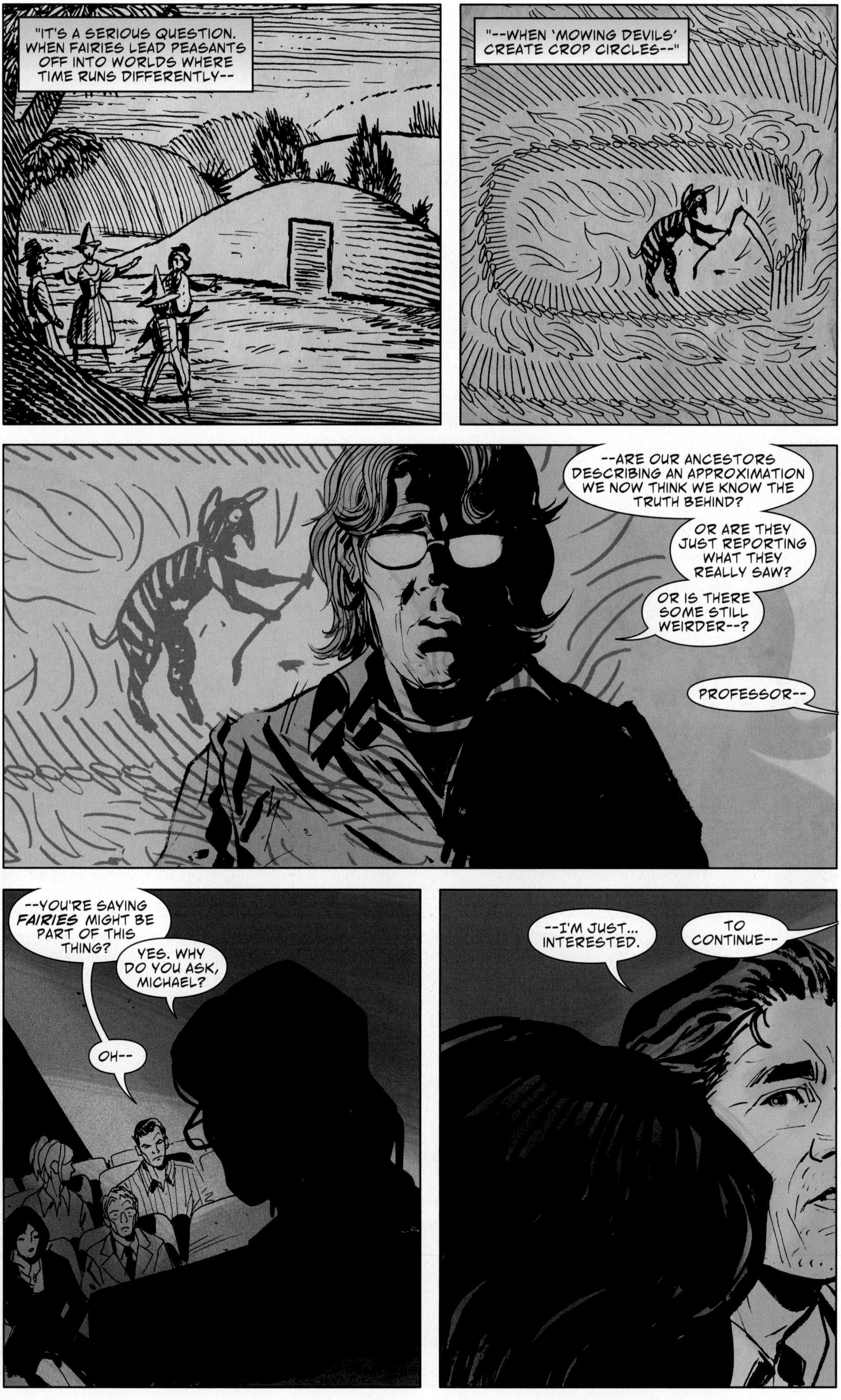
"IT'S A SERIOUS QUESTION. WHEN FAIRIES LEAD PEASANTS OFF INTO WORLDS WHERE TIME RUNS DIFFERENTLY--
"--WHEN 'MOWING DEVILS' CREATE CROP CIRCLES--"
--ARE OUR ANCESTORS DESCRIBING AN APPROXIMATION WE NOW THINK WE KNOW THE TRUTH BEHIND?
OR ARE THEY JUST REPORTING WHAT THEY REALLY SAW?
OR IS THERE SOME STILL WEIRDER--?
PROFESSOR--
--YOU'RE SAYING FAIRIES MIGHT BE PART OF THIS THING?
YES. WHY DO YOU ASK, MICHAEL?
OH--
--I'M JUST... INTERESTED.
TO CONTINUE--

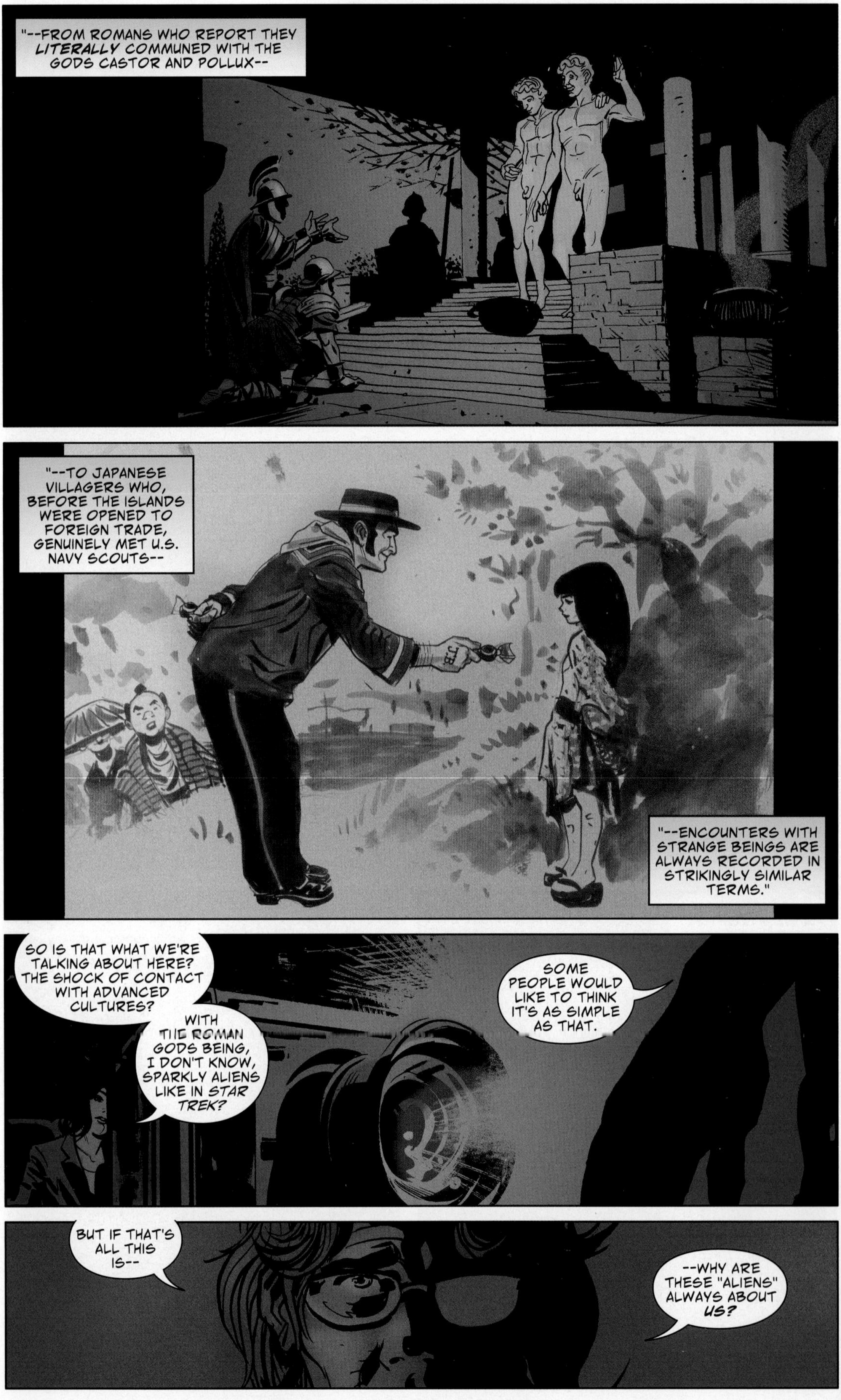
"--FROM ROMANS WHO REPORT THEY *LITERALLY* COMMUNED WITH THE GODS CASTOR AND POLLUX--
"--TO JAPANESE VILLAGERS WHO, BEFORE THE ISLANDS WERE OPENED TO FOREIGN TRADE, GENUINELY MET U.S. NAVY SCOUTS--
"--ENCOUNTERS WITH STRANGE BEINGS ARE ALWAYS RECORDED IN STRIKINGLY SIMILAR TERMS."
SO IS THAT WHAT WE'RE TALKING ABOUT HERE? THE SHOCK OF CONTACT WITH ADVANCED CULTURES?
WITH THE ROMAN GODS BEING, I DON'T KNOW, SPARKLY ALIENS LIKE IN *STAR TREK*?
SOME PEOPLE WOULD LIKE TO THINK IT'S AS SIMPLE AS THAT.
BUT IF THAT'S ALL THIS IS--
--WHY ARE THESE "ALIENS" ALWAYS ABOUT *US?*

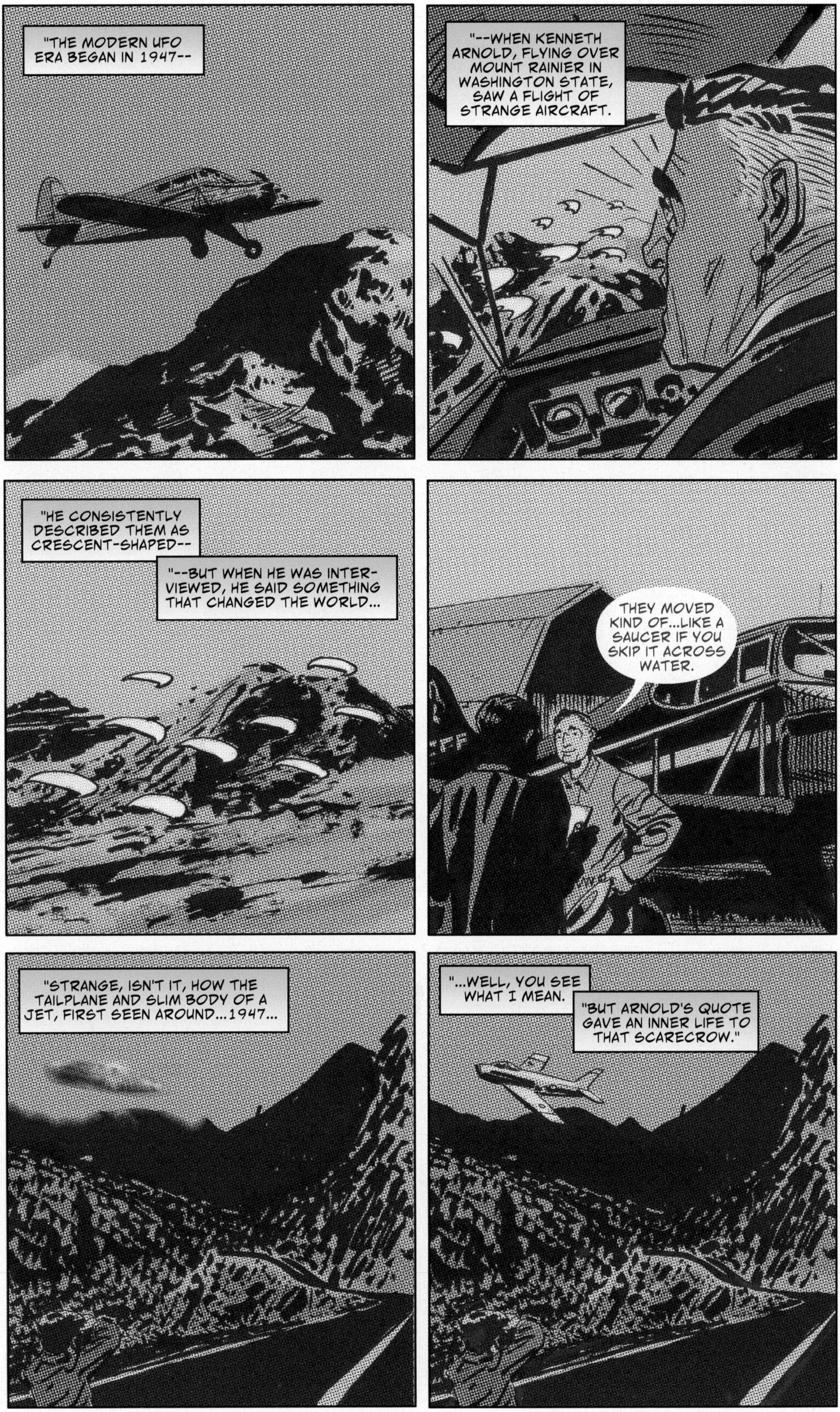
"THE MODERN UFO ERA BEGAN IN 1947--
"--WHEN KENNETH ARNOLD, FLYING OVER MOUNT RAINIER IN WASHINGTON STATE, SAW A FLIGHT OF STRANGE AIRCRAFT.
"HE CONSISTENTLY DESCRIBED THEM AS CRESCENT-SHAPED--
"--BUT WHEN HE WAS INTERVIEWED, HE SAID SOMETHING THAT CHANGED THE WORLD...
THEY MOVED KIND OF...LIKE A SAUCER IF YOU SKIP IT ACROSS WATER.
"STRANGE, ISN'T IT, HOW THE TAILPLANE AND SLIM BODY OF A JET, FIRST SEEN AROUND...1947...
"...WELL, YOU SEE WHAT I MEAN.
"BUT ARNOLD'S QUOTE GAVE AN INNER LIFE TO THAT SCARECROW."

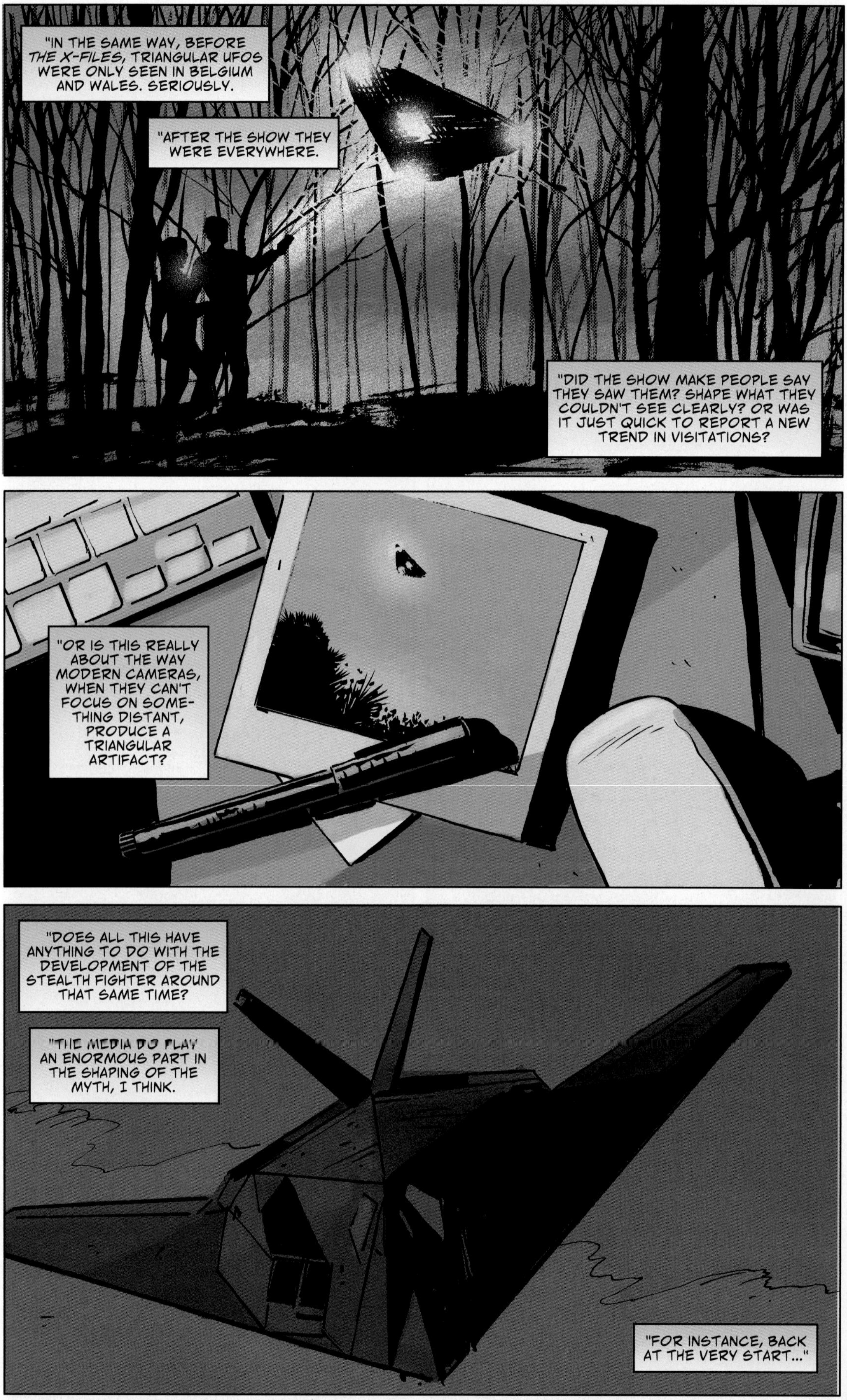
"IN THE SAME WAY, BEFORE *THE X-FILES*, TRIANGULAR UFOS WERE ONLY SEEN IN BELGIUM AND WALES. SERIOUSLY.
"AFTER THE SHOW THEY WERE EVERYWHERE.
"DID THE SHOW MAKE PEOPLE SAY THEY SAW THEM? SHAPE WHAT THEY COULDN'T SEE CLEARLY? OR WAS IT JUST QUICK TO REPORT A NEW TREND IN VISITATIONS?
"OR IS THIS REALLY ABOUT THE WAY MODERN CAMERAS, WHEN THEY CAN'T FOCUS ON SOME-THING DISTANT, PRODUCE A TRIANGULAR ARTIFACT?
"DOES ALL THIS HAVE ANYTHING TO DO WITH THE DEVELOPMENT OF THE STEALTH FIGHTER AROUND THAT SAME TIME?
"THE MEDIA DO PLAY AN ENORMOUS PART IN THE SHAPING OF THE MYTH, I THINK.
"FOR INSTANCE, BACK AT THE VERY START..."

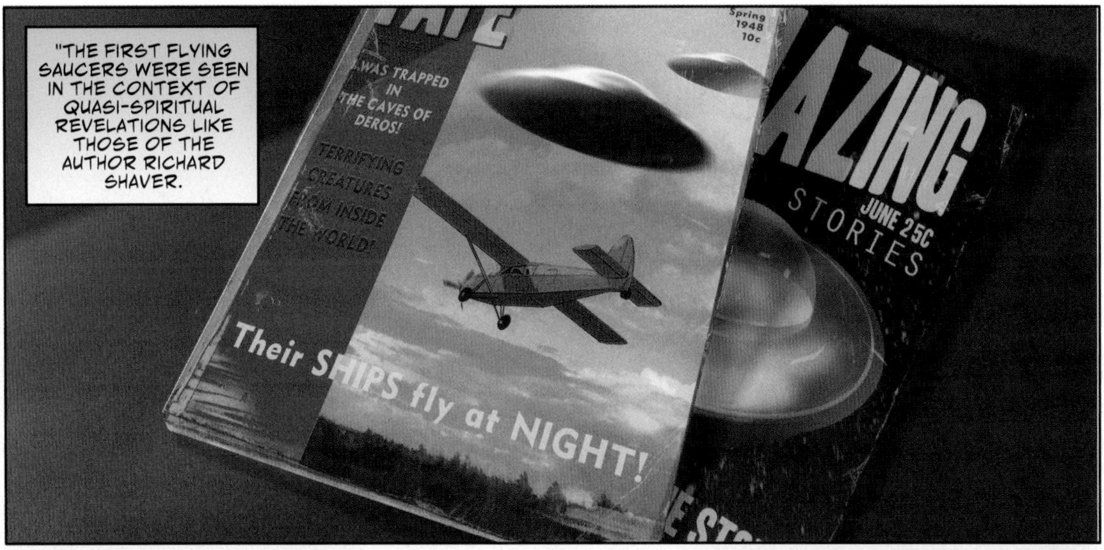
"THE FIRST FLYING SAUCERS WERE SEEN IN THE CONTEXT OF QUASI-SPIRITUAL REVELATIONS LIKE THOSE OF THE AUTHOR RICHARD SHAVER.
Spring 1948 10c
WAS TRAPPED IN THE CAVES OF DEROS!
TERRIFYING CREATURES FROM INSIDE THE WORLD!
Their SHIPS fly at NIGHT!
STORIES
JUNE 25C

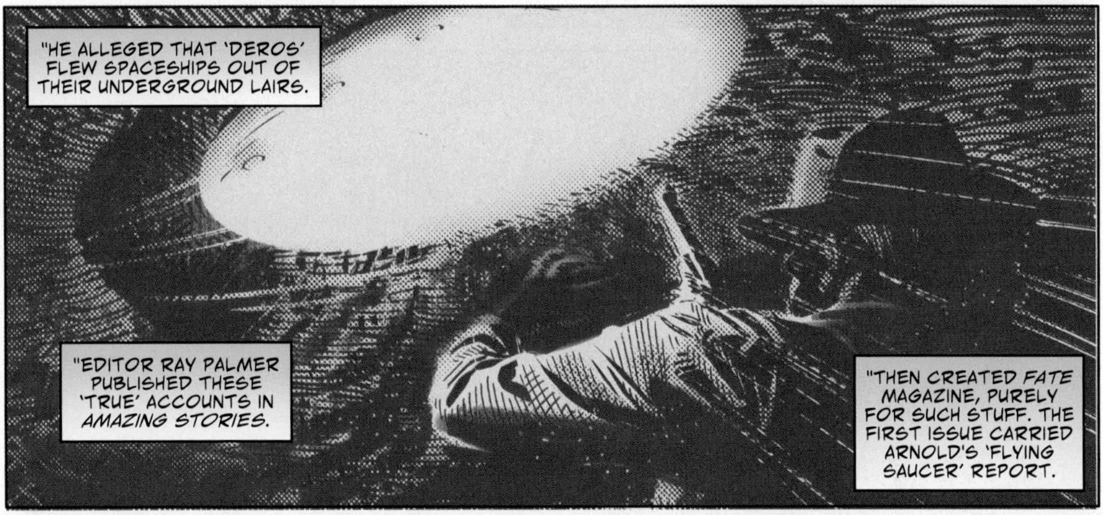
"HE ALLEGED THAT 'DEROS' FLEW SPACESHIPS OUT OF THEIR UNDERGROUND LAIRS.
"EDITOR RAY PALMER PUBLISHED THESE 'TRUE' ACCOUNTS IN *AMAZING STORIES*.
"THEN CREATED *FATE* MAGAZINE, PURELY FOR SUCH STUFF. THE FIRST ISSUE CARRIED ARNOLD'S 'FLYING SAUCER' REPORT.

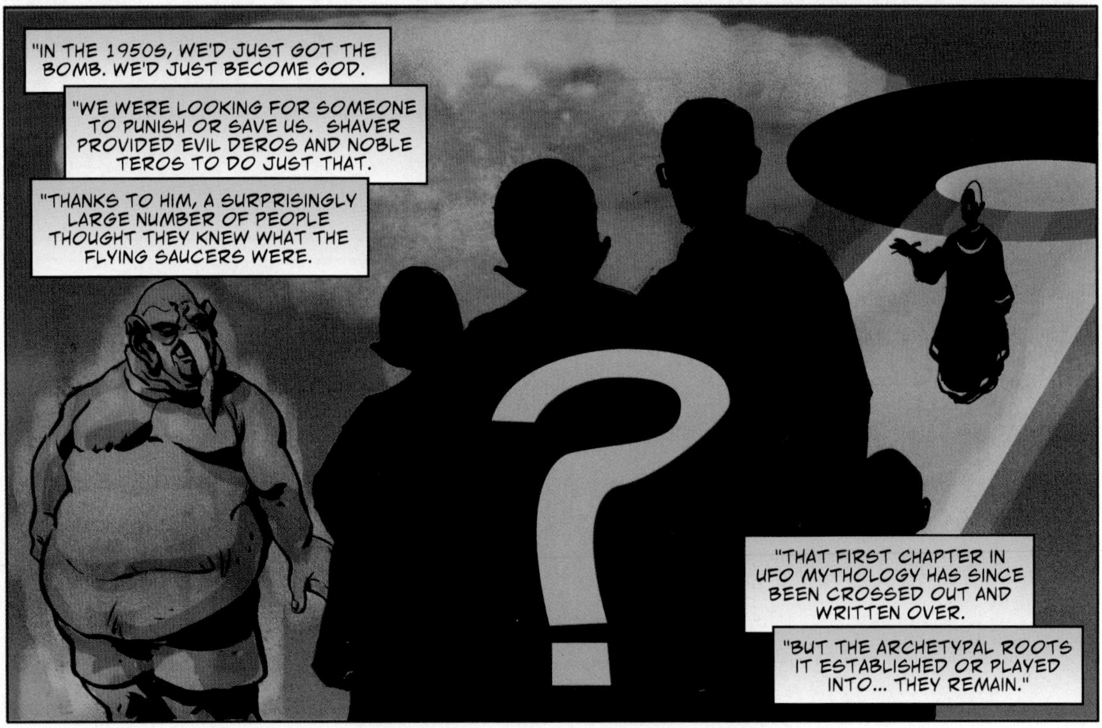
"IN THE 1950S, WE'D JUST GOT THE BOMB. WE'D JUST BECOME GOD.
"WE WERE LOOKING FOR SOMEONE TO PUNISH OR SAVE US. SHAVER PROVIDED EVIL DEROS AND NOBLE TEROS TO DO JUST THAT.
"THANKS TO HIM, A SURPRISINGLY LARGE NUMBER OF PEOPLE THOUGHT THEY KNEW WHAT THE FLYING SAUCERS WERE.
"THAT FIRST CHAPTER IN UFO MYTHOLOGY HAS SINCE BEEN CROSSED OUT AND WRITTEN OVER.
"BUT THE ARCHETYPAL ROOTS IT ESTABLISHED OR PLAYED INTO... THEY REMAIN."

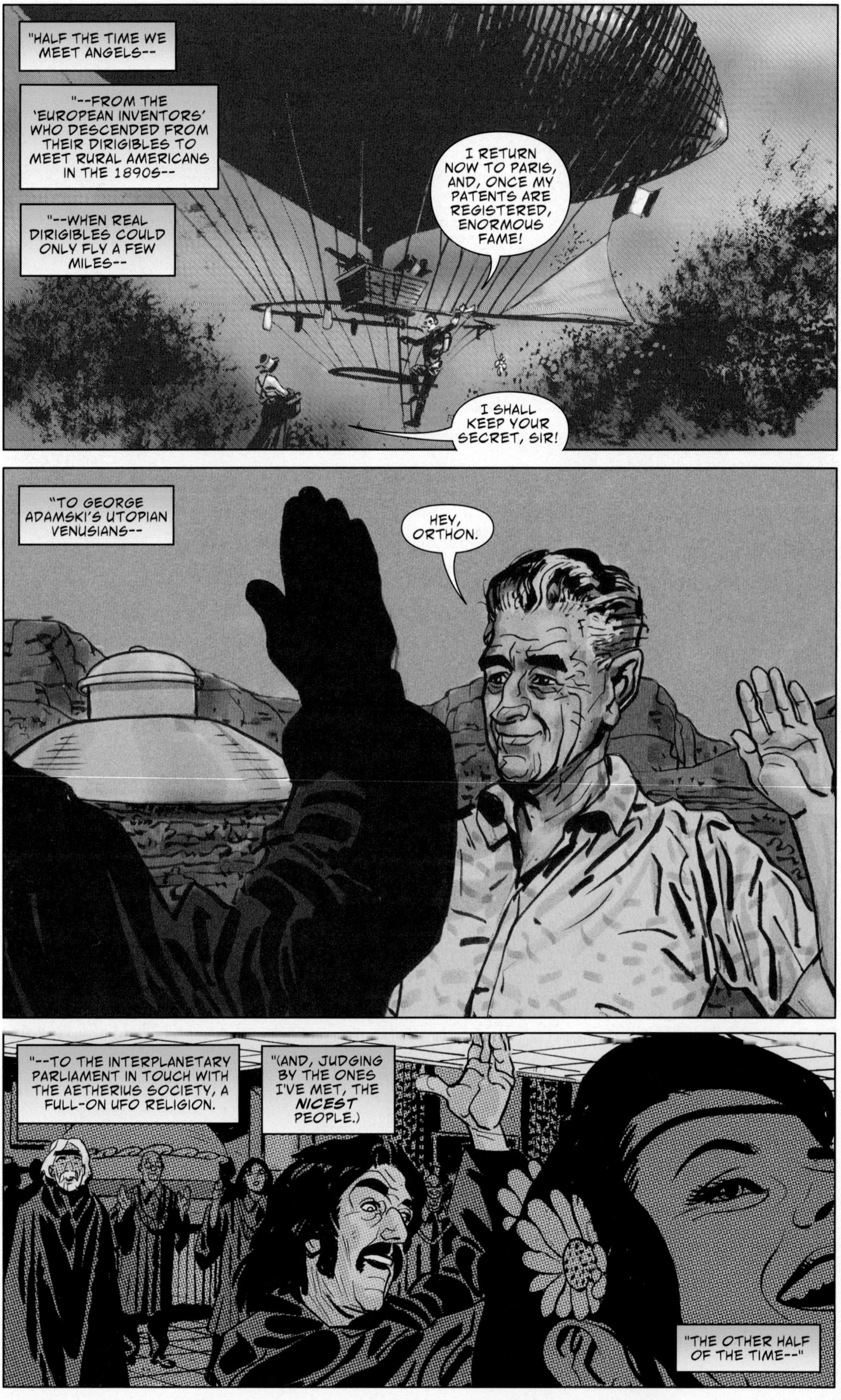
"HALF THE TIME WE MEET ANGELS--
"--FROM THE 'EUROPEAN INVENTORS' WHO DESCENDED FROM THEIR DIRIGIBLES TO MEET RURAL AMERICANS IN THE 1890S--
"--WHEN REAL DIRIGIBLES COULD ONLY FLY A FEW MILES--
I RETURN NOW TO PARIS, AND, ONCE MY PATENTS ARE REGISTERED, ENORMOUS FAME!
I SHALL KEEP YOUR SECRET, SIR!
"TO GEORGE ADAMSKI'S UTOPIAN VENUSIANS--
HEY, ORTHON.
"--TO THE INTERPLANETARY PARLIAMENT IN TOUCH WITH THE AETHERIUS SOCIETY, A FULL-ON UFO RELIGION.
"(AND, JUDGING BY THE ONES I'VE MET, THE *NICEST* PEOPLE.)
"THE OTHER HALF OF THE TIME--"

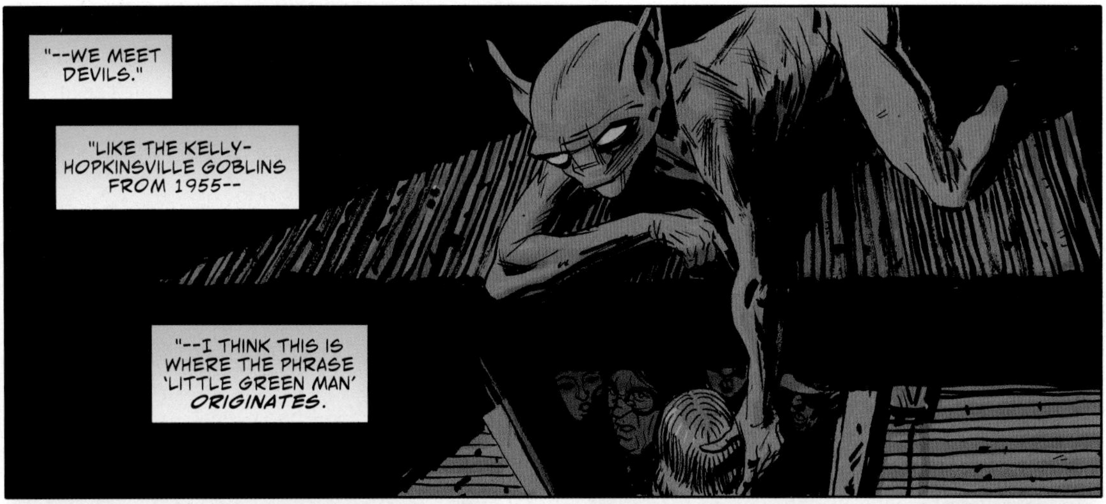
"--WE MEET DEVILS."
"LIKE THE KELLY-HOPKINSVILLE GOBLINS FROM 1955--
"--I THINK THIS IS WHERE THE PHRASE 'LITTLE GREEN MAN' *ORIGINATES*.

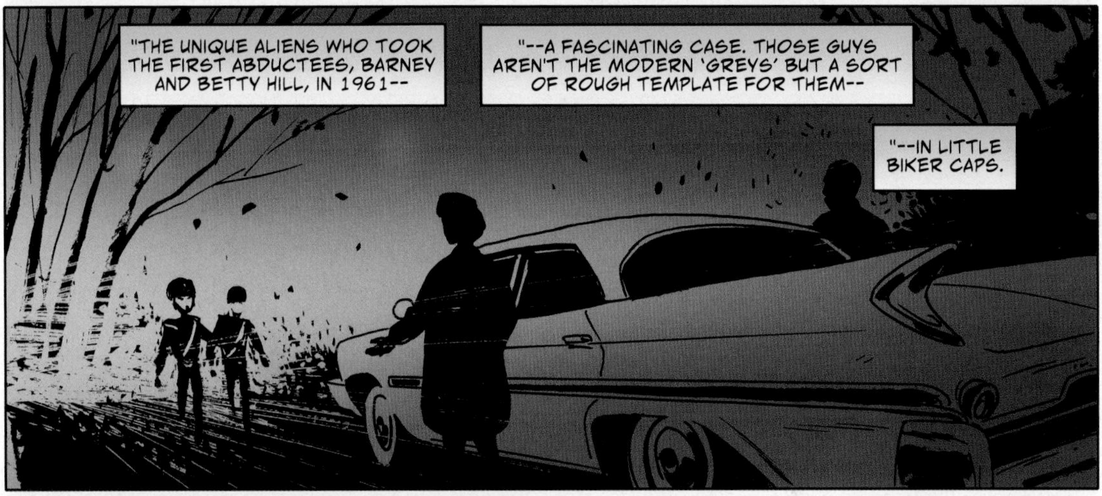
"THE UNIQUE ALIENS WHO TOOK THE FIRST ABDUCTEES, BARNEY AND BETTY HILL, IN 1961--
"--A FASCINATING CASE. THOSE GUYS AREN'T THE MODERN 'GREYS' BUT A SORT OF ROUGH TEMPLATE FOR THEM--
"--IN LITTLE BIKER CAPS.

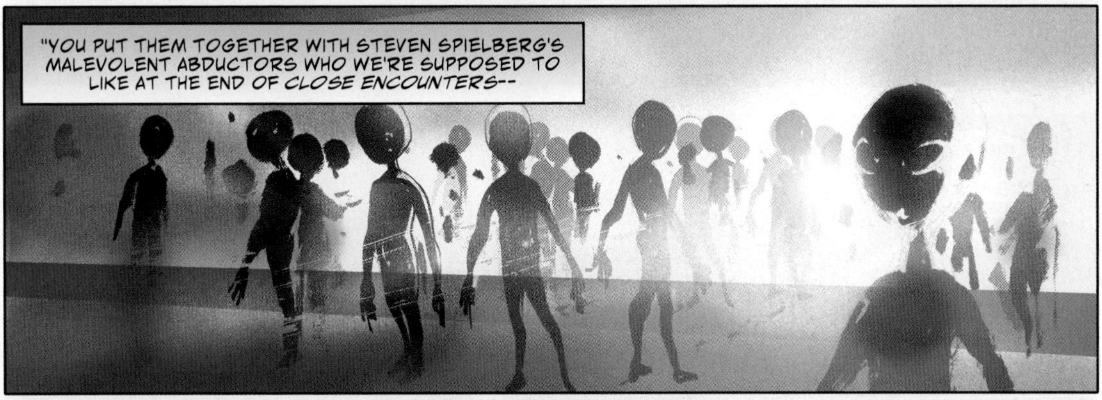
"YOU PUT THEM TOGETHER WITH STEVEN SPIELBERG'S MALEVOLENT ABDUCTORS WHO WE'RE SUPPOSED TO LIKE AT THE END OF *CLOSE ENCOUNTERS*--

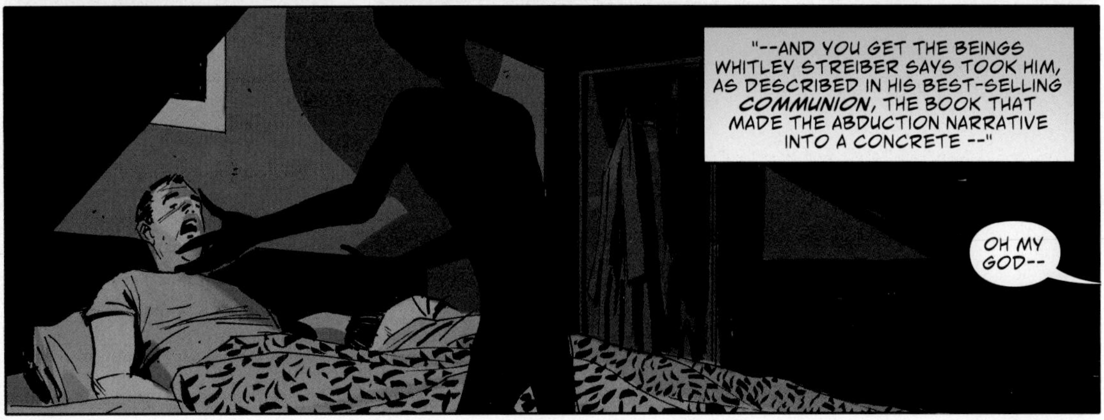
"--AND YOU GET THE BEINGS WHITLEY STREIBER SAYS TOOK HIM, AS DESCRIBED IN HIS BEST-SELLING ***COMMUNION***, THE BOOK THAT MADE THE ABDUCTION NARRATIVE INTO A CONCRETE --"
OH MY GOD--

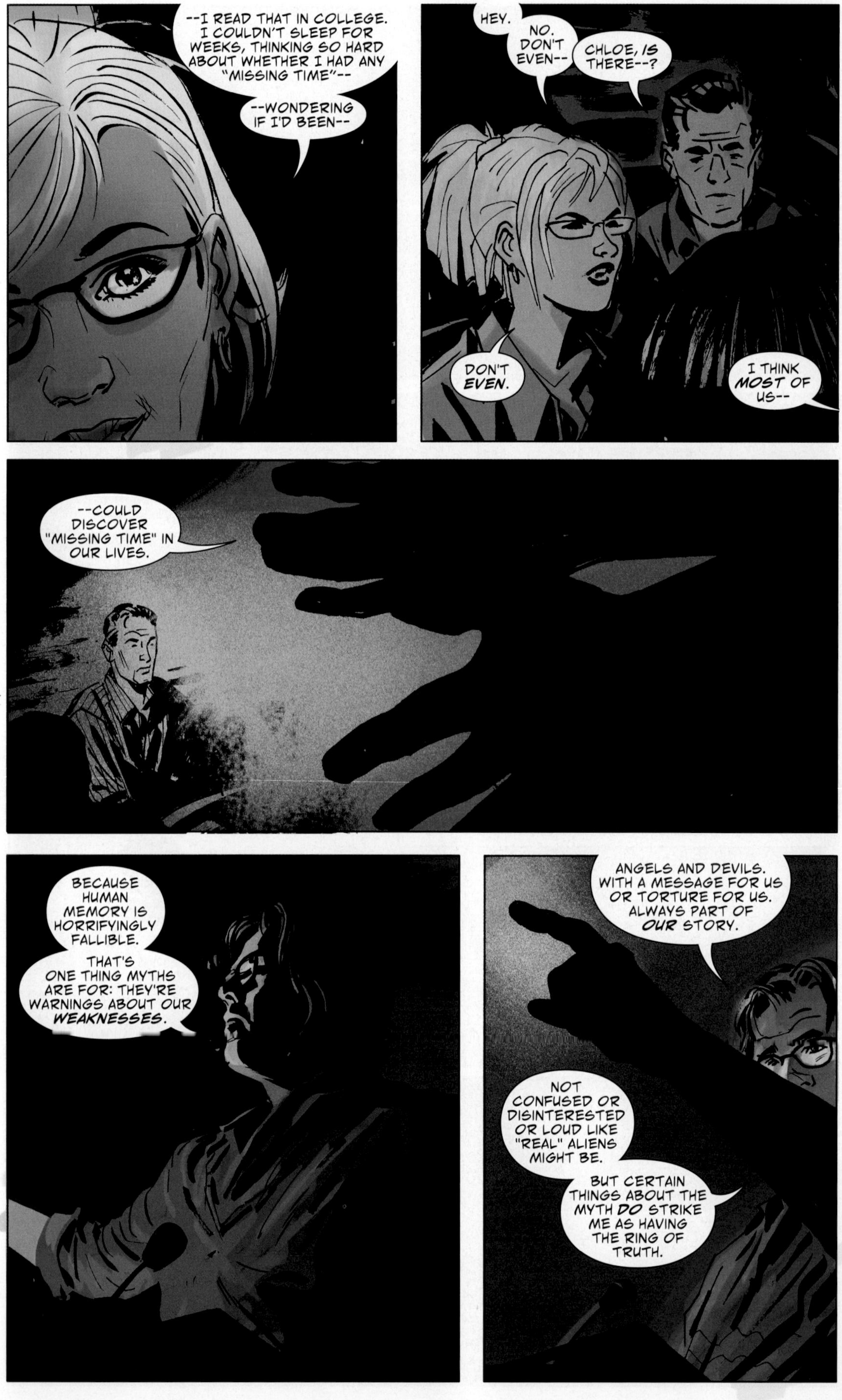
--I READ THAT IN COLLEGE. I COULDN'T SLEEP FOR WEEKS, THINKING SO HARD ABOUT WHETHER I HAD ANY "MISSING TIME"--
--WONDERING IF I'D BEEN--
HEY.
NO. DON'T EVEN--
CHLOE, IS THERE--?
DON'T EVEN.
I THINK MOST OF US--
--COULD DISCOVER "MISSING TIME" IN OUR LIVES.
BECAUSE HUMAN MEMORY IS HORRIFYINGLY FALLIBLE.
THAT'S ONE THING MYTHS ARE FOR: THEY'RE WARNINGS ABOUT OUR WEAKNESSES.
ANGELS AND DEVILS. WITH A MESSAGE FOR US OR TORTURE FOR US. ALWAYS PART OF OUR STORY.
NOT CONFUSED OR DISINTERESTED OR LOUD LIKE "REAL" ALIENS MIGHT BE.
BUT CERTAIN THINGS ABOUT THE MYTH DO STRIKE ME AS HAVING THE RING OF TRUTH.

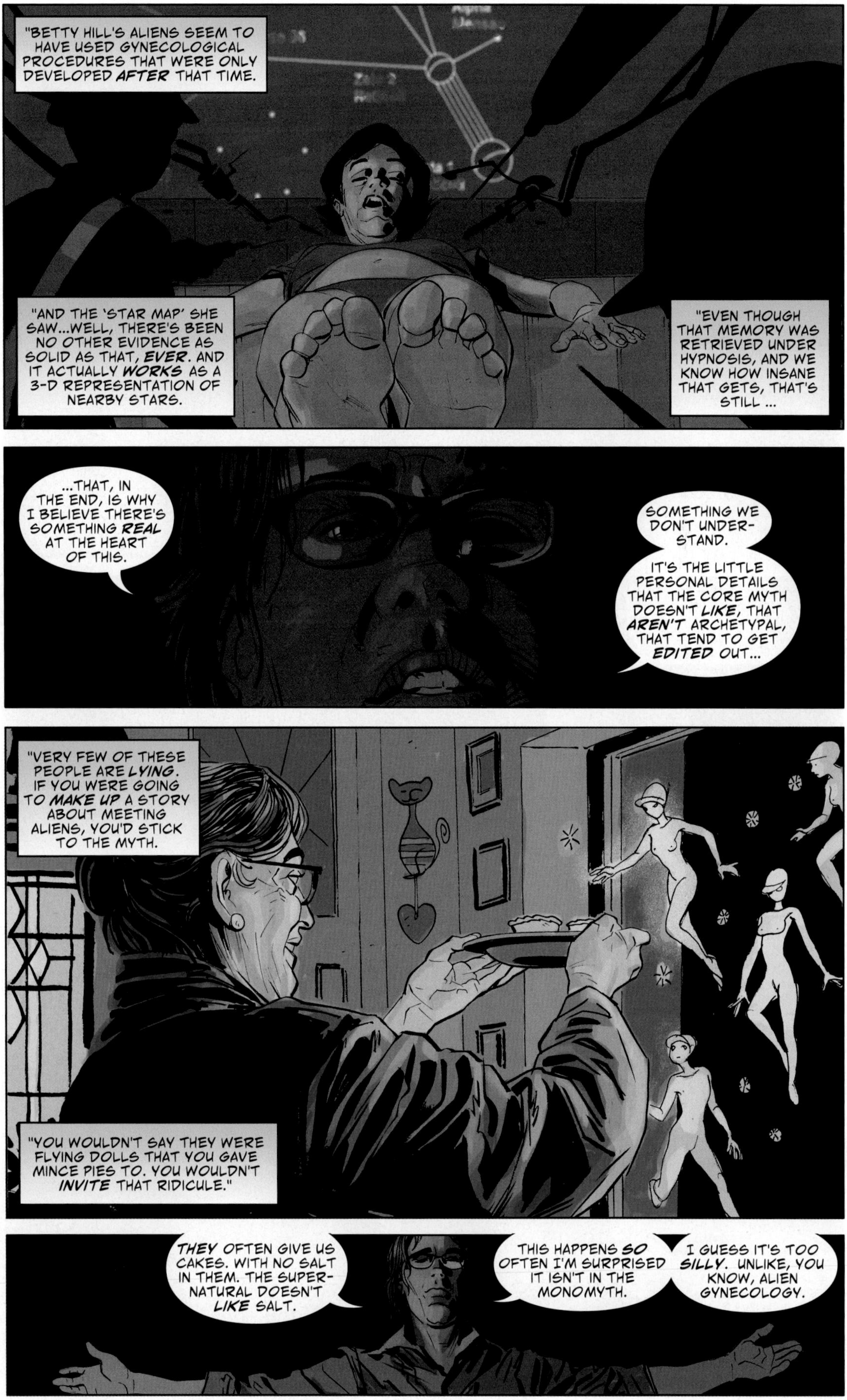
"BETTY HILL'S ALIENS SEEM TO HAVE USED GYNECOLOGICAL PROCEDURES THAT WERE ONLY DEVELOPED AFTER THAT TIME.
"AND THE 'STAR MAP' SHE SAW...WELL, THERE'S BEEN NO OTHER EVIDENCE AS SOLID AS THAT, EVER. AND IT ACTUALLY WORKS AS A 3-D REPRESENTATION OF NEARBY STARS.
"EVEN THOUGH THAT MEMORY WAS RETRIEVED UNDER HYPNOSIS, AND WE KNOW HOW INSANE THAT GETS, THAT'S STILL ...
...THAT, IN THE END, IS WHY I BELIEVE THERE'S SOMETHING REAL AT THE HEART OF THIS.
SOMETHING WE DON'T UNDER-STAND.
IT'S THE LITTLE PERSONAL DETAILS THAT THE CORE MYTH DOESN'T LIKE, THAT AREN'T ARCHETYPAL, THAT TEND TO GET EDITED OUT...
"VERY FEW OF THESE PEOPLE ARE LYING. IF YOU WERE GOING TO MAKE UP A STORY ABOUT MEETING ALIENS, YOU'D STICK TO THE MYTH.
"YOU WOULDN'T SAY THEY WERE FLYING DOLLS THAT YOU GAVE MINCE PIES TO. YOU WOULDN'T INVITE THAT RIDICULE."
THEY OFTEN GIVE US CAKES. WITH NO SALT IN THEM. THE SUPER-NATURAL DOESN'T LIKE SALT.
THIS HAPPENS SO OFTEN I'M SURPRISED IT ISN'T IN THE MONOMYTH.
I GUESS IT'S TOO SILLY. UNLIKE, YOU KNOW, ALIEN GYNECOLOGY.

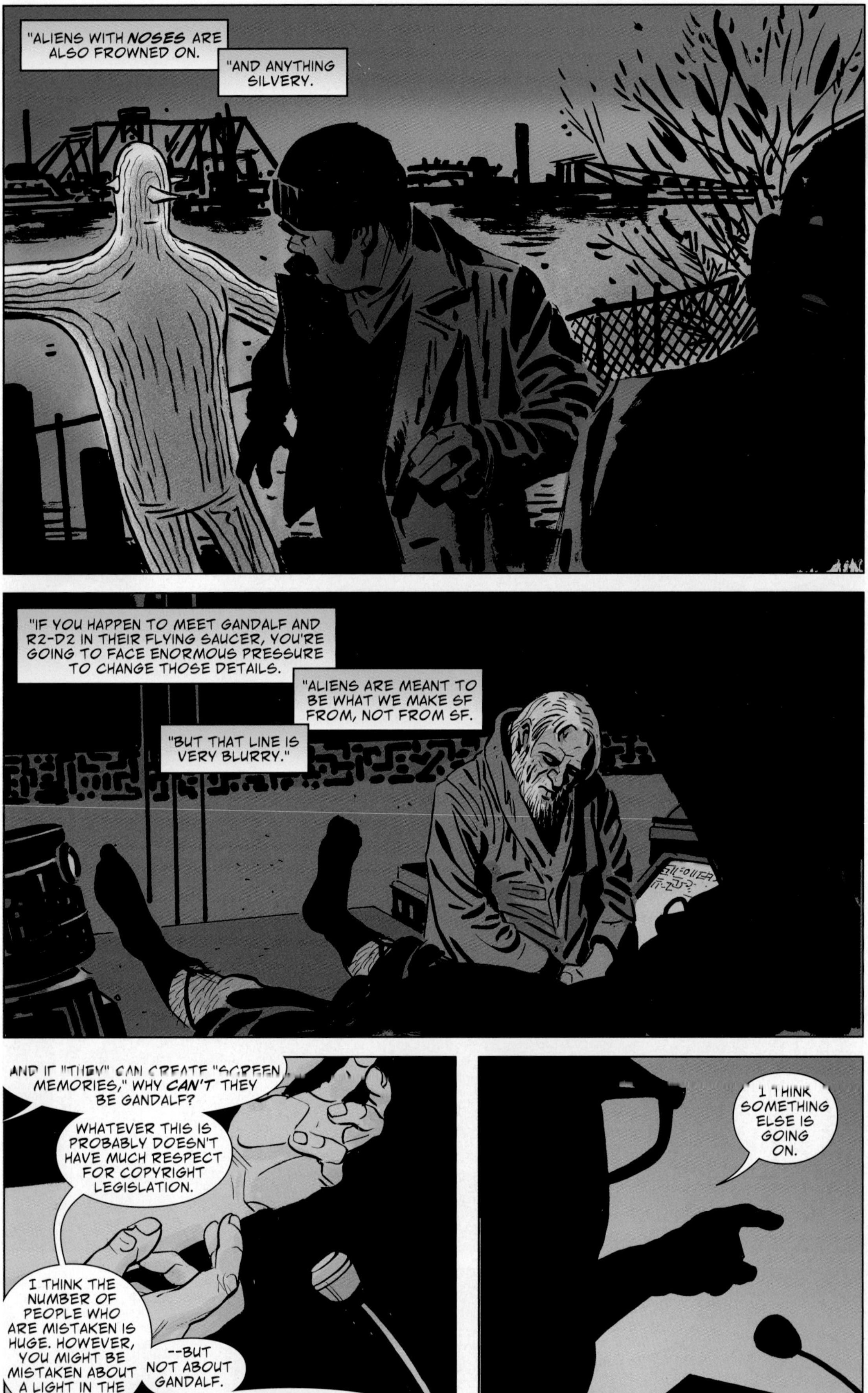
"ALIENS WITH NOSES ARE ALSO FROWNED ON.
"AND ANYTHING SILVERY.
"IF YOU HAPPEN TO MEET GANDALF AND R2-D2 IN THEIR FLYING SAUCER, YOU'RE GOING TO FACE ENORMOUS PRESSURE TO CHANGE THOSE DETAILS.
"ALIENS ARE MEANT TO BE WHAT WE MAKE SF FROM, NOT FROM SF.
"BUT THAT LINE IS VERY BLURRY."
AND IF "THEY" CAN CREATE "SCREEN MEMORIES," WHY CAN'T THEY BE GANDALF?
WHATEVER THIS IS PROBABLY DOESN'T HAVE MUCH RESPECT FOR COPYRIGHT LEGISLATION.
I THINK THE NUMBER OF PEOPLE WHO ARE MISTAKEN IS HUGE. HOWEVER, YOU MIGHT BE MISTAKEN ABOUT A LIGHT IN THE SKY--
--BUT NOT ABOUT GANDALF.
YOU'RE EITHER LYING, OR SOMETHING ELSE IS GOING ON.
I THINK SOMETHING ELSE IS GOING ON.

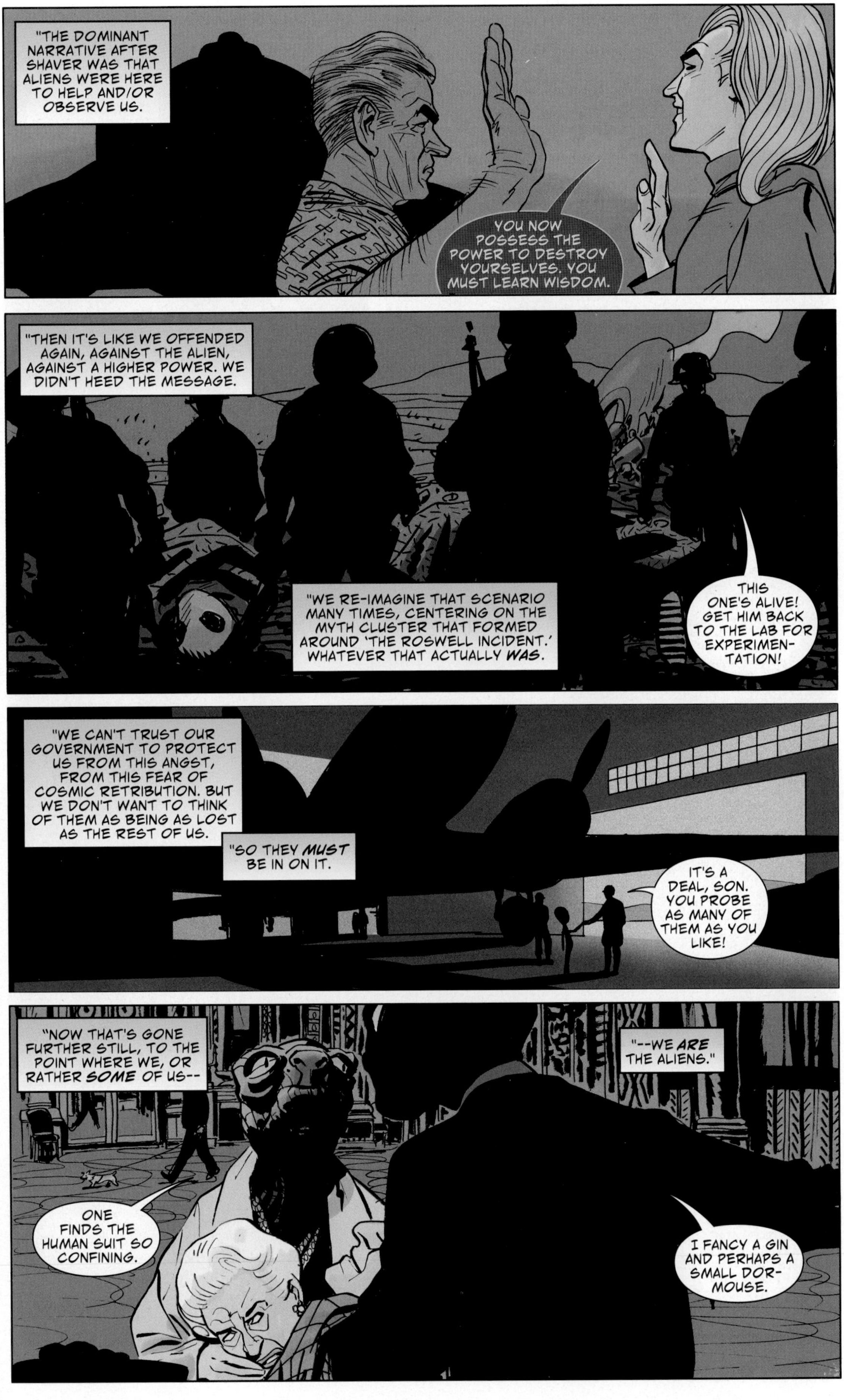
"THE DOMINANT NARRATIVE AFTER SHAVER WAS THAT ALIENS WERE HERE TO HELP AND/OR OBSERVE US.
YOU NOW POSSESS THE POWER TO DESTROY YOURSELVES. YOU MUST LEARN WISDOM.
"THEN IT'S LIKE WE OFFENDED AGAIN, AGAINST THE ALIEN, AGAINST A HIGHER POWER. WE DIDN'T HEED THE MESSAGE.
"WE RE-IMAGINE THAT SCENARIO MANY TIMES, CENTERING ON THE MYTH CLUSTER THAT FORMED AROUND 'THE ROSWELL INCIDENT.' WHATEVER THAT ACTUALLY *WAS*.
THIS ONE'S ALIVE! GET HIM BACK TO THE LAB FOR EXPERIMEN-TATION!
"WE CAN'T TRUST OUR GOVERNMENT TO PROTECT US FROM THIS ANGST, FROM THIS FEAR OF COSMIC RETRIBUTION. BUT WE DON'T WANT TO THINK OF THEM AS BEING AS LOST AS THE REST OF US.
"SO THEY *MUST* BE IN ON IT.
IT'S A DEAL, SON. YOU PROBE AS MANY OF THEM AS YOU LIKE!
"NOW THAT'S GONE FURTHER STILL, TO THE POINT WHERE WE, OR RATHER *SOME* OF US--
"--WE *ARE* THE ALIENS."
ONE FINDS THE HUMAN SUIT SO CONFINING.
I FANCY A GIN AND PERHAPS A SMALL DOR-MOUSE.

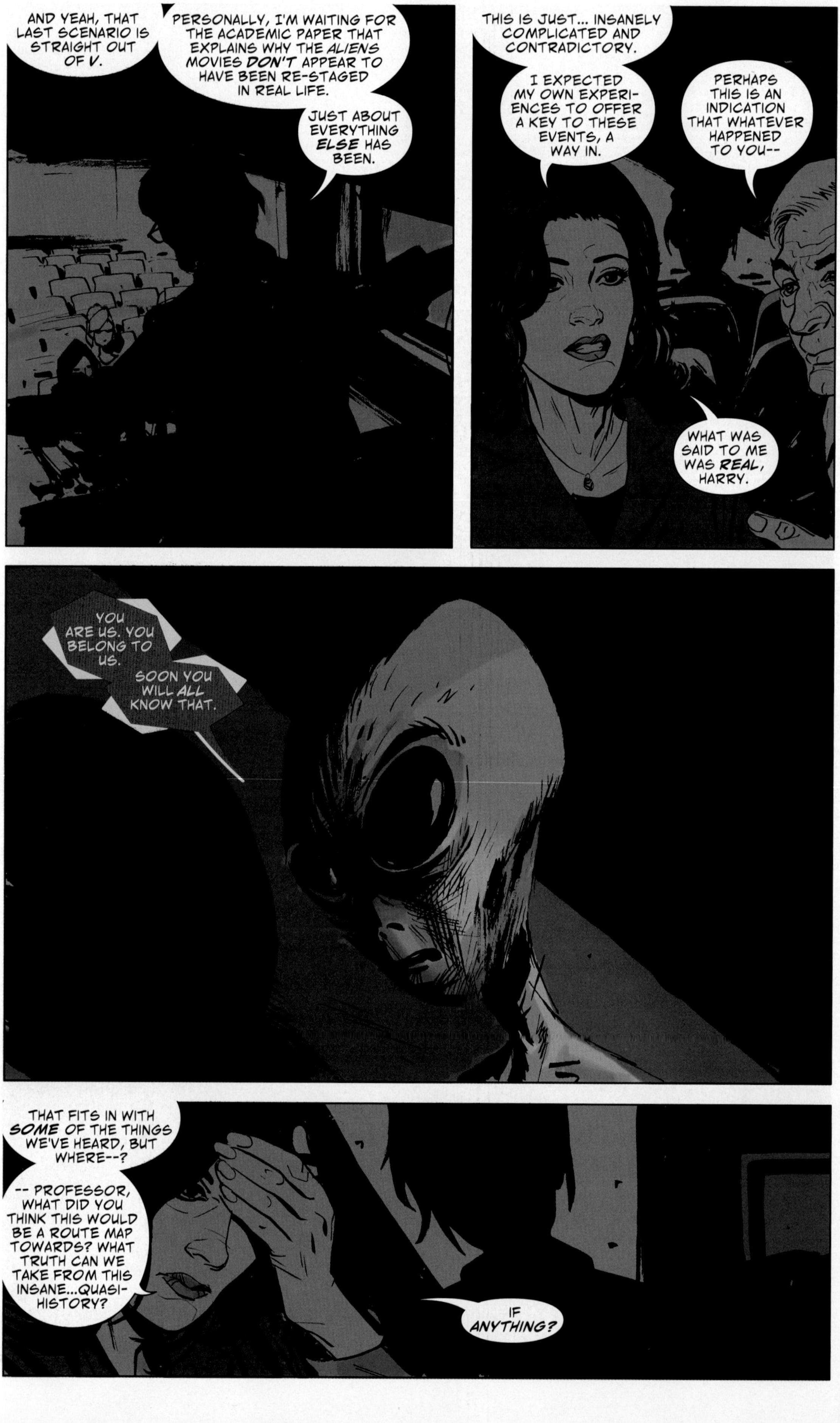
AND YEAH, THAT LAST SCENARIO IS STRAIGHT OUT OF *V*.
PERSONALLY, I'M WAITING FOR THE ACADEMIC PAPER THAT EXPLAINS WHY THE *ALIENS* MOVIES ***DON'T*** APPEAR TO HAVE BEEN RE-STAGED IN REAL LIFE.
JUST ABOUT EVERYTHING ***ELSE*** HAS BEEN.
THIS IS JUST... INSANELY COMPLICATED AND CONTRADICTORY.
I EXPECTED MY OWN EXPERIENCES TO OFFER A KEY TO THESE EVENTS, A WAY IN.
PERHAPS THIS IS AN INDICATION THAT WHATEVER HAPPENED TO YOU--
WHAT WAS SAID TO ME WAS ***REAL***, HARRY.
YOU ARE US. YOU BELONG TO US.
SOON YOU WILL *ALL* KNOW THAT.
THAT FITS IN WITH ***SOME*** OF THE THINGS WE'VE HEARD, BUT WHERE--?
-- PROFESSOR, WHAT DID YOU THINK THIS WOULD BE A ROUTE MAP TOWARDS? WHAT TRUTH CAN WE TAKE FROM THIS INSANE...QUASI-HISTORY?
IF ***ANYTHING?***

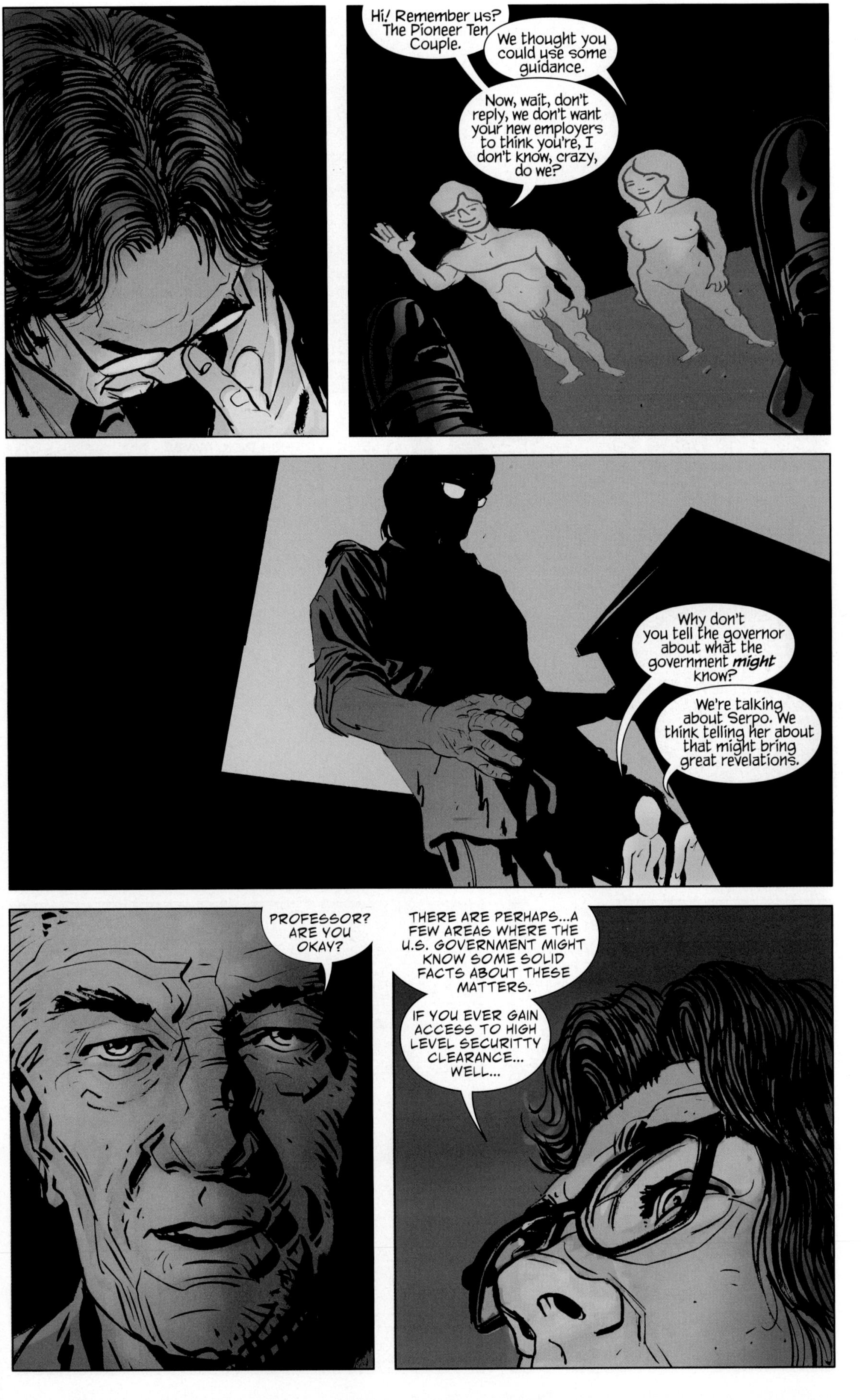
Hi! Remember us? The Pioneer Ten Couple.
We thought you could use some guidance.
Now, wait, don't reply, we don't want your new employers to think you're, I don't know, crazy, do we?
Why don't you tell the governor about what the government *might* know?
We're talking about Serpo. We think telling her about that might bring great revelations.
PROFESSOR? ARE YOU OKAY?
THERE ARE PERHAPS...A FEW AREAS WHERE THE U.S. GOVERNMENT MIGHT KNOW SOME SOLID FACTS ABOUT THESE MATTERS.
IF YOU EVER GAIN ACCESS TO HIGH LEVEL SECURITTY CLEARANCE... WELL...

"IT IS SAID...AND UNTIL... THIS MOMENT...I NEVER REALLY GAVE IT MUCH CREDENCE..."

"THAT THE U.S. HAS AN EXCHANGE PROGRAM WITH AN EXTRASOLAR PLANET, THE NAME OF IT BEING *SERPO*. OR SOMETIMES *SEINU*.

"TWELVE MILITARY PERSONNEL LIVED THERE BETWEEN 1965 AND 1978, THEY SAY.

"AND YES, THIS IS EXACTLY LIKE THE ENDING OF *CLOSE ENCOUNTERS*. AND MORE THAN THAT--

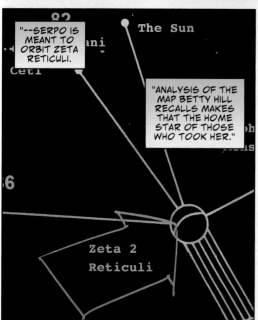

"--SERPO IS MEANT TO ORBIT ZETA RETICULI.

The Sun

"ANALYSIS OF THE MAP BETTY HILL RECALLS MAKES THAT THE HOME STAR OF THOSE WHO TOOK HER."

Zeta 2 Reticuli

THE STAR HAS ALSO BEEN RECENTLY OBSERVED TO HAVE AT LEAST A DEBRIS DISK, MAYBE A PLANETARY SYSTEM, TO BE A GREAT CANDIDATE FOR LIFE --

WAIT, WAIT!

ZETA RETICULI?! THAT'S WHERE THEY FIND THE *ALIEN* IN THE RIDLEY SCOTT MOVIE.

THERE'S YOUR *ALIEN* REFERENCE.

PROFESSOR, ARE YOU *SURE* SOMEONE ISN'T HAVING A JOKE AT YOUR EXPENSE?

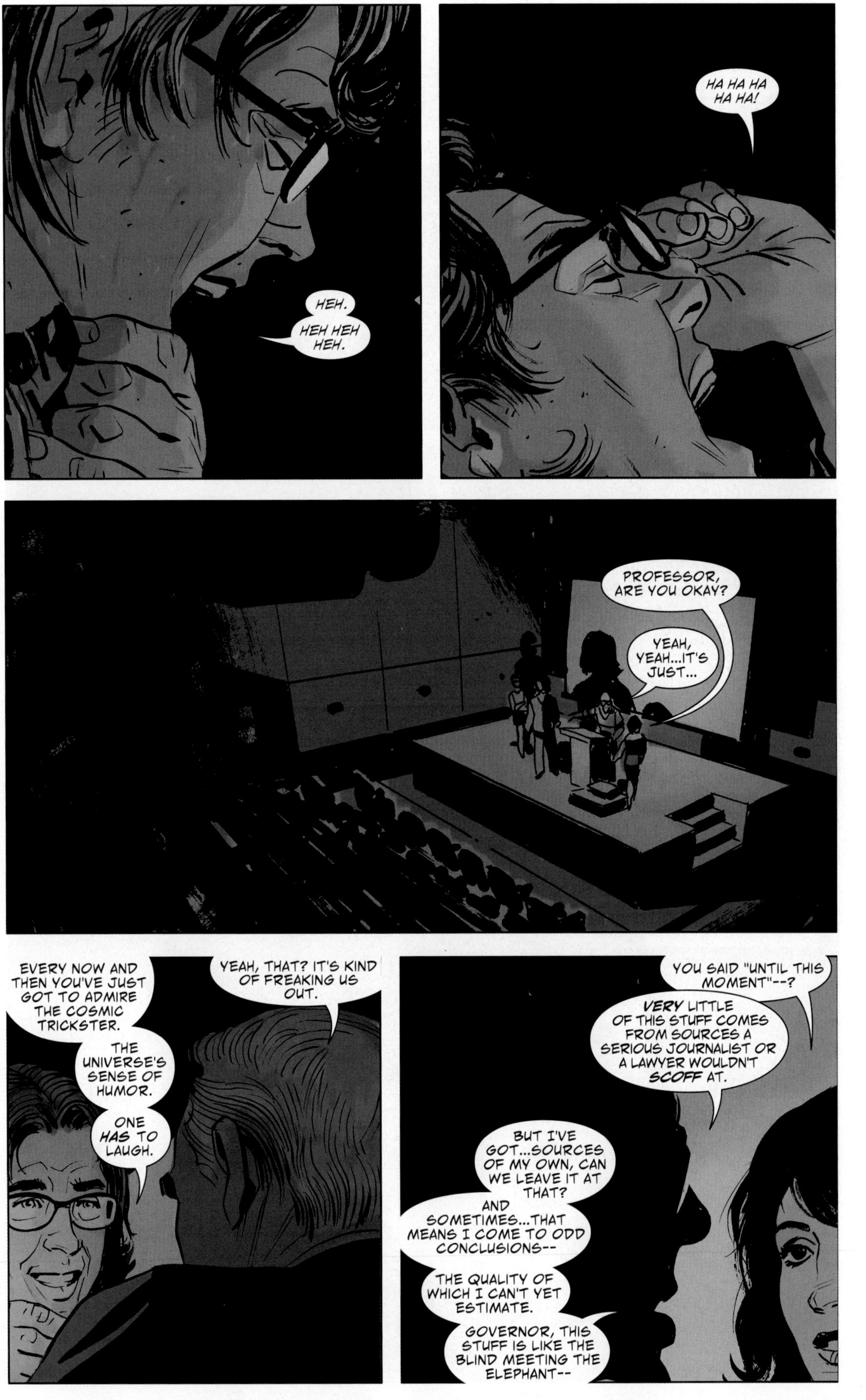
HEH.
HEH HEH HEH.
HA HA HA HA HA!
PROFESSOR, ARE YOU OKAY?
YEAH, YEAH...IT'S JUST...
EVERY NOW AND THEN YOU'VE JUST GOT TO ADMIRE THE COSMIC TRICKSTER.
THE UNIVERSE'S SENSE OF HUMOR.
ONE HAS TO LAUGH.
YEAH, THAT? IT'S KIND OF FREAKING US OUT.
YOU SAID "UNTIL THIS MOMENT"--?
VERY LITTLE OF THIS STUFF COMES FROM SOURCES A SERIOUS JOURNALIST OR A LAWYER WOULDN'T SCOFF AT.
BUT I'VE GOT...SOURCES OF MY OWN, CAN WE LEAVE IT AT THAT?
AND SOMETIMES...THAT MEANS I COME TO ODD CONCLUSIONS--
THE QUALITY OF WHICH I CAN'T YET ESTIMATE.
GOVERNOR, THIS STUFF IS LIKE THE BLIND MEETING THE ELEPHANT--

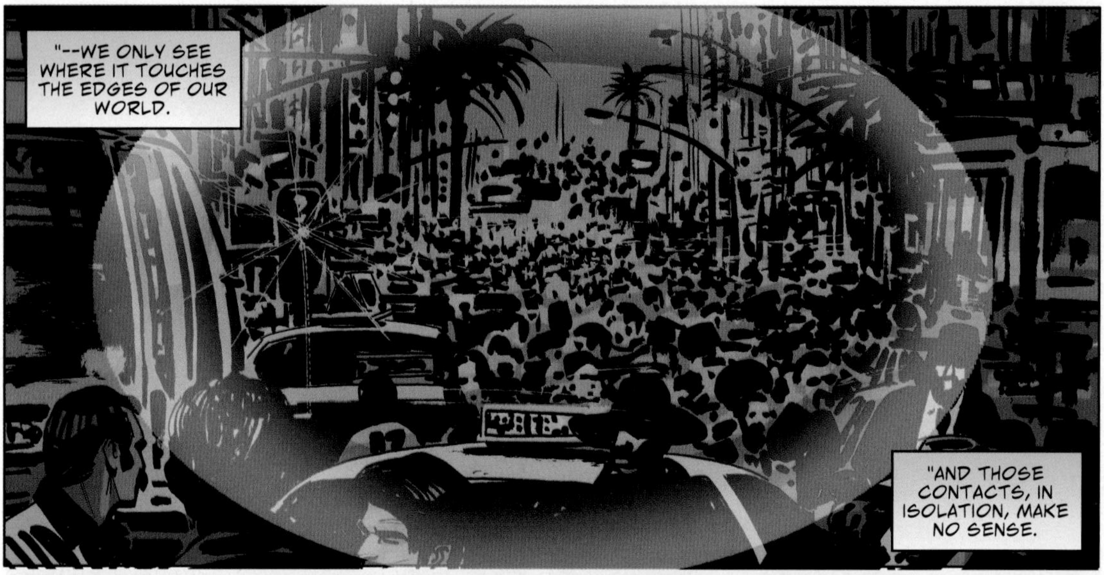
"--WE ONLY SEE WHERE IT TOUCHES THE EDGES OF OUR WORLD.
"AND THOSE CONTACTS, IN ISOLATION, MAKE NO SENSE.

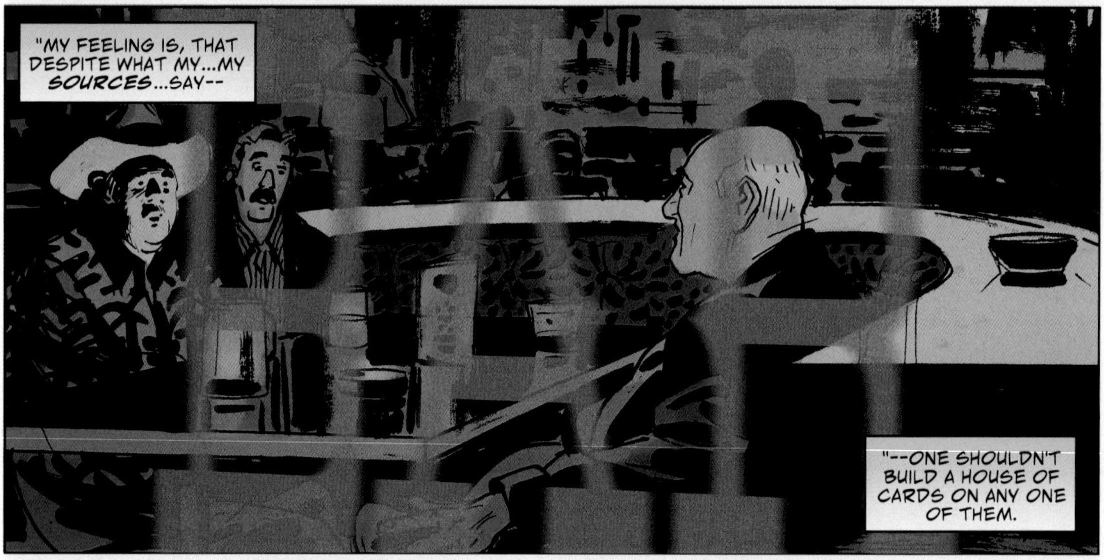
"MY FEELING IS, THAT DESPITE WHAT MY...MY *SOURCES*...SAY--
"--ONE SHOULDN'T BUILD A HOUSE OF CARDS ON ANY ONE OF THEM.

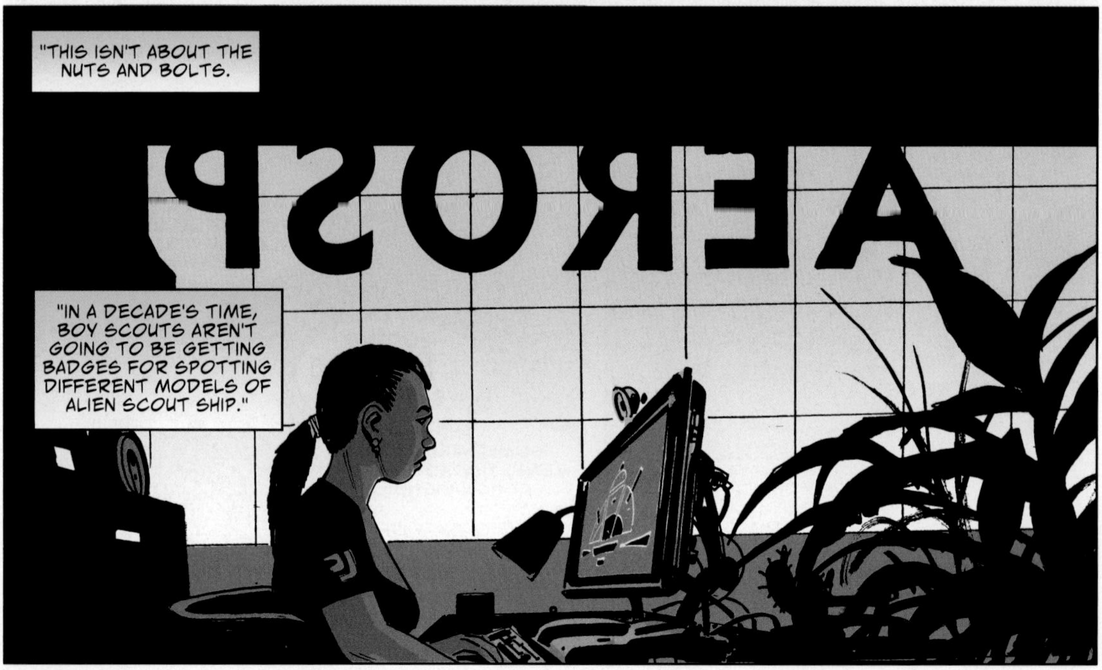
"THIS ISN'T ABOUT THE NUTS AND BOLTS.
"IN A DECADE'S TIME, BOY SCOUTS AREN'T GOING TO BE GETTING BADGES FOR SPOTTING DIFFERENT MODELS OF ALIEN SCOUT SHIP."

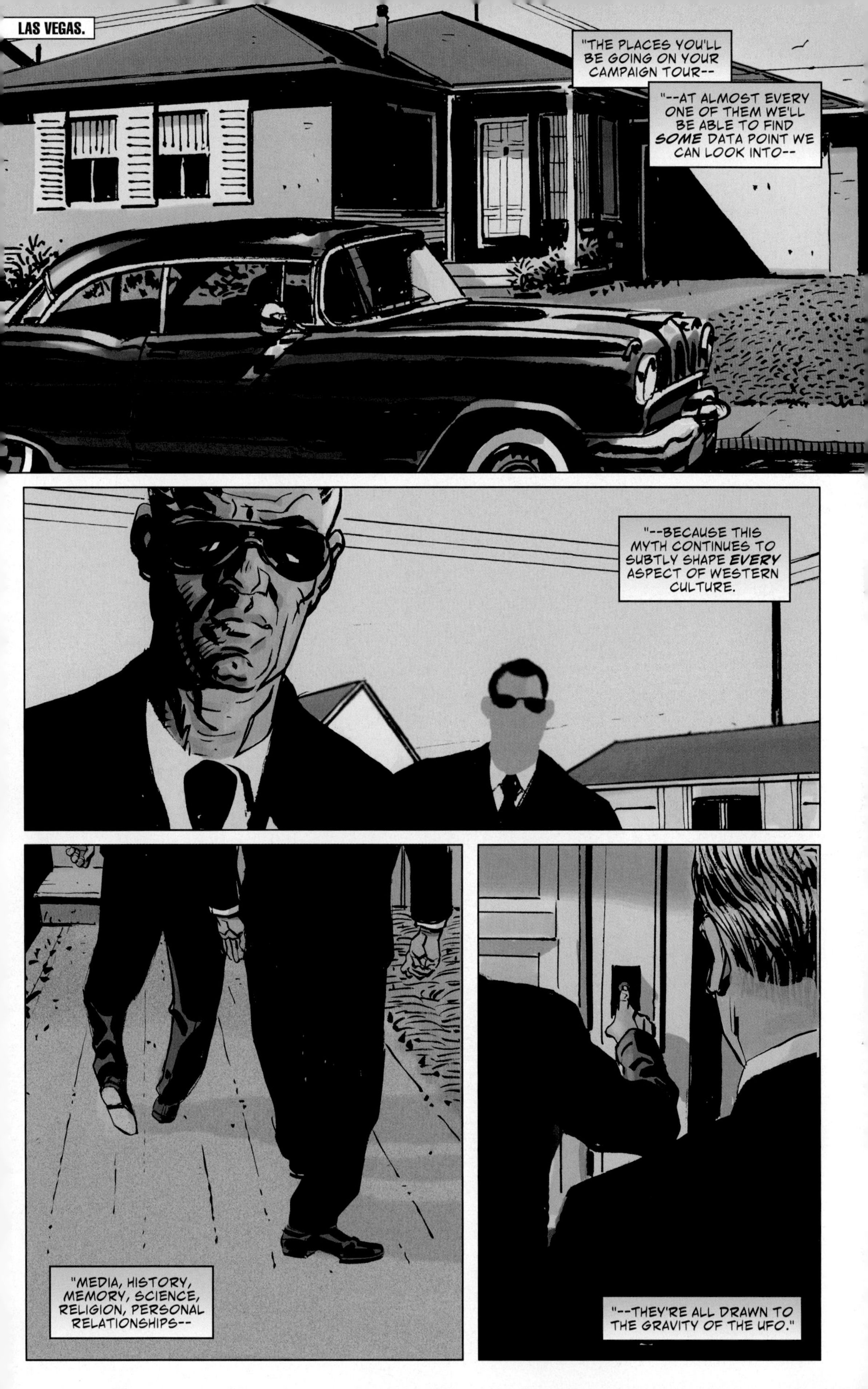
LAS VEGAS.
"THE PLACES YOU'LL BE GOING ON YOUR CAMPAIGN TOUR--
"--AT ALMOST EVERY ONE OF THEM WE'LL BE ABLE TO FIND SOME DATA POINT WE CAN LOOK INTO--
"--BECAUSE THIS MYTH CONTINUES TO SUBTLY SHAPE EVERY ASPECT OF WESTERN CULTURE.
"MEDIA, HISTORY, MEMORY, SCIENCE, RELIGION, PERSONAL RELATIONSHIPS--
"--THEY'RE ALL DRAWN TO THE GRAVITY OF THE UFO."

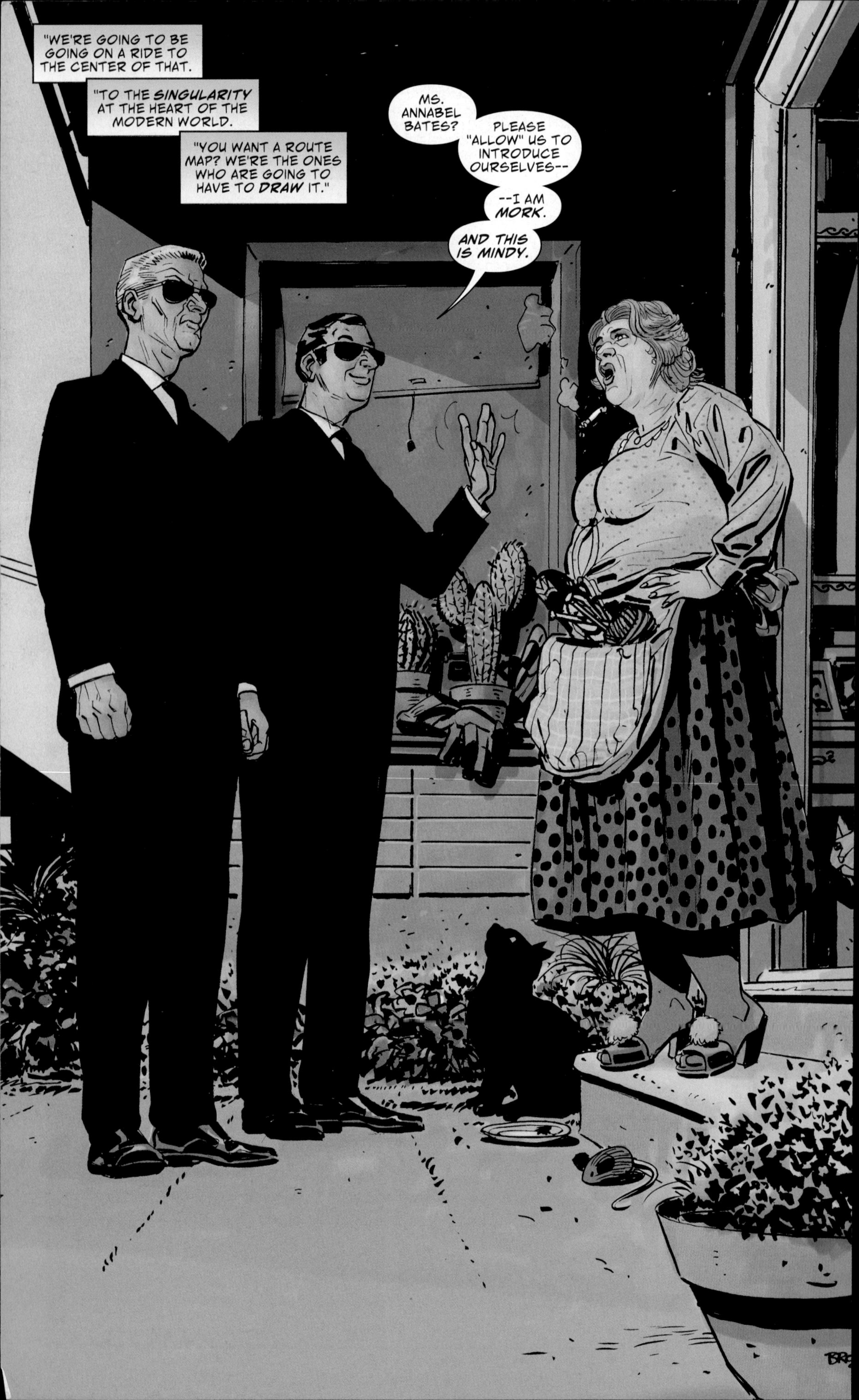
"WE'RE GOING TO BE GOING ON A RIDE TO THE CENTER OF THAT.
"TO THE SINGULARITY AT THE HEART OF THE MODERN WORLD.
"YOU WANT A ROUTE MAP? WE'RE THE ONES WHO ARE GOING TO HAVE TO DRAW IT."
MS. ANNABEL BATES?
PLEASE "ALLOW" US TO INTRODUCE OURSELVES--
--I AM MORK.
AND THIS IS MINDY.

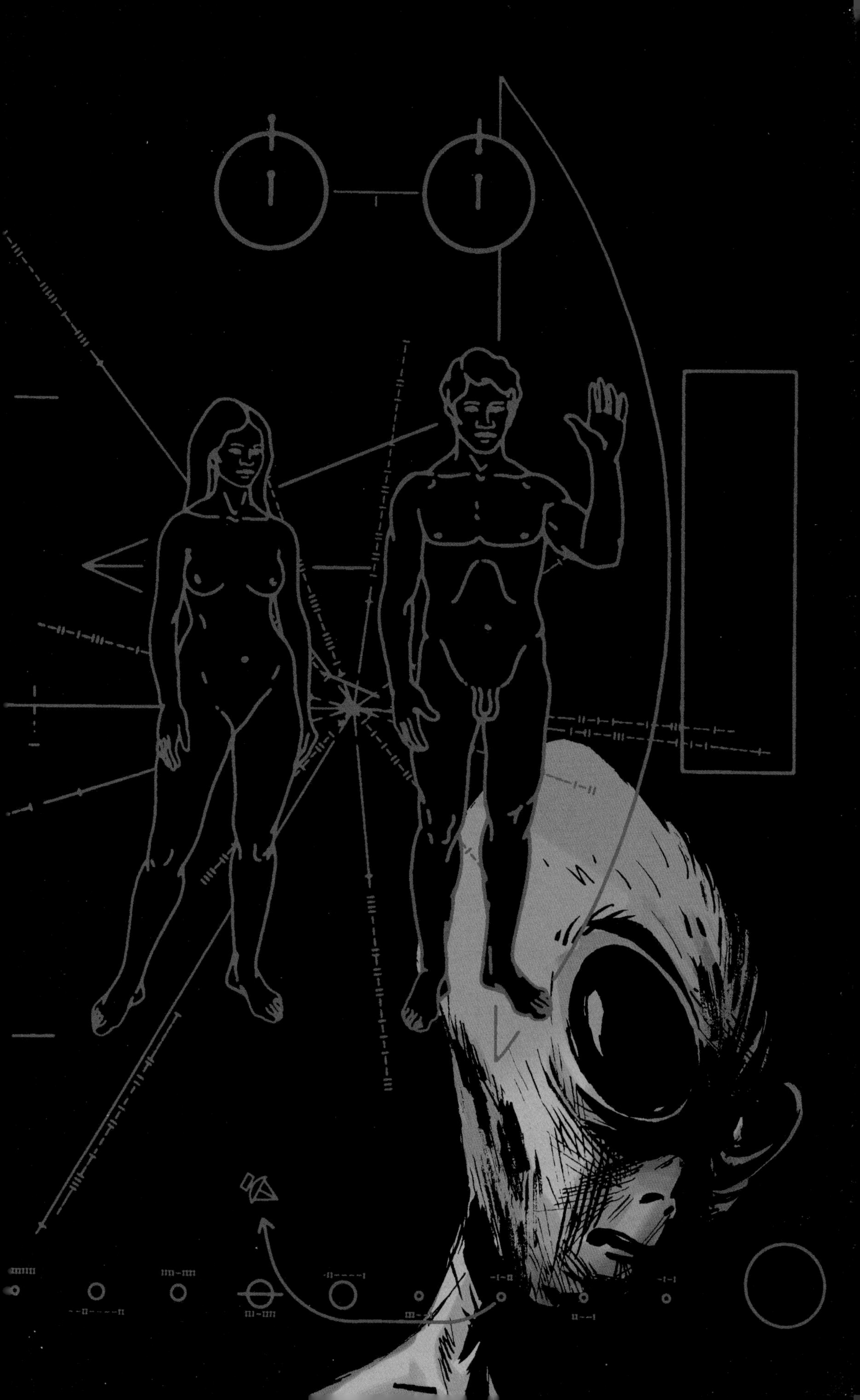

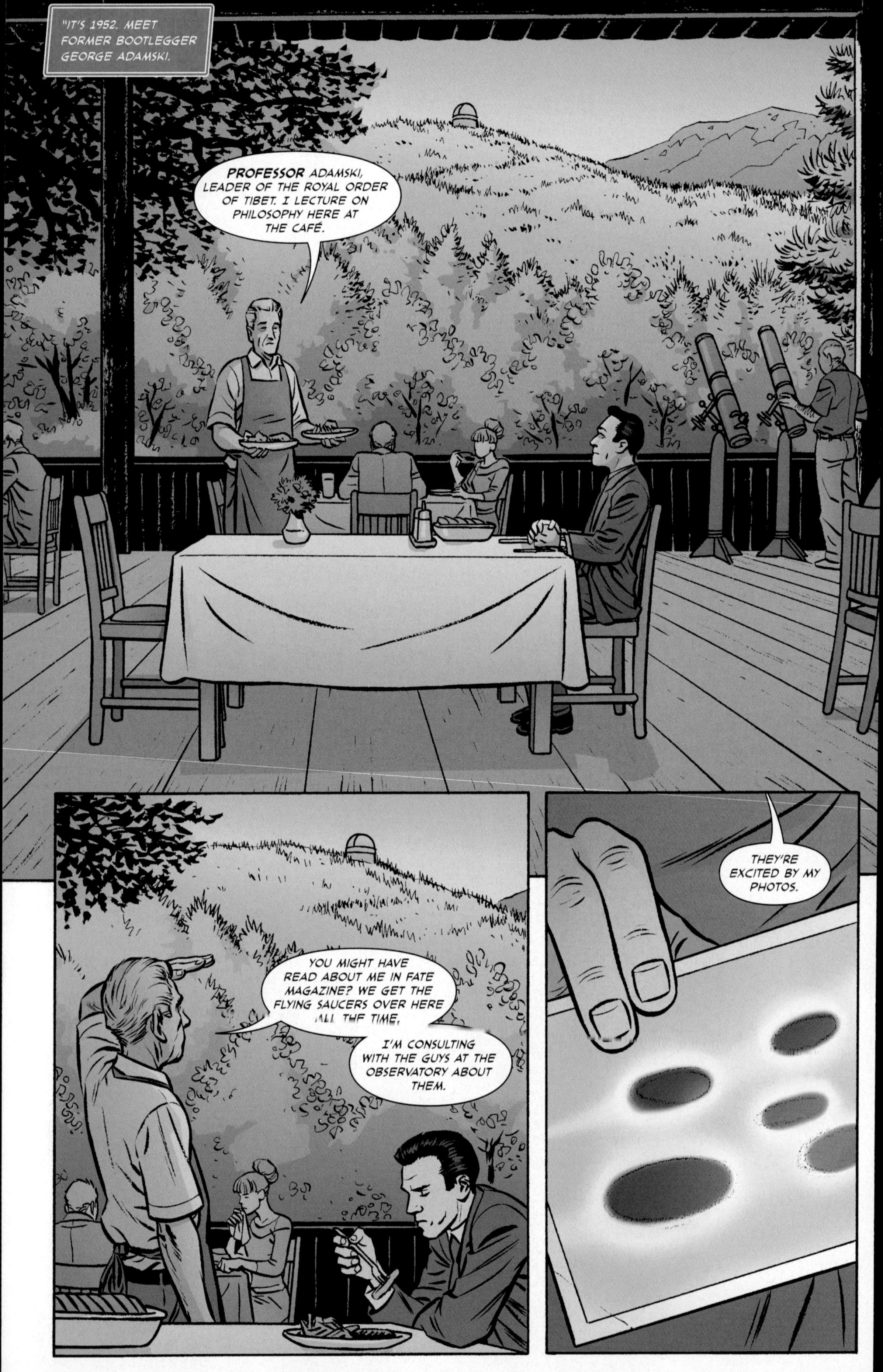
"IT'S 1952. MEET FORMER BOOTLEGGER GEORGE ADAMSKI.
PROFESSOR ADAMSKI, LEADER OF THE ROYAL ORDER OF TIBET. I LECTURE ON PHILOSOPHY HERE AT THE CAFÉ.
YOU MIGHT HAVE READ ABOUT ME IN FATE MAGAZINE? WE GET THE FLYING SAUCERS OVER HERE ALL THE TIME.
I'M CONSULTING WITH THE GUYS AT THE OBSERVATORY ABOUT THEM.
THEY'RE EXCITED BY MY PHOTOS.

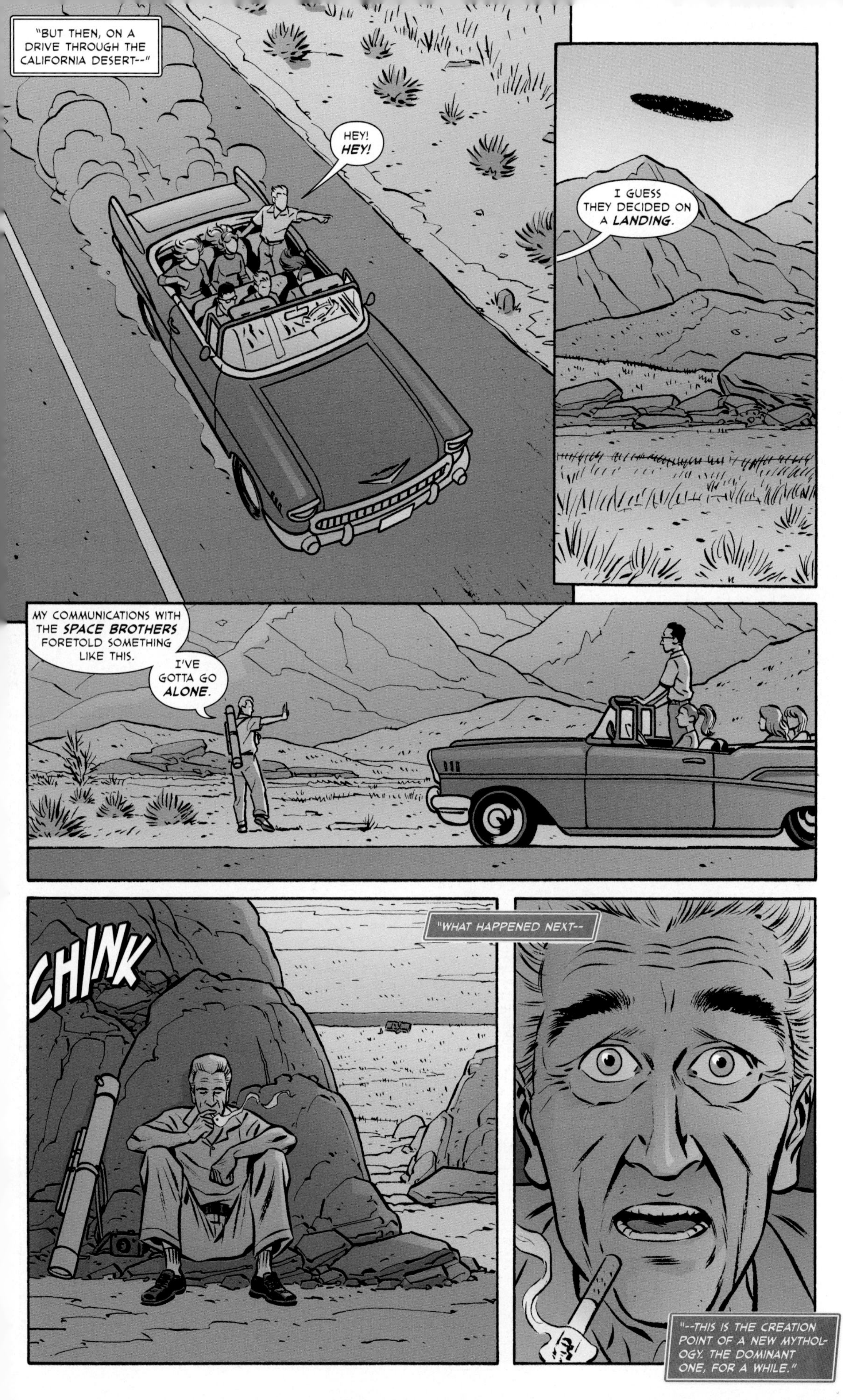
"BUT THEN, ON A DRIVE THROUGH THE CALIFORNIA DESERT--"
HEY! HEY!
I GUESS THEY DECIDED ON A LANDING.
MY COMMUNICATIONS WITH THE SPACE BROTHERS FORETOLD SOMETHING LIKE THIS.
I'VE GOTTA GO ALONE.
CHINK
"WHAT HAPPENED NEXT--
"--THIS IS THE CREATION POINT OF A NEW MYTHOLOGY. THE DOMINANT ONE, FOR A WHILE."

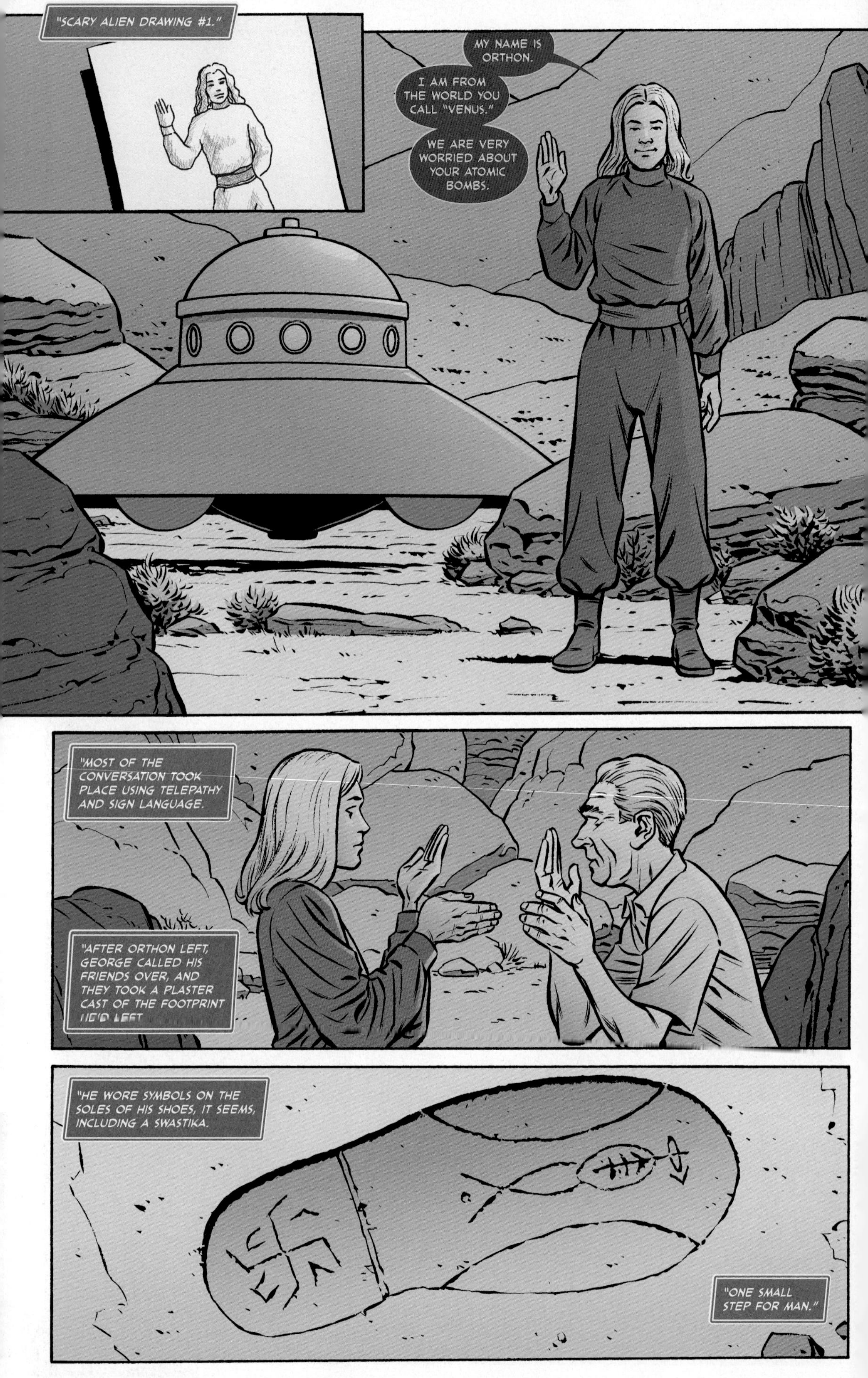
"SCARY ALIEN DRAWING #1."
MY NAME IS ORTHON.
I AM FROM THE WORLD YOU CALL "VENUS."
WE ARE VERY WORRIED ABOUT YOUR ATOMIC BOMBS.
"MOST OF THE CONVERSATION TOOK PLACE USING TELEPATHY AND SIGN LANGUAGE.
"AFTER ORTHON LEFT, GEORGE CALLED HIS FRIENDS OVER, AND THEY TOOK A PLASTER CAST OF THE FOOTPRINT HE'D LEFT.
"HE WORE SYMBOLS ON THE SOLES OF HIS SHOES, IT SEEMS, INCLUDING A SWASTIKA.
"ONE SMALL STEP FOR MAN."

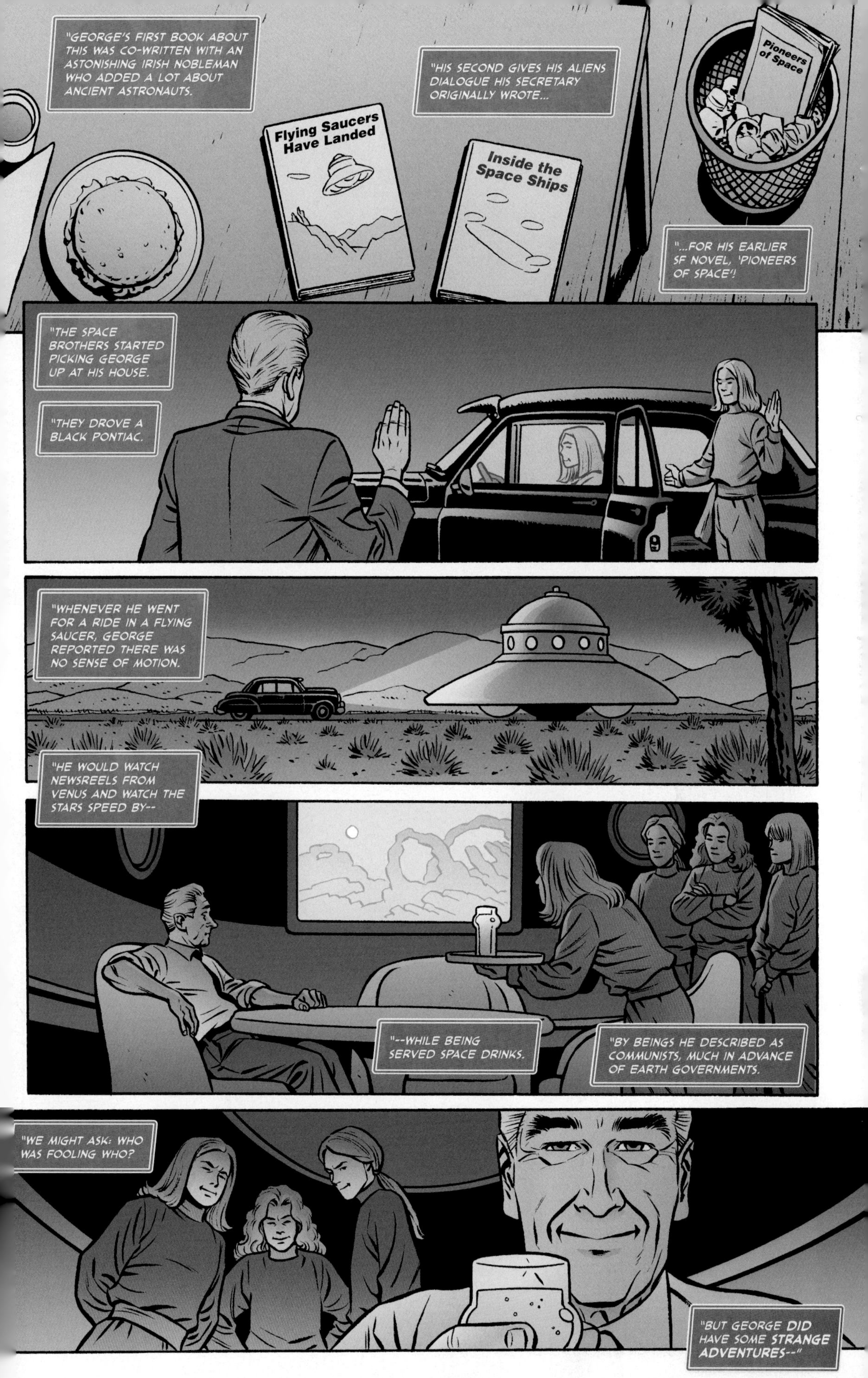
"GEORGE'S FIRST BOOK ABOUT THIS WAS CO-WRITTEN WITH AN ASTONISHING IRISH NOBLEMAN WHO ADDED A LOT ABOUT ANCIENT ASTRONAUTS.
Flying Saucers Have Landed
"HIS SECOND GIVES HIS ALIENS DIALOGUE HIS SECRETARY ORIGINALLY WROTE...
Inside the Space Ships
Pioneers of Space
"...FOR HIS EARLIER SF NOVEL, 'PIONEERS OF SPACE'!
"THE SPACE BROTHERS STARTED PICKING GEORGE UP AT HIS HOUSE.
"THEY DROVE A BLACK PONTIAC.
"WHENEVER HE WENT FOR A RIDE IN A FLYING SAUCER, GEORGE REPORTED THERE WAS NO SENSE OF MOTION.
"HE WOULD WATCH NEWSREELS FROM VENUS AND WATCH THE STARS SPEED BY--
"--WHILE BEING SERVED SPACE DRINKS.
"BY BEINGS HE DESCRIBED AS COMMUNISTS, MUCH IN ADVANCE OF EARTH GOVERNMENTS.
"WE MIGHT ASK: WHO WAS FOOLING WHO?
"BUT GEORGE **DID** HAVE SOME **STRANGE ADVENTURES**--"

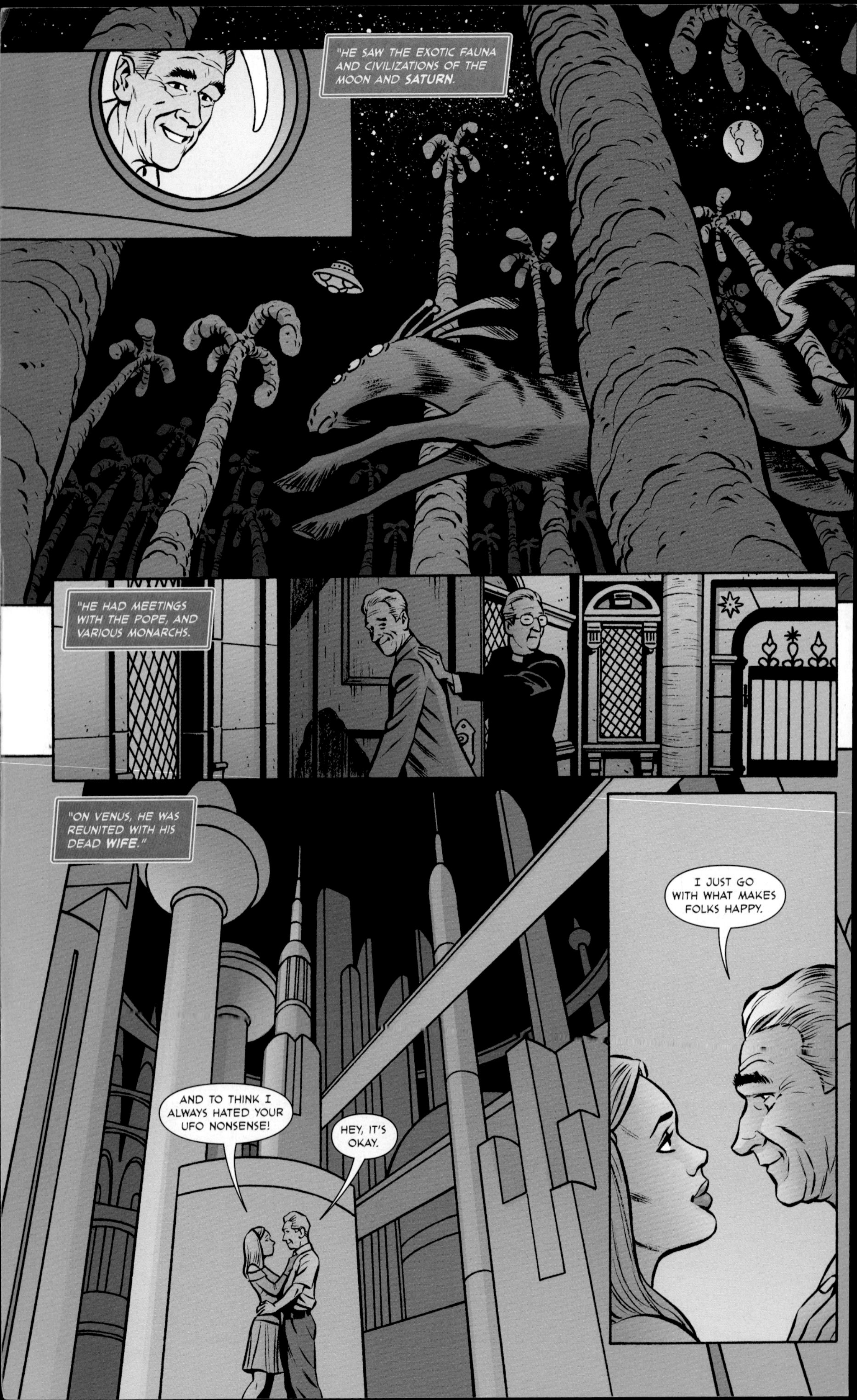
"HE SAW THE EXOTIC FAUNA AND CIVILIZATIONS OF THE MOON AND SATURN.
"HE HAD MEETINGS WITH THE POPE, AND VARIOUS MONARCHS.
"ON VENUS, HE WAS REUNITED WITH HIS DEAD WIFE."
AND TO THINK I ALWAYS HATED YOUR UFO NONSENSE!
HEY, IT'S OKAY.
I JUST GO WITH WHAT MAKES FOLKS HAPPY.

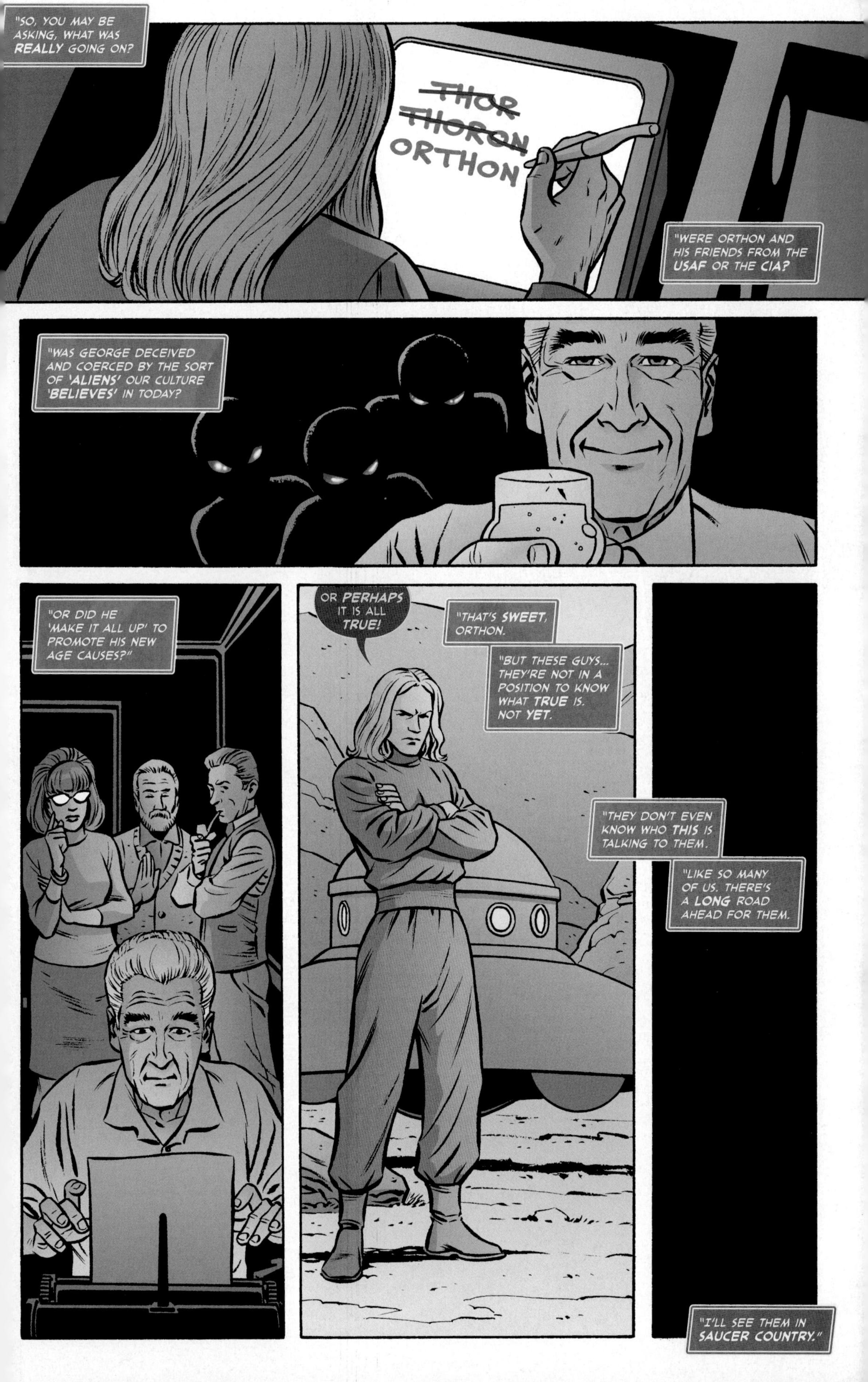
"SO, YOU MAY BE ASKING, WHAT WAS REALLY GOING ON?
THOR
THORON
ORTHON
"WERE ORTHON AND HIS FRIENDS FROM THE USAF OR THE CIA?
"WAS GEORGE DECEIVED AND COERCED BY THE SORT OF 'ALIENS' OUR CULTURE 'BELIEVES' IN TODAY?
"OR DID HE 'MAKE IT ALL UP' TO PROMOTE HIS NEW AGE CAUSES?"
OR PERHAPS IT IS ALL TRUE!
"THAT'S SWEET, ORTHON.
"BUT THESE GUYS... THEY'RE NOT IN A POSITION TO KNOW WHAT TRUE IS. NOT YET.
"THEY DON'T EVEN KNOW WHO THIS IS TALKING TO THEM.
"LIKE SO MANY OF US. THERE'S A LONG ROAD AHEAD FOR THEM.
"I'LL SEE THEM IN SAUCER COUNTRY."

SAUCER COUNTRY #1
variant cover by SEAN MURPHY

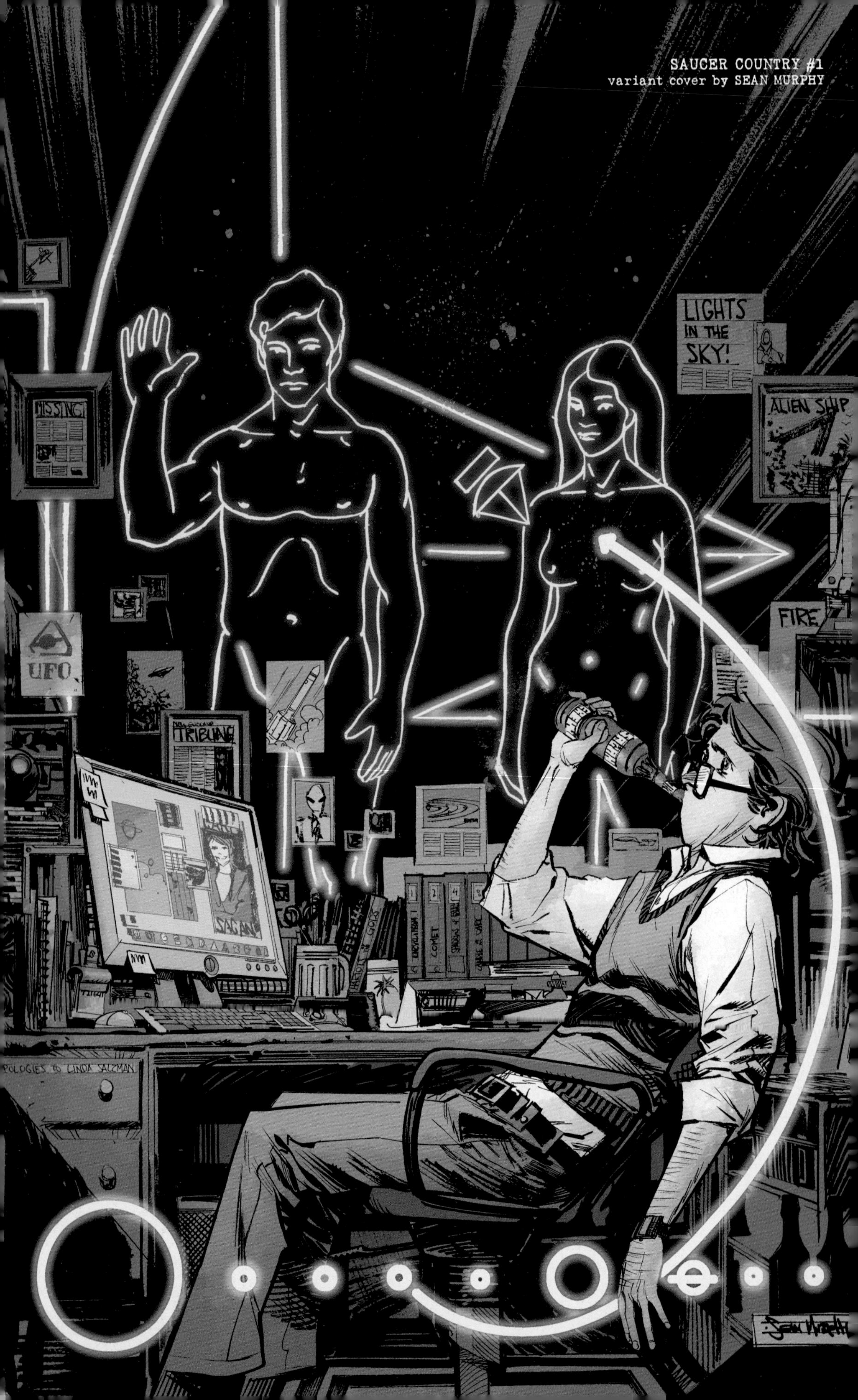
MISSING!
LIGHTS IN THE SKY!
ALIEN SHIP
UFO
FIRE
TRIBUNE
SAGAN
COMET
POLOGIES TO LINDA SALZMAN